King's Lynn . . . . .5 to 8 **PE30**
L
Loddon 66 NR14
Long Stratton 64 NR15
M
Martham 49 NR29
Middleton 8 PE32
Mundesley 23 NR11
Mundford 60 IP26
N
Narborough 11 PE32
New Costessey 37 NR5
Newgate 17 NR25
North End, King's Lynn 9 PE30
North Runcton 8 PE32
North Walsham 22 NR28
North Wootton 6 PE30
Norwich city centre 36 NR1
Norwich . . . . .37 to 46 NR1
O
Old Catton 39,46 NR6

Old Costessey 37 NR5
Ormesby St. Margaret 51 NR29
P
Poringland 48 NR14
R
Reedham 48 NR13
Reepham 26 NR10
S
Scratby 51 NR29
Sheringham 19 NR26
Snettisham 2 PE31
South Lynn 7 PE30
South Wootton 6 PE30
Sprowston 40 NR7
St. James End 9 PE30
Stalham 24 NR12
Sutton 24 NR12
Swaffham 12 PE37
T
Taverham 31 NR8
Terrington St. Clement 3 PE34

Thetford 67 IP24
Thorpe End 41 NR13
Thorpe Marriot 31 NR8
Thorpe St. Andrew 41,46 NR7
Toftwood 25 NR19
Trowse Newton 45 NR14
U
Upper Stoke . . . .
W
Watlington . . . .
Watton . . . .
Wells next the Sea . . . .
West Lynn . . . .
West Runton . . . .
West Winch . . . .
Winterton on Sea . . . .
Wiveton . . . .
Wroxham . . . .
Wymondham 62 NR18

G000108946

Mapping sourced from **Ordnance Survey**

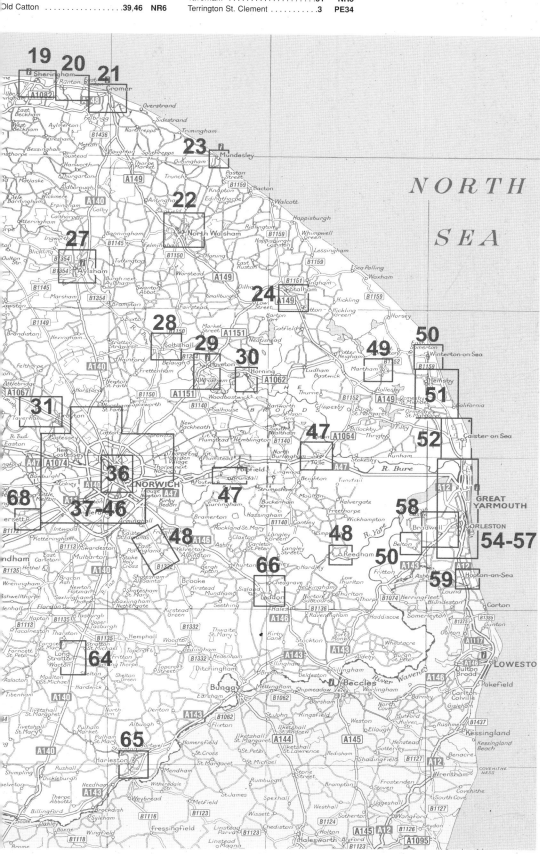

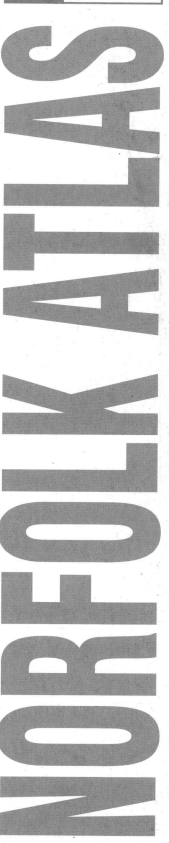

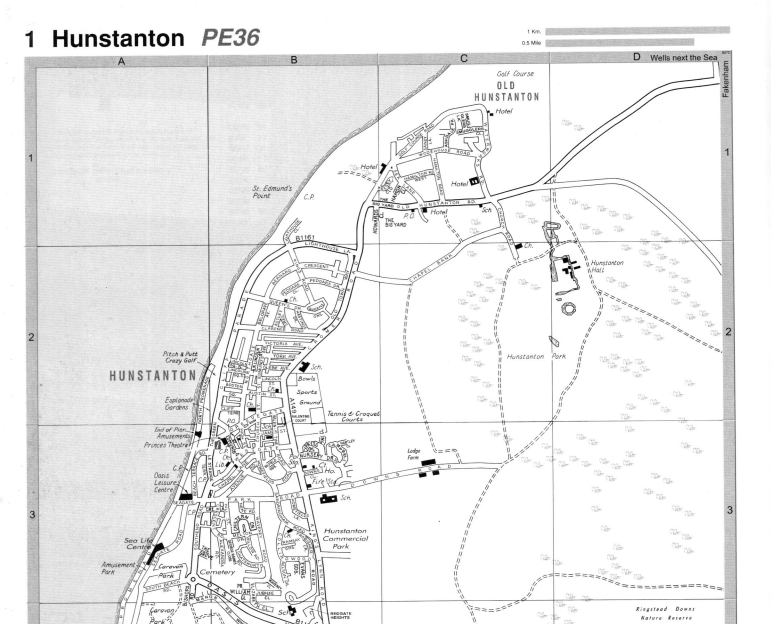

ALEXANDRA ROAD B.3	CRESCENT ROAD B.3	HOMEFIELDS ROAD ..B.3	NURSERY DRIVE B.3	SEA WORLD A.3
AMUSEMENT PARK ...A.3	CROMER ROAD B.2	HOWARDS CL. B.1		SEAGATE A.3
ANDREWS PLACE B.4	CYPRESS PLACE B.3	HUNSTANTON HALL ..D.2	OASIS LEISURE CNT. ..A.3	SEAGATE ROAD A.3
ANNES DRIVE B.4		HUNSTANTON PARK ..C.2	OLD HUNSTANTON RD .C.2	SILFIELD GARDENS ...B.3
ASHDALE PARK C.1	DIANAS GROVE B.4		OLD TOWN WAY B.2	SMUGGLER'S CL. C.1
ASTLEY CRESCENT ..B.2	DOWNS CL. B.3	JAMES STREET B.3		SMUGGLER'S LANE ...C.1
AUSTIN STREET B.2	DOWNS ROAD B.3	JUBILEE CL. B.3	PARK ROAD B.3	SOUTH BEACH ROAD ..A.4
AVENUE ROAD B.3	ELIZABETH CL. B.3		PEDDARS CL. B.2	SOUTH PROMENADE ..A.4
	ESPLANADE GDNS A.2	KELSEY CL. C.1	PEDDARS DRIVE B.2	SOUTHEND ROAD A.3
BEACH TERRACE RD ..A.3	EVANS GARDENS B.3	KING'S LYNN ROAD ..B.3	PHILIPS CHASE B.4	
BELGRAVE AVENUE ...B.2		KINGS ROAD B.2	PIER END A.3	THE BIG YARD C.1
BENNET CL. B.4	FIRE STATION B.3	LE STRANGE TERR. ..B.3	PINE CL. B.3	THE GREEN B.3
BERNARD CRESCENT ..B.2	FROBISHER CR. B.3		PRINCE WILLIAM CL. ..B.3	THE GROVE A.3
BISHOPS ROAD A.3		LIBRARY B.3	PRINCES THEATRE ...B.3	TUDOR CRESCENT ...B.4
BOSTON SQUARE B.2	GEORGE RAINES CL. ..B.3	LIGHTHOUSE CL. B.1	PRINCES DRIVE B.4	
	GLEBE AVENUE B.2	LIGHTHOUSE LANE ...B.1		VALENTINE COURT ...B.3
CAMPBELL CL. B.3	GOLF COURSE C.1	LINCOLN SQ. NORTH ..B.2	QUEEN'S DRIVE B.2	VALENTINE ROAD B.2
CHAPEL BANK B.2	GOLF COURSE ROAD ..C.1	LINCOLN SQ. SOUTH ..B.2	QUEEN'S GARDENS ..B.2	VICTORIA AVENUE ...B.2
CHAPEL LANE B.3	GREEVEGATE B.3	LINCOLN STREET B.2		
CHARLES ROAD B.4		LOWER LINCOLN ST. ..B.2	RAMSAY GARDENS ...B.3	WATERWORKS ROAD .C.1
CHATSWORTH ROAD ..B.3	HAMILTON ROAD C.1		REDGATE HILL B.4	WAVENEY CL. B.3
CHILTERN CR. B.3	HAMILTON RD WEST ..C.1	MANOR ROAD A.3		WAVENEY ROAD B.3
CHURCH ROAD C.1	HAMON CL. B.3	MARGARETS CL. B.4	ST. EDMUND'S AVENUE B.2	WESTGATE B.3
CHURCH STREET B.3	HARRY'S WAY B.4	MELTON DRIVE B.3	ST. EDMUND'S POINT ..B.1	WILLOW ROAD B.3
CLARENCE ROAD B.2	HARTLEY CL. B.3		ST. EDMUND'S TERR. ..B.3	WINDSOR RISE B.4
CLIFF PARADE B.2	HASTINGS DRIVE B.2	NELSON DRIVE B.3	SANDRINGHAM ROAD ..B.3	WODEHOUSE ROAD ..C.1
CLIFF TERRACE B.2	HIGH STREET B.3	NENE ROAD B.3	SANDY LANE C.1	
COLLINGWOOD D B.3	HILL STREET B.3	NORTH PROMENADE ..A.2	SARAHS ROAD B.4	YORK AVENUE B.2
CRESCENT LANE B.3	HOMEFIELDS LANE ...B.3	NORTHGATE B.2	SEA LANE C.1	

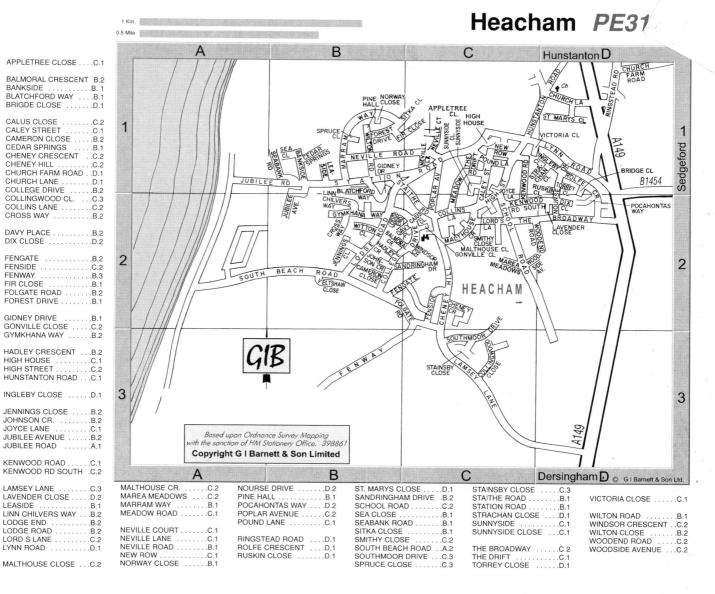

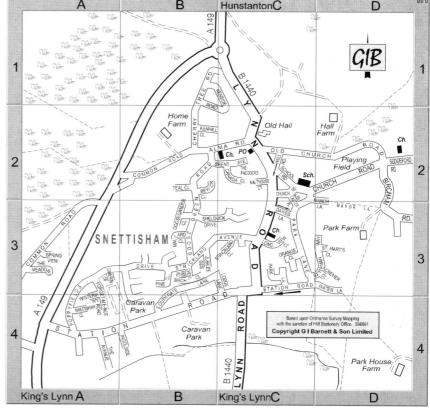

Dersingham *PE31*

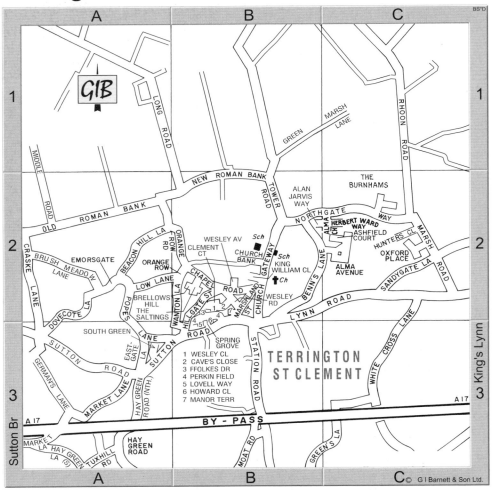

Terrington St. Clement *PE34*

Dersingham index

ALEXANDRA CL A.1

BALMORAL CL B.3
BALMORAL WEST B.3
BANK ROAD B.3
BEECH DRIFT B.3
BROADLANDS CL. A.2
BROOK ROAD B.3
BURMAH CL. A.2
BUSH CL. B.2

CENTRE CR. B.2
CENTRE VALE R.D B.2
CHAPEL R.D B.2
CHESTNUT CL. B.2
CHURCH LANE C.2
CLAYTON CL. B.2
CREST ROAD A.1
CRISP CL. A.2

DODDSHILL R.D C.3
DUCK DECOY CL. A.3

EARL CL. A.2
EDINGBURGH WAY B.2

FERN HILL B.2

GELHAM COURT A.2
GELHAM MANOR B.2
GLEBE CL. B.1
GLEBE ROAD B.1
GREENWICH CL. B.3

HAWTHORN DRIVE . . . B.1
HEATH ROAD B.3
HIPKIN ROAD A.2
HOLYROOD DRIVE B.3
HUNSTANTON ROAD . . . B.1

IVEAGH CL. B.3

JUBILEE COURT B.2
JUBILEE DRIVE A.1

KERRICH CL. A.2
KINGS CROFT B.2

LYNN ROAD B.3

MANOR ROAD C.2
MANOR ROAD B.3
MANORSIDE B.3
MILL ROAD C.1
MOUNTBATTEN RD A.2

OLD HALL DR. B.2
ONEDINE CL. A.1
ORCHARD CL. B.2

PAKENHAM DR. A.2
PANSEY DRIVE A.1
PARK HILL B.2
PELL ROAD B.2
PHILIP NURSE ROAD . . . A.2
POST OFFICE R.D B.2
PRINCE ANDREW DR . . B.2
PRINCE CHARLES CL . B.2
QUEEN ELIZABETH DR . B.2

REG HOUCHEN R.D . . . B.2
REYNOLDS WAY A.2
ROBERT BALDING RD . . A.2

ST. NICHOLAS CL. . . . B.2
SANDRINGHAM R.D . . . B.3
SAXON WAY B.3
SENTERS ROAD B.3
SHERNBOURNE ROAD C.2
SHOULDHAM CL. A.2
SILVER DRIVE A.1
STANTON WAY A.2
STATION ROAD A.2
STRATFORD CL. C.2
SUGAR LANE C.2

THE GREEN B.1
THOMAS DREW CL. . . A.2
TUDOR WAY B.2

VALLEY RISE A.1
VICEROY CL. A.2

WALLACE TWITE WAY . A.2
WEST HALL ROAD . . . B.2
WEST ROAD B.2
WHITE HORSE DRIVE . B.2
WICLEWOOD WAY . . . A.2
WILLOW DRIVE B.3
WINDSOR DR. B.2
WOODSIDE AVE. B.1
WOODSIDE CL. B.1

Terrington St. Clement index

ALAN JARVIS WAY . . . B.2
ALMA AVENUE C.2
ALMA CHASE C.2
ASHFIELD COURT C.2

BEACON HILL LANE . . A.2
BENN'S LANE B.2
BRELLOWS HILL B.2
BRUSH MEADOW LA . . A.2

CAVES CLOSE B.2
CHAPEL ROAD B.2
CHURCH BANK B.2
CHURCH GATEWAY . . B.2
CLEMENT COURT . . . B.2
CRASKE LANE A.2

DOVECOTE LANE . . . A.2

EASTGATE LANE A.3
EMORSGATE A.2

FFOLKES DRIVE B.2

GERMAN'S LANE A.3
GREEN MARSH LANE . B.1
GREEN'S LANE C.3

HAY GREEN ROAD . . . A.3
HAY GREEN ROAD
(NORTH) A.3
HAY GREEN RD (STH) . A.3
HERBERT WARD WAY . C.2
HILLGATE STREET . . . B.2
HOWARD CLOSE B.2
HUNTERS CLOSE . . . C.2

KING WILLIAM CLOSE . B.2

LONG ROAD A.1
LOVELL WAY B.3
LOW LANE A.2
LYNN ROAD B.2

MANOR TERRACE . . . B.2
MARKET LANE A.3
MARSH ROAD C.2
MARSHLAND STREET . B.2
MIDDLE ROAD A.1
MOAT ROAD B.3

NEW ROMAN BANK . . B.2

NORTHGATE WAY . . . B.2

OLD ROMAN BANK . . A.2
ORANGE ROW B.2
ORANGE ROW ROAD . B.2
OXFORD PLACE C.2

POPES LANE A.2
PERKIN FIELD B.2
RHOON ROAD C.1

SANDYGATE LANE . . . C.2
SOUTH GREEN A.3
SPRING GROVE B.3
STATION ROAD B.3
SUTTON ROAD A.3

THE BURNHAMS C.2
THE SALTINGS B.2
TOWER ROAD B.2
TUXHILL ROAD A.3

WANTON LANE B.2
WESLEY AVENUE B.2
WESLEY CLOSE B.2
WESLEY ROAD B.2
WHITECROSS LANE . . C.3

ABERDEEN ST. B.4
ACER RD. A.5
ACONITE C.3
ADA COXON CL. B.3
ADAM CL. C.4
ADELAIDE AVE. C.3
AILMAR CL. C.4
ALBAN RD. C.1
ALBERT AVE. B.4
ALBERT ST. B.4
ALBION ST. B.4
ALEXANDRA DOCK A.3
ALICE FISHER CR. ...B.3
ALL SAINTS DRIVE ...C.1
ALL SAINTS ST. B.4
ANDERSON CL. B.3
ANNES CL. D.2
APPLEDORE CL. C.2
ARCHDALE CL. B.6
ARCHDALE ST. B.3
ARGYLE ST. B.4
ARLINGTON PK RD. ..D.6
ARUNDEL DRIVE C.2
ASH GROVE (INSET) ..B.7
ASHBEY RD. D.3
ASHBY HILL D.4
ASHFIELD HILL C.4
ATBARA TERRACE B.5
AUSTIN FIELDS B.3
AUSTIN ST. B.4
AVE. RD. B.4
AVON RD. C.2
AYRE WAY D.3

BACK LANE B.6
BACTON CL. C.2
BADER CL. C.4
BAGGE RD. C.4
BAILEY LANE A.3
BAINES RD. B.5
BAKER CL. B.5
BAKER LANE B.4
BALDOCK DRIVE C.3
BALDWIN RD. C.3
BALMORAL RD. C.3
BANKSIDE A.4
BARNWELL RD. C.3
BARRETT CL. D.4
BARSHAM DRIVE D.2
BARTON CL. C.3
BARTON'S COURT C.2
BAYFIELD CL. C.4
BEAMONT WAY C.4
BECKETT CL. C.1
BEDE CL. C.1
BEDFORD DRIVE C.2
BEECH AVE. D.2
BEECH CRESCENT ...B.7
BEECH RD. B.4
BELOE CRESCENT B.5
BENTICK DOCK A.3
BENTICK WAY A.3
BERGEN WAY B.3
BEULAH ST. C.3
BEVERIDGE WAY B.5
BEVIS WAY C.3
BINHAM RD. C.2
BIRCH CL. D.4
BIRCH GR. (INSET) ..B.7
BIRCHGROVE RD. C.1
BIRCHWOOD ST. B.3
BIRDCAGE WALK B.4
BIRKBECK CL. C.2
BISHOP'S RD. C.4
BISHOPS PARK C.4
BISHOPS TERRACE ...C.3
BLACKFRIARS RD. B.4
BLACKFRIARS ST. B.4
BLACKTHORN RD. B.2
BLENHEIM RD. C.3
BLICK CL. (INSET) ...B.7
BLICKLING CL. C.3
BLUEBELL WALK C.4
BOAL ST. B.4
BOURNE CL. C.2
BRACKEN RD. C.2
BRAMBLE DRIVE C.2
BRANCASTER CL. C.3
BRANSBY CL. B.4
BRETT WAY C.3
BREYDON RD. D.4
BRIAR CL. C.2
BRIDGE ST. B.4
BRIDGE WAY C.4
BRD. ST. B.4
BRD. WALK B.4
BROCKLEY GREEN ...C.4
BROOKWELL SPRINGS D.6
BROWNING PLACE ...C.3
BRUMMELL CL. C.4
BRYGGEN RD. B.3
BRYONY COURT C.2
BUCKINGHAM CL. C.1
BUNNETT AVE. B.5
BURE CL. D.4
BURGH CORNER D.3
BURGHLEY RD. D.2
BURKITT ST. B.3
BURNEY RD. B.5
BURNHAM AVE. C.3
BURNS COURT C.3
BUTTERWICK C.4

CALAMINT RD. C.3
CAMBRIDGE RD. C.1
CAMFREY C.3
CAMPDEN HILL D.4

CAPGRAVE AVE. B.3
CARLTON DRIVE C.1
CARTER'S CL. C.2
CASTLE CL. C.3
CASTLE RISING D.1
CASTLE RISING RD. ..C.2
CASTLEACRE CL. C.2
CAVENDISH CL. D.6
CAXTON COURT C.4
CEDAR GROVE C.6
CEDAR WAY A.4
CENTRAL RD. B.3
CENTRE POINT C.4
CHADWICK SQ B.3
CHAPEL LANE B.6
CHAPEL ST. B.4
CHARLES ST. B.4
CHARLOCK B.3
CHASE AVE. B.4
CHECKER ST. B.4
CHEQUERS LA (INSET) C.7
CHERRY TREE DR. ...A.4
CHESTNUT AVE. B.7
CHEW COURT D.3
CHOLMONDLEY WY
(INSET) B.7
CHURCH CL. A.4
CHURCH CROFTS E.1
CHURCH LANE C.2
CHURCH LEAS EST. ..C.1
CHURCH ST. B.4
CLARE RD. C.1
CLARKE'S LA (INSET) .B.6
CLENCHWARTON RD. .A.4
CLIFFORD BURMAN CL.C.2
CLIFTON CL. C.2
CLOUGH LANE B.4
COBURG ST. B.4
COCKLESHELL WALK .B.4
COLLEGE LANE B.4
COLNEY RD. D.4
COLUMBIA WAY B.3
COMMON CL. B.6
COMMON LANE C.2
CONISTON CL. C.3
CONSTITUTION HILL ..C.5
COPPERFIELD C.4
CORBYN SHAW RD. ..D.4
CORONATION AVE. ...C.6
CORONATION RD. B.4
COTMAN WAY C.4
COULTON CL. B.3
COUNTY COURT RD. ..B.4
COURTNELL PLACE ..C.3
CRABTREE WAY C.4
CRANMER CL. C.1
CRESSWELL ST. B.3
CROSS BANK RD. A.3
CROWN SQUARE B.3
CULEY CL. C.4
CUTHBERT CL. C.1

DASELEY'S CL. C.2
DAWBER CL. C.4
DAWNAY AVE. C.4
DE GREY RD. C.4
DENMARK RD. C.4
DENNEY RD. C.4
DERWENT AVE. D.2
DEVON CRESCENT ...C.1
DEVONSHIRE CT C.3
DIAMOND ST. B.4
DOBBY DRIVE B.3
DOHAMERO LANE ...B.7
DRAYCOTE CL. C.4
DRIFTWAY C.2

EARSHAM DRIVE C.3
EASTCOTT WAY C.4
EASTFIELD CL. C.4
EASTFIELDS C.4
EASTGATE ST. B.3
EBBLE CL. C.2
EDINBURGH WAY C.3
EDMA ST. C.3
EDWARD BENEFER WY B.3
ELDERBERRY WALK ..C.4
ELLER DR (INSET) B.7
ELM CL. A.5
ELM TREE GROVE B.7
ELMHURST DRIVE ...C.2
ELMSTEAD RD. C.4
ELSING DRIVE C.3
ELVINGTON C.3
EMPIRE AVE. B.4
ENNERDALE DRIVE ..D.2
ENTERPRISE WAY ...B.5
ESTUARY CL. B.3
ESTUARY RD. B.3
EUSTON WAY D.2
EVELYN WAY C.4

EXETER CRESCENT ..C.1
EXTON'S PLACE B.4
EXTON'S RD. B.4

FAIRFIELD RD. D.6
FAIRSTEAD ESTATE ..C.4
FAIRWICK PATH C.4
FELBRIGG CL. D.2
FEN LANE C.2
FENLAND RD. C.4
FERMOY AVE. B.3
FERNLEA RD. B.3
FERRY LANE A.4
FERRY RD. A.3
FERRY SQUARE A.3

FERRY ST. A.4
FESTIVAL CL. C.2
FIELD END CL. C.3
FIELD LANE C.3
FIELD RD. C.3
FILBERTS C.4
FINCHDALE CL. C.1
FIR TREE DRIVE B.7
FIVE ELMS C.4
FFOLKES DRIVE C.2
FOLLY COURT C.4
FOLLY GROVE CL. ...C.3
FORD AVE. C.1
FOUNTAINE GROVE ..C.1
FOX'S LANE A.3
FOXDALE WAY C.4
FREDERICK CL. C.1
FREEBRIDGE HAVEN .C.6
FREISTON C.4
FRIARS ST. B.4
FRONT WAY B.3
FULLER CL. (INSET) ..B.7
FURNESS CL. D.2

GALYON RD. C.3
GARDEN COURT B.3
GARWOOD CL. D.4
GASKELL WAY C.2
GATE HOUSE LANE ..C.1
GAYTON RD. C.3
GAYWOOD C.4
GAYWOOD HALL DR ..C.4
GAYWOOD RD. C.4
GENERALS WALK C.4
GEORGE ST. B.3
GLADSTONE RD. B.4
GLAVEN C.3
GLOUCESTER RD. C.3
GOLF CL. C.4
GOODWIN'S RD. B.4
GRAFTON CL. C.3
GRAFTON RD. C.3
GRAHAM DRIVE D.6
GRAHAM ST. B.4
GRANTLY COURT C.3
GRAVELHILL LANE ...B.7
GREEN ACRES CL. ...C.3
GREEN LANE D.2
GREENLAND AVE. ...B.3
GREENPARK AVE. B.3
GREGORY CL. C.1
GRESHAM CL. C.3
GREYSEDGE C.3
GRIMSTON RD. D.2
GUANOCK TERRACE .B.4

HALL DRIVE C.6
HALL LANE (INSET) ..B.7
HALL ORCHARDS D.6
HALL RD. C.2
HALL VIEW RD. C.4
HAMBURG WAY B.3
HAMLIN WAY B.5
HANOVER COURT ...C.4
HANSA RD. B.5
HARDWICK C.5
HARDWICK RD. B.4
HARECROFT GDS. ...B.3
HARECROFT PARADE B.3
HAREWOOD DRIVE ..B.3
HAREWOOD PARADE .B.3
HARROW CL. A.4
HAWTHORNS C.4
HEATH CL. D.1
HEATH WALK C.4-D.4
HEATHER WALK C.4
HEMINGTON CL. D.3
HENRY BELL CL. C.4
HEREFORD WAY B.5
HEXTABLE RD. B.3
HICKLING C.4
HICKORY RD. C.4
HIGH ST. B.4
HIGHAM GREEN C.4
HIGHFIELD C.4
HIGHGATE B.4
HILL RD., KING'S LYNN C.3
HILL RD., MIDDLETON .D.6
HILLEN RD. A.5
HILLINGDON SQ B.4
HILLSIDE CL. D.6
HINCHINGBROOK CL. .D.2
HOCKHAM ST. B.4
HOLECOMBE CL. C.4
HOLLY CL., S. WTTON .D.2
HOLLY CL.(INSET) B.7
HOMELAND RD. B.3
HOPE COURT B.3
HORSLEYS CHASE ...B.5
HORSLEYS FIELDS ...B.4
HORTON RD. D.3
HOSPITAL WALK B.4
HOUGHTON AVE. C.2
HOVETON CL. C.4
HOWARDS ESTATE ...C.1
HUGH CL. C.1
HULTON RD. C.4

ICKWORTH CL. D.2
INGLEBY CL. C.4

JAMES CL. C.2
JARVIS RD. B.3
JEFFERY CL. B.3
JERMYN RD. C.3
JOHN KENNEDY RD. ..B.3
JUBILEE BANK RD. ...A.4
JULIAN RD. C.1

KATHERINE PLACE ...D.4
KEBLE CL. C.1
KEENE RD. B.5
KEMPE RD. A.4
KENDLE WAY D.3
KENSINGTON RD. C.3
KENT RD. C.3
KESWICK D.4
KETTLEWELL LANE ..B.3
KETTS CROSS C.4
KILHAMS WAY B.3
KING CUP C.2
KING GEORGE V AVE. .B.4
KING JOHN AVE. C.4
KING ST. B.4
KING'S AVE. B.4
KING'S GREEN C.4
KING'S LYNN BY-PASS .C.5
KING'S LYNN STATION .B.4
KING'S STAITHE LANE .A.4
KINGSWAY B.3
KIRBY ST. B.4
KIRKSTEAD D.4
KIRKSTONE GR D.2
KITCHENER ST. B.5

LADBROOKE WAY C.4
LADY JANE GREY RD. .B.3
LAMBOURN WAY C.4
LAMPORT COURT ...D.3
LANCASTER RD. C.4
LANGHAM ST. B.4
LANGLAND C.3
LANGLEY RD. D.2
LANPORT D.3
LANSDOWNE ST. B.3
LARCH CL. C.2
LARCH RD. A.6
LAUREL GROVE B.7
LAVENDER COURT ...C.3
LAVENDER RD. C.3
LE STRANGE AVE. ...B.3
LEA WAY C.3
LEAFIELD RD. C.4
LEETE WAY (INSET) ..B.7
LEICESTER AVE. C.4
LEONARD CL. C.3
LEVERS CL. C.3
LEXHAM RD. D.3
LILAC WOOD C.3
LINDENS C.4
LING COMMON RD. ..C.1
LITTLE CARR RD. D.1
LT. WALLSINGHAM CL. .C.2
LITTLEPORT ST. B.4
LODGE LANE E.2
LOKE RD. B.3
LONDON RD. B.4
LONG LANE B.7
LONG SUTTON RD. ..A.4
LOSINGA RD. B.3
LOW RD. C.2
LOWFIELD C.4
LYNN RD., N. WTTON .D.1
LYNN RD., GAYWOOD .C.3
LYNN RD., MIDDLETN .D.6

MAIN RD. B.6
MALLOW WAY C.4
MALVERN PL. D.2
MANNINGTON PL D.2
MANOR RD. C.1
MAPLE DRIVE D.2
MAPLE RD. A.5
MAPPLEBECK CL. D.4
MARGARET ROSE CL. .D.4
MARHAM CL. A.4
MARINERS WAY B.3
MARKET LANE B.4
MARKET ST. B.4
MARSH LANE C.2
MARSH LANE C.2
MARSH RD. C.1
MAYFIELD WAY C.4-D.4
MAYFLOWER AVE. ...B.3
MEADOW CL. C.1
MEADOW RD. C.2
MEADOW WAY A.4
MEADOWVALE GDS. .C.3
MELFORD RD. D.2
METCALFE AVE. B.5
METHUEN AVE. C.3
MIDDLETON E.6
MIDDLEWOOD C.4
MILL DROVE E.6
MILL LA., KING'S LYNN C.3
MILL LA. (INSET) B.6
MILLENNIUM WAY ...A.4
MILLFIELD LANE B.6
MILLFIELDS C.4
MILLFLEET B.4
MILLHOUSES B.3
MILTON AVE. B.4
MINSTER COURT C.4
MONKS HOOD C.2
MONTGOMERY WAY ..D.4
MOUNT PARK CL. ...D.6
MOUNT ST. C.4
MULBERRY RD. C.4

NAPIER CL. C.4
NELSON ST. B.4
NEW CONDUIT ST. ...B.4
NEW RD. C.3
NEW RD., N. RUNCTON C.6
NEW ST. C.3
NEWBY RD. D.3

NEWLANDS AVE. B.3
NORFOLK ST. B.4
NORMAN WAY C.4
NORTH EVERARD ST. .B.4
NORTH LYNN IND EST .B.3
NORTH RUNCTON D.6
NORTH ST. C.2
NORTH WAY B.3
NORTH WOOTTON C.1
NOTHALL CRESCENT .C.3
NOTTINGHAM RD. B.3
NURSERY CL. C.2
NURSERY LANE C.2

OAK AVE., S. WTTON ..C.2
OAK AVE. (INSET) C.7
OAK CIRCLE C.6
OLD KILN RD. (INSET) .C.7
OLD MANOR CL. C.1
OLD RECTORY CL. ...C.1
OLD SOUTH C.4
OLD SUNWAY B.4
OLDMEADOW RD. B.5
ORCHARD GDS. C.3
ORCHARD GR., W. LNN A.4
ORCHARD GR., W. WH .B.3
ORCHARD LANE C.3
ORFORD CL. (INSET) .C.7
ORMESBY D.4
ORWELL CL. D.4
OTLEY WAY C.4
OUSE AVE. B.4
OXBOROUGH DRIVE ..D.2

PAGE STAIR LANE A.3
PANDORA D.4
PANTON CL. B.5
PARADISE RD. B.4
PARK AVE. C.4
PARK WAY C.4
PARKHILL D.6
PAUL DRIVE D.6
PAXMAN RD. B.5
PAXTON TERRACE ...B.4
PECKOVER WAY D.3
PECKS MEADOW D.2
PEEL PLACE (INSET) ..B.7
PEEL ST. B.4
PENROSE CL. C.3
PEPPERS GREEN C.2
PERSIMMON C.2
PETERSCOURT C.3
PILOT ST. B.3
PINE RD. D.2
PINE TREE CHASE ...B.7
PINNYS WAY A.3
PIPER RD. B.5
PLANTATION WAY ...C.4
PLEASANCE CL. C.4
PLOUGHMAN RD. C.4
POPLAR AVE. C.3
POPLAR DRIVE D.2
POPLAR RD. B.7
PORTLAND PLACE ...B.4
PORTLAND ST. B.4
POST MILL C.4
PRINCES WAY B.4
PRIORY LA., KS LYNN .B.4
PRIORY LA., N. WTTN .C.1
PRIORY RD. C.1
PROCTORS A.5
PROVIDENCE ST. C.4
PULLOVER RD. A.5
PURFLEET B.4
PURFLEET ST. B.4

QN. ELIZABETH AVE. ..C.3
QN. ELIZABETH WY ...D.3
QUEEN MARY RD. C.4
QUEEN ST. B.4
QUEEN'S AVE. B.4
QUEENS RD. A.4
QUEENSWAY C.3

RABY AVE. B.3
RADCLIFFE WAY C.4
RAILWAY RD. B.4
RAINSTHORPE D.3
RALEIGH RD. C.4
RANWORTH D.4
RAYNHAM CL. C.4
RECTORY LANE C.4
REDFERN CL. C.3
REEVES AVE. C.3
REFFLEY AVE. C.2
REGENCY AVE. C.4
REGENT WAY C.4
REGENTS PARK C.4
REID WAY B.3
RILL CL. C.1
RIVER LANE C.3
RIVER WALK A.3
RIVERSIDE B.4
RIVERSWAY B.3
ROBERTS ST. B.4
RODINGHEAD C.3
ROLLESBY RD. C.4
ROMAN WAY C.4
ROSE CL. B.3
ROSEBAY C.2
ROSEBERRY AVE. C.3
ROSSER HILL B.7
ROWAN RD. A.5
RUSHMEAD CL. C.2
RUSSELL ST. B.4
RUSSETT CL. C.3
RYALLA DRIFT C.2

RYELANDS RD. C.1
RYLEY CL. D.3

SADDLE BOW RD. B.5
SADLER CL. B.3
SALTERS AVE. B.3
SALTERS RD. C.3
SAMPHIRE C.3
SANDALE RD. C.4
SANDOVER CL. (INSET) B.7
SANDRINGHAM CR. ..C.1
SANDRINGHAM RD. ..C.3
SANDY LA., S. WTTN ..D.3
SAWSTON D.3
SAXON WAY C.4
SCANIA WAY C.5
SCHOOL LANE C.6
SCHOOL RD. D.6
SCULTHORPE AVE. ...A.4
SEA BANK WAY B.3
SEABANK ESTATE ...B.2
SEATHWAITE RD. D.3
SEGRAVE RD. C.4
SHELFORD DRIVE ...C.3
SHEPHERDS WAY C.4
SHEPLEY CORNER ...D.3
SHEPLEY CRESCENT .D.4
SHIRE GREEN C.4
SIDNEY ST. B.4
SILFIELD TERRACE ...B.4
SILVER GREEN C.4
SILVER HILL C.3
SILVERTREES WAY ..B.7
SIMON SCOTLAND RD. .B.4
SIR LEWIS ST. B.3
SMITH AVE. B.3
SOMERSBY CL. C.3
SOMERVILLE RD. B.4
SORREL COURT C.3
SOUTH EVERARD ST. .B.4
SOUTH LYNN B.5
SOUTH ST. B.4
SOUTH WOOTTON C.2
SOUTH WOOTTON LA. .C.2
SOUTHERN BY-PASS ..A.5
SOUTHFIELD DR B.7
SOUTHFIELDS C.3
SOUTHGATE ST. B.4
SPENSER RD. C.2
SPINNEY CL. C.2
SPRING CL. C.2
SPRING LANE C.3
SPRINGHEAD C.3
SPRINGWOOD EST. ..D.3
ST. ANDREWS RD. ...C.4
ST. ANN'S ST. B.3
ST. AUGUSTINES WAY .C.2
ST. BENNETTS CL. ...C.2
ST. BOTOLPHS CL. ...C.4
ST. EDMUNDSBURY RD.B.3
ST. FAITH'S DRIVE ...C.3
ST. JAMES RD. B.4
ST. JAMES ST. B.4
ST. JOHN'S TERRACE .B.4
ST. JOHNS WALK B.4
ST. LAWRENCE RD. ..B.3
ST. MARGARET'S LA. .B.4
ST. MARY'S CL. C.2
ST. MICHAELS RD. ...B.5
ST. NICHOLAS ST. ...B.3
ST. PETER'S CL. A.4
ST. PETER'S RD. A.4
ST. VALERY LANE A.5
STAG PLACE C.3
STATION RD., MIDDLTN D.6
STATION RD., N. WTTN .C.1
STOCK LEA CL. C.1
STOCK LEA RD. C.1
STODY DRIVE D.2
SUFFIELD WAY C.2
SUFFOLK RD. C.3
SURRY ST. B.4
SWALLOWFIELD RD. .C.4
SWAN LANE C.3
SYCAMORE CL. C.2
SYDNEY TERRACE ...B.5

TAMARISK C.2
TAWNYSEDGE C.3
TELFORD CL. C.4
TEMPLE RD. D.2
TENNYSON AVE. B.4
TENNYSON RD. B.4
THE ALLEY D.7
THE BIRCHES C.1
THE BOLTONS C.2
THE CEDARS D.2
THE FRIARS B.4
THE GABLES C.2
THE HOWARDS C.1
THE MEADOWS C.2
THE PINGLES ESTATE .C.1
THE WALKS B.4
THETFORD WAY C.3
THORASBY AVE. C.4
THREE OAKS C.4
THURLIN RD. C.4
THURNE D.4
TINTERN GROVE C.1
TOWER END D.5
TOWER LANE E.5
TOWER PLACE B.4
TOWER ST. B.4
TOWNSEND TER. B.3
TURBUS RD. B.3
TWO ACRES D.6
TYNDALE C.1

ULLSWATER AVE. D.2

VALINGERS RD. B.4
VANCOUVER AVE. B.4
VICTORIA PLACE B.3
VICTORIA TERR. A.4
VIKING WAY C.4
VINERY CL. A.3

WALKER ST. B.3
WALLACE CL. C.4
WALNUT AVE. B.7
WALNUT AVE. N. B.7
WALPOLE RD. B.4
WALPOLE WAY (INSET) B.7
WALSHAM CL. C.4
WALTON CL. C.1
WATER LANE, W. LYNN A.4
WATERDEN CL. C.3
WATERHOWES CR. ...D.6
WATERING LANE B.6
WATERLOO ST. B.3
WATERSIDE B.3
WAVENEY RD. D.4
WEEDON WAY D.4
WELLESLEY ST. B.4
WESLEY RD. C.1
WEST LYNN A.4
WEST WINCH C.6
WEST WINCH RD. C.5
WESTFIELDS C.4
WESTHORPE CL. C.3
WESTLAND CR B.7
WESTMARK C.4
WHEATLEY DRIVE ...C.1
WHEELWRIGHT RD. ..C.4
WHISSON CL. C.3
WHITEFRIARS TERR. .B.4
WHITEHALL DRIVE ...A.4
WHITESEDGE C.3
WILD BRIAR CL. B.7
WILLIAM BOOTH RD. .B.4
WILLIAM ST. B.4
WILLOW CL. D.6
WILLOW CRESCENT ..C.7
WILLOW DRIVE C.5
WILLOW PARK C.2
WILLOW RD. D.2
WILTON CRESCENT ..C.1
WIMPOLE DRIVE D.2
WINDERMERE RD. ...D.2
WINDSOR RD. B.4
WINDSOR TERR. B.4
WINFATHING AVE. ...B.4
WINGFIELD D.4
WINKFIELD RD. D.4
WINSTN. CHRCHLL DR.C.4
WOLLSTENCROFT AVE. B.3
WOOD ST. B.4
WOODBRIDGE WAY ..D.4
WOODLAND GDS. C.1
WOODSIDE C.4
WOODWARK AVE. B.3
WOOTTON RD. C.3
WYATT ST. B.4

YORK RD. B.4

0.5 Km
0.25 Mile

A   B

1

Barnett's
Street plan of
KING'S LYNN

Based on the Ordnance Survey map
with the sanction of the Controller, Her Majesty's Stationery Office.

Copyright G.I. Barnett & Son.

© 398861   Crown Copyright.

MARSH

CHUR...
E...

2

South Outmarsh

SO...
WO...

1 CHARLOCK
2 CLIFFORD BURMAN CL.
3 TAMARISK
4 CARTERS CL
5 MONKS HOOD

A.1078

BENEFER   WAY
BERGEN
SPENSER

Clock Case

North Fm

North Lynn Fm

Riverside Industrial Est.

St. Edmunds School

Fire Sta.

JEFFERY CL.
KILHAMS

WESTHORPE CL.
SOMERSBY CL.
Industrial Estate
KINGSWAY
GREENLAND AV.
MARINERS
NOTTINGHAM RD.
JARVIS ROAD
Riversway
HAMBURG RD.
REID WAY

River   Great   Ouse

ESTUARY

3

PINNYS WAY

BAILEY LA.

Bentinck Dock

Dobby Dr.

CROSS BANK RD.

EDWARD

TURBUS Ing CL
LOSINGA RD.
ANDERSON CL.
SALTERS RD.
GREENPARK AVENUE
Lynnsport & Leisure Park
YMCA
MILLHOUSES
SALTERS RD.
CHADWICK SQ.

B1148

Highgate Sch.

GAYWOOD
LYNN RD.
ROAD

Alexandra Dock

FERRY ROAD

VINERY CL.
BENTINCK WAY
FOXS LANE
Harvey House

WEST LYNN

PAGE STAIR L.
WATER L.
Mkt. Pl.
FERRY ST.
St. NICHOLAS
St. ANN'S
AUSTIN
St.
NORTH ST.

Sports Hall
Norfolk Coll. of Arts & Technology
King Edward VII Sch.
Playing Fields

MILTON AV.
TENNYSON
GEORGE V AVE.

4

LONG SUTTON ROAD

JUBILEE
MILLENNIUM WAY
BANK ROAD
CORONATION RD.
QUEENS RD.

ST. PETERS ROAD
West Lynn Sch.
BANKSIDE
FERRY SQ.
VICTORIA TER.

Town Hall
NEW CONDUIT
HIGH ST.
NORFOLK ST.
Mus.
Station
BLACKFRIARS
St. JOHN'S
WALK
TENNYSON RD.

Gaywood Park High Sch.
PARK

Playing Field

A   B

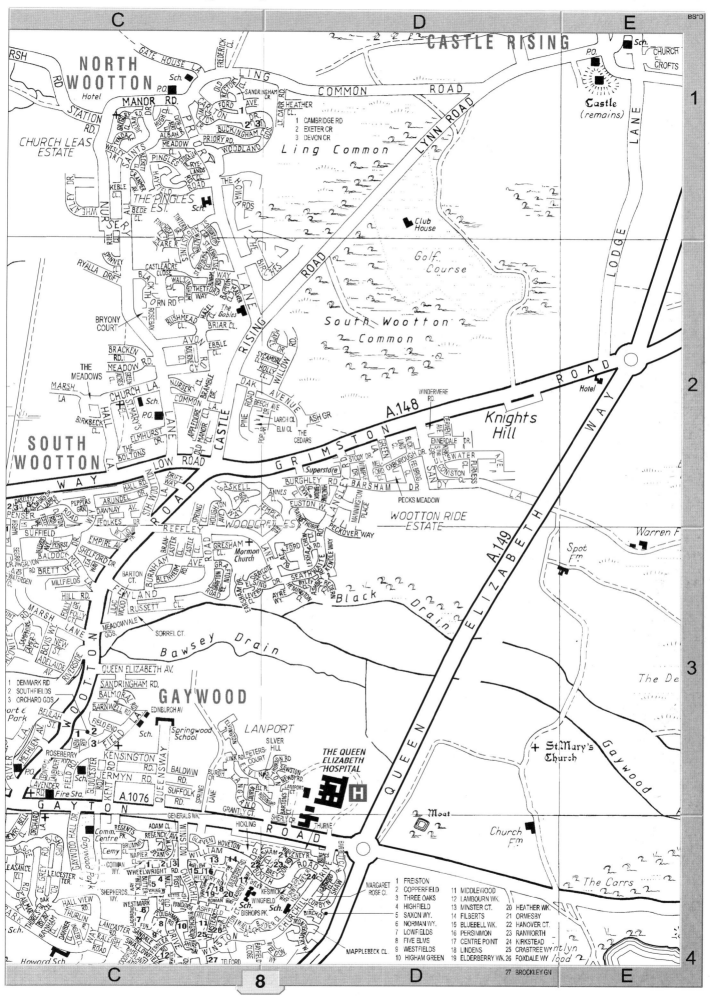

BS"D

CASTLE RISING

NORTH WOOTTON
Hotel

STATION RD.
CHURCH LEAS ESTATE
MANOR RD.
GATE HOUSE LA.
FREDERICK CL.
Sch.
P.O.

OLD RECTORY
CARLTON
SANDRINGHAM CR.
AVE.
FORD
DR.
BUCKINGHAM GDS.
PRIORY RD.
WOODLAND

HEATHER CL.
1 CAMBRIDGE RD
2 EXETER CR
3 DEVON CR

COMMON ROAD

Ling Common

LYNN ROAD

LODGE LANE

Castle (remains)

P.O.
Sch.
CHURCH CROFTS

THE PINGLES EST.
Sch.

Club House

Golf Course

South Wootton Common

LING RISING LANE ROAD

BRYONY COURT
BRACKEN RD.
THE MEADOWS
MARSH LA.
BIRKBECK CL.

RYALLA DRIFT

The Goblets
BRIAR CL.
AVON
EBBLE CL.

SYCAMORE
HOLLY
WILLOW
OAK AVENUE
BEECH AVE.
LARCH CL.
ELM CL.
ASH GR.
THE CEDARS
PINE RD.
POPLAR

WINDERMERE RD.

Knights Hill

A.148 GRIMSTON ROAD

Hotel

SOUTH WOOTTON
WAY
CHURCH LA.
HALL RD.
St.Mary's
Sch.
P.O.
ELMHURST DR.
THE BOLTONS

DRIFT WAY
STH. WOOTTON ROAD
LOW ROAD

Superstore
BURGHLEY RD.
BARSHAM
PECKS MEADOW
WOOTTON RIDE ESTATE

A.149 QUEEN ELIZABETH WAY

Warren F.
Spot Fm

GAYWOOD

1 DENMARK RD
2 SOUTHFIELDS
3 ORCHARD GDS.

QUEEN ELIZABETH AV.
SANDRINGHAM RD.
BALMORAL RD.
BARNWELL RD.
EDINBURGH AV.
Sch.

Black Drain

Bawsey Drain

MARSH LANE
MEADOWVALE GDS.
SORREL CT.
RUSSETT CL.

The De

St.Mary's Church

Gaywood

WOOTTON ROAD
RIVERSIDE
Park
BEULAH ST.
ROSEBERY
KENSINGTON RD.
BALDWIN RD.
JERMYN RD.
SUFFOLK RD.
GLOUCESTER
KENT
Fire Sta.
A.1076
GAYTON ROAD
LAVENDER
P.O.

Springwood School
LANPORT
SILVER HILL
EVINGTON
PETERS COURT
SAWSTON RD.

THE QUEEN ELIZABETH HOSPITAL H

Moat

Church Fm

GENERALS WK.
HICKLING
GLAVEN
HOVETON
WAVENEY R.
THURNE
SHEPLY RD.

Comm. Centre
Cemy
REGENCY AV.
ADAM CL.
GAYWOOD HALL DR.
GAYWOOD PARK
NAPIER
COTMAN WY.
WHEELWRIGHT RD.
WILLIAM
WINSTON
CHURCHILL
BISHOPS PK.
WESTMARK
HALL VIEW
SWALLOWFIELD ROAD
LANCASTER WAY
RALEIGH ROAD
TELFORD

Howard Sch.

Margaret Rose Cl.

MAPPLEBECK CL.

1 FREISTON
2 COPPERFIELD
3 THREE OAKS
4 HIGHFIELD
5 SAXON WY.
6 NORMAN WY.
7 LOWFIELDS
8 FIVE ELMS
9 WESTFIELDS
10 HIGHAM GREEN
11 MIDDLEWOOD
12 LAMBOURN WK.
13 MINSTER CT.
14 FILBERTS
15 BLUEBELL WK.
16 PERSIMMON
17 CENTRE POINT
18 LINDENS
19 ELDERBERRY WK.
20 HEATHER WK.
21 ORMESBY
22 HANOVER CT.
23 RANWORTH
24 KIRKSTEAD
25 CRABTREE WY.
26 FOXDALE WY.
27 BROCKLEY GN

The Carrs

C D E

1 2 3 4

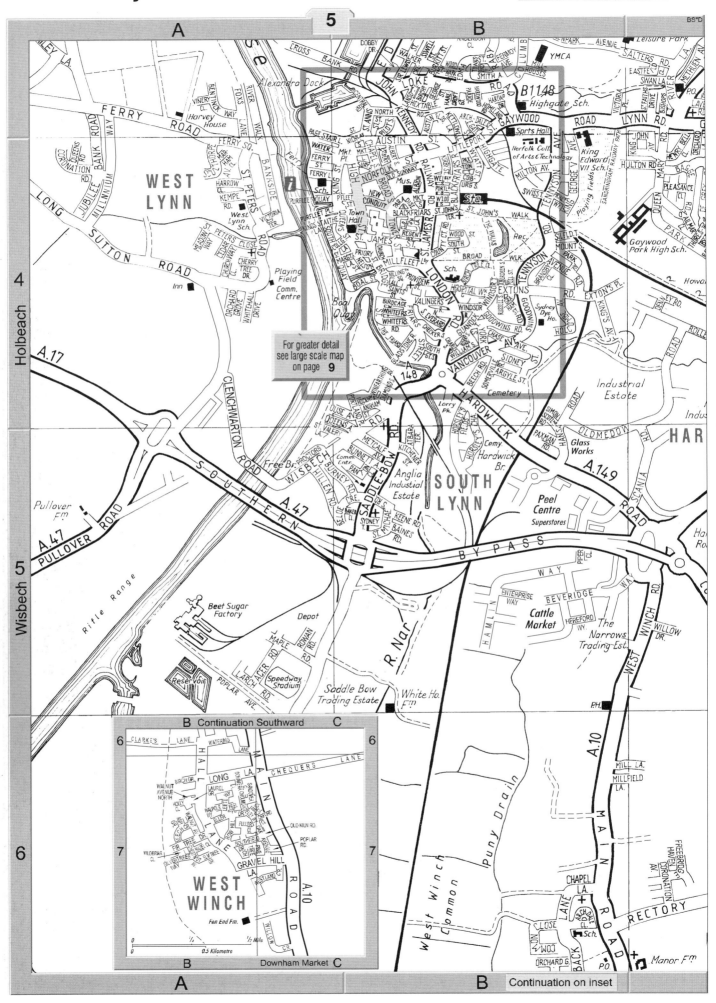

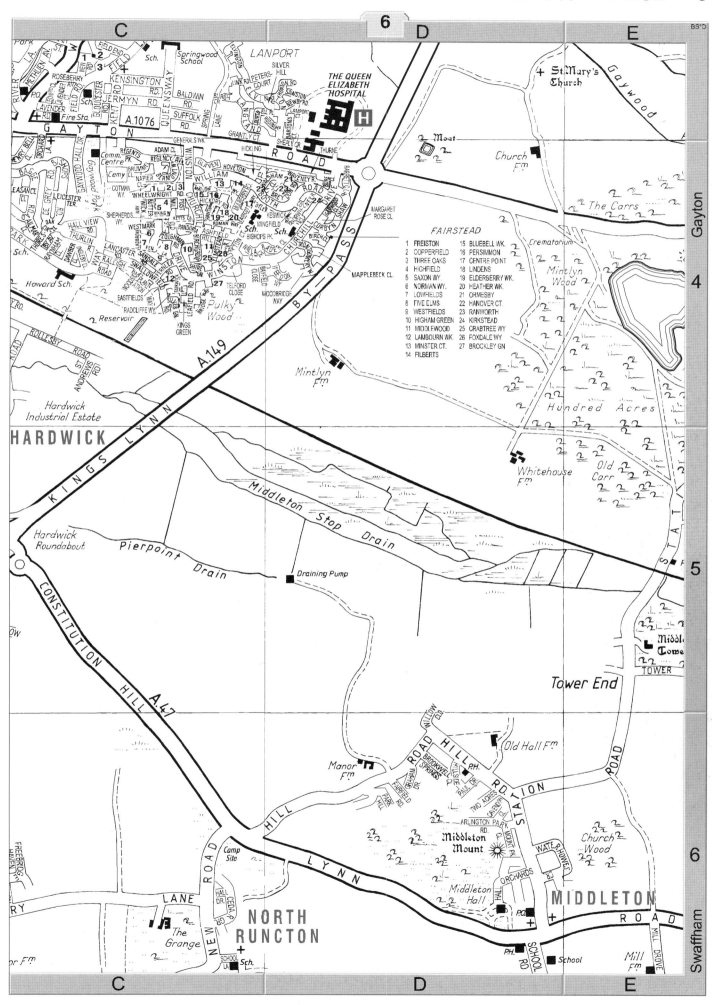

FAIRSTEAD

1 FREISTON		15 BLUEBELL WK.	
2 COPPERFIELD		16 PERSIMMON	
3 THREE OAKS		17 CENTRE POINT	
4 HIGHFIELD		18 LINDENS	
5 SAXON WY.		19 ELDERBERRY WK.	
6 NORMAN WY.		20 HEATHER WK.	
7 LOWFIELDS		21 ORMESBY	
8 FIVE ELMS		22 HANOVER CT.	
9 WESTFIELDS		23 RANWORTH	
10 HIGHAM GREEN		24 KIRKSTEAD	
11 MIDDLEWOOD		25 CRABTREE WY.	
12 LAMBOURN WK.		26 FOXDALE WY	
13 MINSTER CT.		27 BROCKLEY GN	
14 FILBERTS			

0.25 Km
0.125 Mile

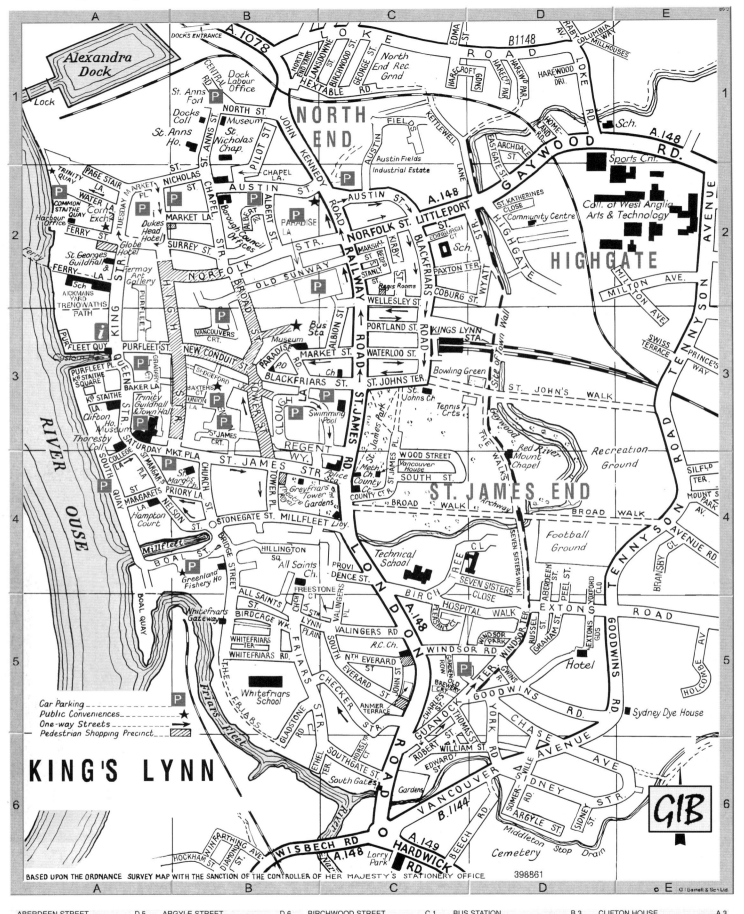

KING'S LYNN

Car Parking _____
Public Conveniences _____ ★
One-way Streets _____ →
Pedestrian Shopping Precinct ////

BASED UPON THE ORDNANCE SURVEY MAP WITH THE SANCTION OF THE CONTROLLER OF HER MAJESTY'S STATIONERY OFFICE

398861

© G I Barnett & Son Ltd.

ABERDEEN STREET D.5	ARGYLE STREET D.6	BIRCHWOOD STREET C.1	BUS STATION B.3	CLIFTON HOUSE A.3
AICKMANS YARD A.2	AUSTIN FIELDS C.2	BIRDCAGE WALK B.5		CLOUGH LANE B.3
ALBERT AVENUE B.2	AUSTIN FIELDS INDUSTRIAL	BLACKFRIARS ROAD C.2	CEMETERY D.6	COBURG STREET C.2
ALBERT STREET B.2	ESTATE C.1	BLACKFRIARS STREET B.3	CENTRAL ROAD B.1	COCKLESHELL WALK C.5
ALBION STREET C.3	AUSTIN STREET B.2	BOAL QUAY A.5	CHAPEL LANE B.2	COLLEGE LANE A.4
ALEXANDRA DOCK A.1	AVENUE ROAD E.4	BOAL STREET A.4	CHAPEL STREET B.2	COLLEGE OF WEST ANGLIA ..D,E.3
ALL SAINTS CHURCH B.4		BOWLING GREEN C.3	CHARLES STREET C.5	COLUMBIA WAY D.1
ALL SAINTS STREET B.4	BAKER LANE A.3	BRANSBY CLOSE E.4	CHASE AVENUE D.5	COMMON STAITHE QUAY A.2
ANMER TERRACE C.5	BAXTERS COURT B.3	BRIDGE STREET B.4	CHECKER STREET C.5	COMMUNITY CENTRE D.2
ARCHDALE STREET D.1	BEDFORD STREET C.2	BROAD STREET B.2	CHURCH LANE B.5	CORN EXCHANGE A.2
ARCHWAY D.4	BEECH ROAD C.6	BROAD WALK C.4	CHURCH STREET B.4	COUNTY COURT C.4

COUNTY COURT ROAD C.4
CUSTOM HOUSE A.3

DIAMOND STREET B.6
DOCK LABOUR OFFICE B.1
DOCKS COLLEGE B.1
DOCKS ENTRANCE B.1
DUKES HEAD HOTEL A.2

EASTGATE STREET D.1
EDINBURGH COURT C.2
EDMA STREET C.1
EDWARD STREET C.6
ETHEL TERRACE B.6
EXTONS GARDENS D.5
EXTONS ROAD D.5

FERMOY ART GALLERY A.2
FERRY .A.2
FERRY LANE A.2
FERRY STREET A.2
FOOTBALL GROUND D.4
FREESTONE COURT C.5
FRIARS FLEET B.5
FRIARS STREET B.5

GARDEN ROW C.5
GAYWOOD RIVER D.3
GAYWOOD ROAD D.2
GEORGE STREET C.1
GLADSTONE ROAD B.6
GLOBE HOTEL A.2
GOODWINS ROAD D.5
GRAHAM STREET D.5
GREENLAND FISHERY A.4
GREYFRIARS TOWER B.4
GUANOCK TERRACE C.6

HAMPTON COURT A.4
HARBOUR OFFICE A.2
HARDWICK ROAD C.6

HARECROFT GARDENS C.1
HARECROFT PARADE D.1
HAREWOOD DRIVE D.1
HAREWOOD PARADE D.1
HEXTABLE ROAD B.1
HIGH STREET A.2
HIGHGATE; D.2
HIGHGATE D.2
HILLINGTON SQUARE B.4
HOCKHAM STREET B.6
HOLCOMBE AVENUE E.5
HOMELAND ROAD D.1
HORSLEYS COURT C.6
HOSPITAL WALK C.4

JOHN KENNEDY ROAD B.1
JOHN STREET C.5

KETTLEWELL LANE C.1
KING STAITHE LANE A.3
KING STAITHE SQUARE A.3
KING STREET A.3
KING'S LYNN HIGH SCHOOL A.2
KING'S LYNN STATION C.3
KIRBY STREET C.2

LANSDOWNE STREET B.1
LIBRARY C.4
LITTLEPORT STREET C.2
LODGE LANE E.2
LOKE ROAD C.1
LONDON ROAD C.4

MARKET LANE A.2
MARKET STREET B.3
MARSH ROAD C.1
MARSHALL STREET C.2
MAYOR'S WALK D.4
METHODIST CHURCH C.4
MILLFIELDS C.3
MILLFLEET B.4

MILLHOUSES D.1
MILTON AVENUE D.2
MOUNT STREET E.4
MUSEUM B.3

NELSON STREET A.4
NEW CONDUIT STREET B.3
NORFOLK STREET B.3
NORTH END; B.1
NORTH EVERARD STREET C.5
NORTH STREET B.1

OLD BREWERY COURT C.5
OLD SUNWAY B.2

PAGE STAIR LANE A.2
PARADISE LANE B.2
PARADISE ROAD B.3
PARK AVENUE E.4
PAXTON TERRACE C.2
PEEL STREET D.5
PILOT STREET B.2
PLEASANT COURT C.5
POLICE STATION C.4
PORTLAND STREET B.3
PRINCE'S WAY E.3
PRIORY LANE A.4
PROVIDENCE STREET C.4
PURFLEET A.2
PURFLEET PLACE A.3
PURFLEET QUAY A.3
PURFLEET STREET A.3

QUEEN STREET A.3

RABY AVENUE D.1
RAILWAY ROAD C.2
RED MOUNT CHAPEL D.3
REGENT WAY B.3
ROBERT STREET C.6
ROMAN CATHOLIC CHURCH C.5

RUSSELL STREET D.5

ST. ANDREWS ROAD C.4
ST. ANNS FORT B.1
ST. ANNS HOUSE B.1
ST. ANNS STREET B.2
ST. GEORGES GUILDHALL A.2
ST. JAMES COURT B.3
ST. JAMES' END; C.4
ST. JAMES' PARK C.4
ST. JAMES' STREET B.4
ST. JOHNS CHURCH C.3
ST. JOHNS TERRACE C.3
ST. JOHNS WALK D.3
ST. MARGARETS CHURCH A.4
ST. MARGARETS LANE A.4
ST. MARGARETS PLACE A.4
ST. NICHOLAS CHAPEL B.1
ST. NICHOLAS STREET B.2
SATURDAY MARKET PLACE A.3
SEDGEFORD LANE B.3
SEVEN SISTERS CLOSE C.4
SEVEN SISTERS WALK D.4
SIDNEY DYE HOUSE E.5
SIDNEY STREET D.6
SILFIELD TERRACE E.4
SITE OF TOWN WALL D.3
SOMERVILLE ROAD D.6
SOUTH EVERARD STREET C.5
SOUTH GATES C.6
SOUTH LYNN PLAIN B.5
SOUTH QUAY A.4
SOUTH STREET C.4
SOUTHGATE STREET C.6
SPORTS HALL D.2
STANLEY STREET C.2
STONEGATE STREET B.4
SURREY STREET A.2
SWISS TERRACE E.3

TECHNICAL SCHOOL C.4

TENNIS COURTS C.3
TENNYSON AVENUE E.3
TENNYSON ROAD D.4
THE FRIARS B.5
THE WALKS D.3
THEATRE ROYAL B.4
THOMAS STREET C.5
THORESBY COLLEGE A.3
TOWER PLACE B.4
TOWER STREET B.3
TRENOWATHS PATH A.2
TUESDAY MARKET PLACE A.2

UNION LANE A.4

VALINGERS PLACE C.5
VALINGERS ROAD C.5
VANCOUVER AVENUE C.6
VANCOUVER HOUSE C.4
VANCOUVERS COURT B.3

WATER LANE A.2
WATERLOO STREET C.3
WELLESLEY STREET C.2
WHITEFRIARS GATEWAY B.5
WHITEFRIARS ROAD B.5
WHITEFRIARS SCHOOL B.5
WHITEFRIARS TERRACE B.5
WILLIAM STREET C.6
WINDSOR PARK D.5
WINDSOR ROAD C.5
WINDSOR TERRACE D.5
WINFARTHING AVENUE B.6
WISBECH ROAD B.6
WOOD STREET C.4
WOOTTON DRIFT C.2
WYATT STREET D.2

YORK ROAD D.5
YOXFORD CLOSE D.5

Watlington PE33

BABINGLEY CL. A1
BARNARDS LA. A1
BEECHWOOD CL. B2
BENNETT CL. A2
BRITTON CL. A1
BURE CL. A1

CECIL CL. A1
CHESTNUT CL. A2
CHURCH LA. B1
CHURCH RD. B1

DOWNHAM RD. B2

FAIRFIELD LA. A1
FEN RD. A2

GIPSY LA. A2
GLEBE AVE. B2
HAWTHORN CL. B2

JOHN DAVIS WAY A1

LACEY CL. A1
LARK RD. A1
LYNN RD. B1
MILL RD. B2

NENE RD. A1

ORCHARD CL. B2

PAIGE CL. A2
PLOUGH LA. B2

RECTORY LA. A2
ROWAN CL. B2

SCHOOL RD. A1
ST. PETERS RD. A1
STATION RD. A1
STIFFKEY CL. A1
STONE CL. A1

THIEVES' BRIDGE RD. B2
THOMAS CL. A2

WARREN CL. B2
WENSUM CL. A1

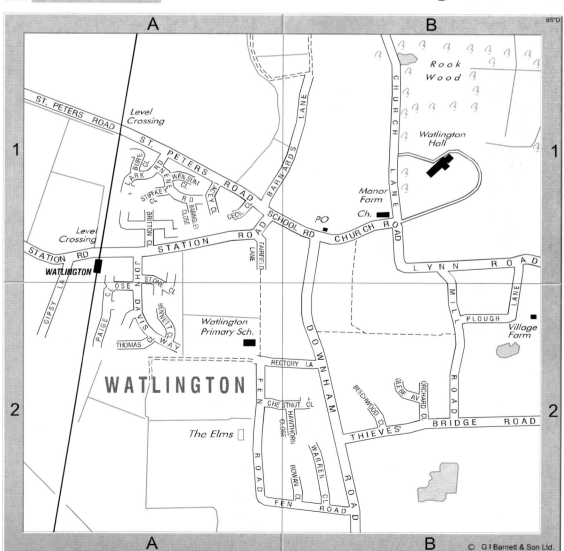

0.5 Km
0.25 Mile

King's Lynn

NARBOROUGH

BLACKSMITHS WAY A.1

CHALK LANE B.2

DENNY'S WALK A.1
DENNY'S WALK A.2
DOWNHAM DROVE B.1

EASTFIELDS B.2

LOW ROAD B.2

MAIN ROAD A.1
MEADOW CLOSE A.1
MEADOW ROAD A.2

NARBOROUGH ROAD A.1
NARFORD ROAD B.1

OLD VICARAGE PARK A.1

RIVER CLOSE A.1

WESTFIELDS A.2

© G I Barnett & Son Ltd.

Swaffham....*map on facing page*

ADASTRAL PLACE C.3
ADMIRALS WAY D.5
ALDISS CLOSE D.5
AMHERST CLOSE C.5
ASH CLOSE B.3

BACK TERRACE B.2
BARTON CLOSE C.6
BEACHAMWELL ROAD A.5
BEARS LANE B.2
BEECH CLOSE C.4
BLAKE COURT C.5
BOTWRIGHT DRIVE C.5
BRADEWELL PLACE C.4
BRANCASTER WAY B.6
BRANDON CLOSE C.5
BRANDON ROAD C.6
BROCKS ROAD B.2
BUCKENHAM ROAD B.6

CAPTAIN CLOSE C.3
CARTER CLOSE C.5
CASTLE ACRE ROAD B.1
CLEY ROAD A.6-B.5
COPPER HALL B.4
CORONATION GROVE B.3
COUHE CLOSE C.2
COURT FIELDS B.5
CROMWELL CLOSE D.5
CYGNET WALK C.5

DULGATE LANE D.4

FILBY ROAD B.6

GLASBURY WALK C.5
GLOBE HILL B.4
GOODRICK PLACE C.4
GORDON TERRACE C.4
GREEN WAY B.2
GREENHOE PLACE B.4

HAMILTON CLOSE C.4
HASPALLS ROAD B.4
HEATHLANDS D.5
HICKLING CLOSE C.6
HILLSIDE D.4
HILTON COURT C.3
HOLKHAM AVENUE B.6
HOLLYWELL GARDENS B.3
HOVETON DRIVE B.6

ICENI DRIVE C.5

KESTREL CLOSE C.5
KING STREET B.3

LAWRENCE WAY A.3
LEE WARNER ROAD C.5
LONDON STREET C.4
LONG LANE C.3
LONGFIELDS C.3
LOVE LANE C.3
LOW ROAD A.2
LYNN ROAD A.3
LYNN STREET B.3

MANGATE STREET C.3
MANOR WAY C.2
MARKET PLACE B.3
MERRYWEATHER ROAD C.5
MILL FARM NURSERIES B.5
MILL LANE C.5
MONTAGU CLOSE C.4
MOUNT CLOSE A.3

NELSON CRESCENT D.5
NEW SPORLE ROAD C.1
NICHOLAS HAMMOND WAY C.4
NORTH PICKENHAM ROAD C.4
NORTHFIELD ROAD C.2
NORTHWELL PLACE C.2
NORTHWELL POOL ROAD C.3
NORWICH ROAD C.3

OAKLEIGH DR. A.3
OAKS CLOSE C.5
OAKS DRIVE C.5
ORCHARD PLACE B.4
ORFORD ROAD C.2
ORMESBY DRIVE B.6
OULTON CLOSE B.6

PARTRIDGE GROVE C.5
PEDDARS VALE D.4
PEDLAR'S GROVE C.3
PIT LANE C.3
PLEASANT ROW C.4
PLOWRIGHT PLACE B.3
POINT DRIVE C.5

PRINCESS STREET A.3
PROVIDENCE TERRACE B.3

QUEEN STREET B.4

RANWORTH CLOSE B.6
ROCKLAND CLOSE B.6
ROLLESBY AVENUE B.6
ROMAN CRESCENT C.5

SALHOUSE DRIVE B.6
SANDRINGHAM WAY C.5
SAXON COURT D.5
SHEPHERDS FOLD C.5
SHOEMAKERS LANE A.4
SHOULDHAM LANE A.3
SOUTHLANDS B.5
SPINNERS CLOSE B.3
SPINNERS LANE B.2
SPORLE ROAD C.3
ST. GUTHAC CLOSE C.1
ST. JOHN'S COURT C.4
ST. MAGDALEN WAY C.5
STATION STREET B.2
STATION YARD B.2
STEEPLE VIEW B.4
STRATTON CLOSE C.5
SURLINGHAM DRIVE B.6
SUTTON ROAD B.6
SWAFFHAM BY-PASS B.1

THE CRESCENT C.4
THE OAKLANDS C.5

THE PADDOCKS B.4
THE PIGHTLE C.4
THEATRE STREET B.4
TOWER MEADOW C.2
TUMBLER HILL C.2
TURBINE WAY B.1

UPTON DRIVE B.6

VALENTINE BARKER COURT B.5
VIKING CLOSE D.5

WARSTADE WAY B.4
WATTON ROAD C.5
WEST ACRE ROAD A.1
WEST FIELD ROAD B.4
WHITE CROSS ROAD B.4
WHITSANDS ROAD A.3
WOLFERTON DRIVE B.6
WROXHAM AVENUE C.6

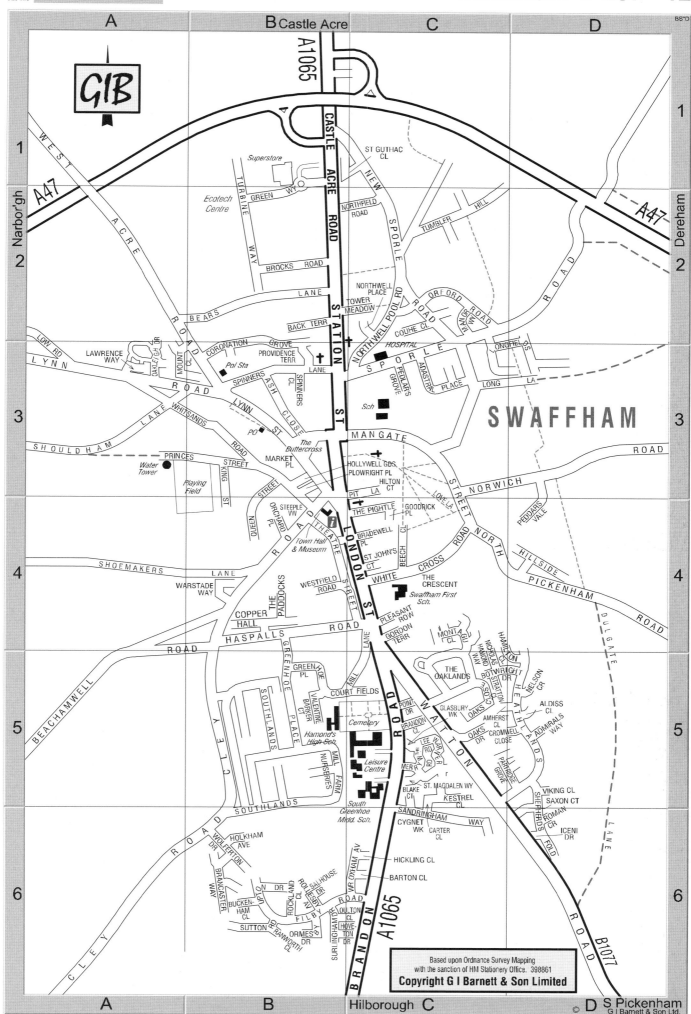

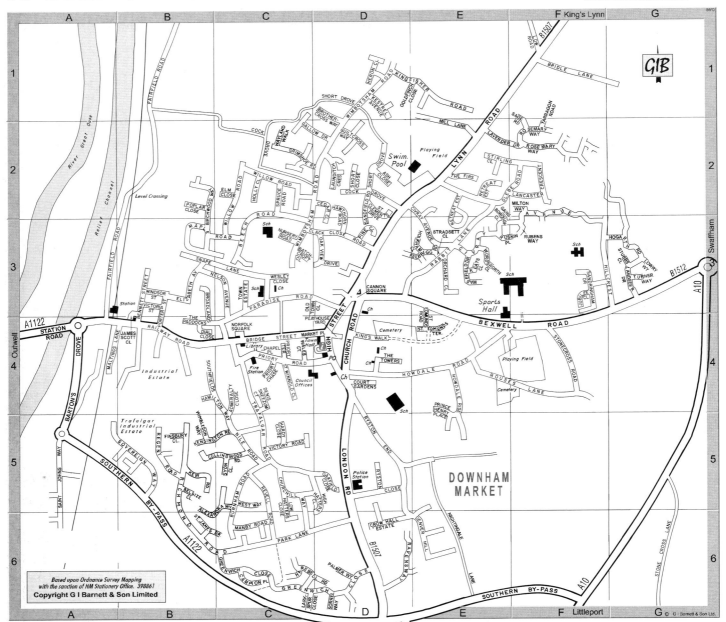

ADMIRALTY CLOSE C.4	FAIRFIELD ROAD B.1	LONDON ROAD D.5	RABBIT LANE E.3	STUBBS CLOSE G.3
ALEXANDRA WAY B.5	FELBRIGG ROAD E.3	LOW HATTERS CLOSE C.5	RAILWAY ROAD B.4	SYON CLOSE C.5
ASH CLOSE D.2	FINSBURY CLOSE B.5	LOW ROAD F.1	RAVENSWAY WAY D.6	
	GAINSBOROUGH CLOSE E.2	LOWRY WAY G.3	REGENT CLOSE B.5	TARRAGON ROAD F.2
BARTONS DROVE A.5	GALLOW DRIVE D.2	LYNN ROAD E.2	RETREAT ESTATE E.2	THE FIRS E.2
BATCHCROFT CLOSE C.3	GLEBE ROAD E.2		REVELL ROAD C.5	THE PADDOCKS B.4
BEECH ROAD C.3	GOLDFINCH CLOSE E.1	MALTINGS LANE A.4	RICHMOND ROAD B.5	THE TOWERS D.4
BELSIZE CLOSE B.5	GREENWICH CLOSE C.6	MANBY ROAD C.6	ROSEMARY WAY F.2	TOWN ESTATE C.3
BENNETT STREET B.3	GRIMSHOE ROAD C.2	MAPLE ROAD B.3	ROUSES LANE E.4	TRAFALGER ROAD C.5
BEXWELL ROAD E.4	GUILTCROSS WAY D.2	MARKET PLACE D.4	RUBENS WAY F.3	TURNER WAY G.3
BIRCHWOOD WAY B.2		MILL LANE E.2	RUSKIN PLACE E.3	
BRIDGE STREET C.4	HAMILTON WAY C.4	MILTON WAY F.2	RYSTON CLOSE D.5	VICTORIA STREET B.3
BRIDLE LANE F.1	HARDY CLOSE C.5		RYSTON END D.5	VICTORY ROAD C.5
BROADLANDS B.3	HAWTHORN ROAD D.3	NELSON AVENUE C.3		
BROTHERCROSS WAY D.1	HERON CLOSE D.1	NIGHTINGALE LANE E.6	ST. CLEMENTS DNVE D.2	WALES COURT C.4
BURNHAM ROAD C.5	HIGH HATTERS CLOSE C.5	NILE ROAD C.5	ST. EDMUNDS ROAD E.4	WAYLAND WALK C.2
	HIGH STREET D.4	NORFOLK SQUARE C.4	ST. EDMUNDS TERRACE E.4	WESLEY CLOSE C.3
CAMPION PLACE C.6	HILLCREST G.3	NURSERY ROAD C.3	ST. JAMES DRIVE B.6	WEST WAY C.5
CANNON SQUARE D.2	HOGARTH ROAD G.3		ST. JOHNS WAY A.5	WILLOW ROAD C.2
CEDAR CLOSE D.2	HOLLY CLOSE C.2	OAK VIEW DRIVE D.3	ST. WINNOLD CLOSE C.4	WIMBLEDON WAY B.5
CHAPEL PLACE C.4	HOWDALE RISE E.4	OAKFIELD CLOSE D.5	SAGE ROAD F.1	WIMBOTSHAM ROAD D.1
CHURCH ROAD D.4	HOWDALE ROAD E.4	OLD TOWN CLOSE C.3	SANDFIELD ROAD D.2	WINDSOR STREET B.3
CHURCHILL WAY C.5		ORCHARD CLOSE E.3	SANDRINGHAM DNVE F.3	WORDSWORTH CLOSE E.3
CIVRAY AVENUE E.2	JAMES SCOTT CLOSE B.3		SHORT CLOSE D.2	
CLACK CLOSE ROAD D.3	JUBILEE CLOSE F.3	PALMER WAY D.6	SHORT DROVE D.2	
COCK DROVE D.2		PARADISE ROAD C.3	SNAPE LANE B.3	
COLLINGWOOD ROAD C.5	KEATS CLOSE E.3	PARK LANE C.5	SORREL WAY D.6	
COURT GARDENS D.4	KENSINGTON ROAD B.5	PINE CLOSE D.3	SOUTHERN BY-PASS B.5	
CROW HALL ESTATE D.6	KESTREL AVENUE D.1	PLAYHOUSE YARD D.4	SOUTHFIELDS B.4	
	KEW ROAD B.5	POPLAR CLOSE B.2	SOVEREIGN WAY B.5	
DENIS SNEEZUM COURT C.4	KINGFISHER ROAD D.1	PORTER STREET B.3	SPRUCE ROAD C.2	
DENVER HILL E.6	KINGS WALK D.4	PRINCE HENRY PLACE E.4	STATION ROAD A.4	
DIAL CLOSE B.4		PRIORY CHASE C.4	STIRLING CLOSE E.2	
ELIZABETH AVENUE B.3	LANCASTER CRESCENT F.2	PRIORY ROAD C.4	STONE CROSS LANE G.6	
ELM CLOSE C.2	LANDSEER DRIVE G.3	PRIORY TERRACE C.4	STONECROSS ROAD F.4	
	LAUNDITCH CRESENT D.2		STRADSETT CLOSE E.3	

0.5 Km
0.25 Mile

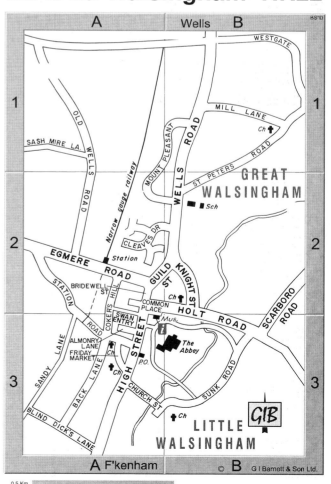

Based upon Ordnance Survey Mapping with the sanction of HM Stationery Office. 398861
Copyright G I Barnett & Son Limited

© G I Barnett & Son Ltd.

Gt. & Lt. Walsingham *NR22*

© G I Barnett & Son Ltd.

0.5 Km
0.25 Mile

0.5 Km
0.25 Mile

ANCHOR LANE B.2	CROWN LANE C.3	GROVE ROAD D.4	MARKET LANE B.4	POLKA PLACE C.4	STRATTON PLACE C.2
			MARSH LANE C.3	POLKA ROAD C.3	
BASES LANE A.2	DOGGER LANE B.2	HIGH STREET C.3	MARYLAND C.3		TEMPLES COURT A.2
BEACH ROAD B.1	EAGLES COURT (4) ...B.2	HOLKHAM ROAD A.2	MASSEYS YARD C.4	RAMMS COURT C.3	THE BOWLING GREEN .C.4
BLACKHORSE YARD ...B.2	EAST END C.2	HONEYMOON ROW ...C.3	MILL COURT B.3	RED LION YARD (1) ...B.2	THE BUTTLANDS B.3
BLUEBELL GARDENS ...C.3			MILL ROAD A.3	ROSE S COURT C.3	THE QUAY B.2
BOATMANS ROW B.2	FAKENHAM ROAD B.4	INVADERS COURT C.2	MINDHAMS YARD B.2	RUSSELL CLOSE A.3	THEATRE ROAD B.2
BOLTS CLOSE C.3	FLINT DRIFT B.4				TUNNS YARD B.2
BRIGG SQUARE B.2	FREEMAN STREET B.2	JICKLINGS YARD B.2	NEILSON CLOSE D.3	SHOP LANE C.2	TWO FURLONG HILL ...B.3
BURNT STREET B.4		JOLLY SAILOR YARD ..C.2	NEWGATES LANE B.2	SOUTHGATE CLOSE ...B.3	
	GALES COURT B.3		NORTHFIELD AVENUE ..C.3	STAITHE STREET C.2	WARHAM ROAD D.4
CHANCERY LANE C.3	GALES ROAD B.2	KNITTING NEEDLE LANE C.3	NORTHFIELD CRESCENT D.3	STANDARD ROAD C.2	WAVENEY CLOSE C.4
CHAPEL YARD B.2	GAMLE SQUARE (3) ...B.2		NORTHFIELD LANE C.3	STANDARD YARD C.2	WESTFIELD AVENUE ..A.3
CHURCH PLAIN C.3	GLEBE ROAD B.2	LEYLANDS YARD A.2	NORTHFIELD WAYE ...D.2	STAR YARD B.2	WHALEBONE YARD ...C.3
CHURCH STREET C.4	GREAT EASTERN WAY .C.3	LUGGER YARD B.2		STATION ROAD C.3	
CLUBB LANE B.2	GREEN DRAGON LANE ..C.3		PARK ROAD B.3	STEARMANS YARD B.2	
CROFT YARD C.2	GREENWAY LANE B.3	MALTHOUSE PLACE (2) .B.2	PLUMMERS HILL B.3	STIFFKEY ROAD D.4	

Fakenham....*map on facing page*

ARTHUR ROAD A.1	CASLON CLOSE B.2	CRAMER COURT C.2	FAYRE GREEN C.3	GREAT EASTERN WAY ..C.3	HAYES LANE A.3
	CATTLE MARKET ST. ...B.4		FIELD LANE B.2	GREEN COURT D.3	HEATH LANE E.3
BACK STREET A.4	CHAPPEL HILL A.2	DAIRY FARM CLOSE ...B.2	FISHER ROAD A.2	GREENWAY CLOSE B.2	HEATH RISE D.3
BARBERS LANE E.3	CHARLES ROAD C.2	DEREHAM ROAD A.4	FOLLY COURT D.3	GREENWAY LANE B.2	HEATH WAY E.3
BARONS CLOSE C.3	CHURCH LANES B.3	DIGBY DRIVE B.2	FOXGLOVE CLOSE E.4	GREENWAY PARK B.2	HEATHER BARROW CT. .D.3
BARONS HALL LANE ...A.2	CLARENDON ROAD ...A.2	DRIFTLANDS C.2		GROVE LANE C.1	HEMPTON ROAD B.4
BRACKEN CLOSE E.3	CLAYPIT LANE B.2	ECKERSLEY DRIVE A.1	GARROOD DRIVE D.2	GWYN CRESCENT E.2	HERON CLOSE D.3
BRAMBLE COURT D.4	CLIPBUSH LANE E.2	EDINBURGH DRIVE ...C.2	GEORGE EDWARDS RD .D.2		HIGH TERRACE B.2
BRIDGE STREET B.3	CLOVER WAY D.3	EDMONDSON WALK ..D.3	GLADSTONE ROAD B.3	HALL CLOSE C.3	HIGHFIELD ROAD B.3
BUCKENHAM CLOSE ...C.2	CONSTITUTION HILL ...B.3	ELIZABETH AVENUE ...C.2	GOGGS MILL ROAD ...A.3	HALL STAITHE B.3	HOLT ROAD C.3
BUTCHERS LANE B.3	COPPER BEECH CL. C.2	ENTERPRISE WAY D.2	GORSE CLOSE E.4	HARP CLOSE B.2	HORNS ROW A.4

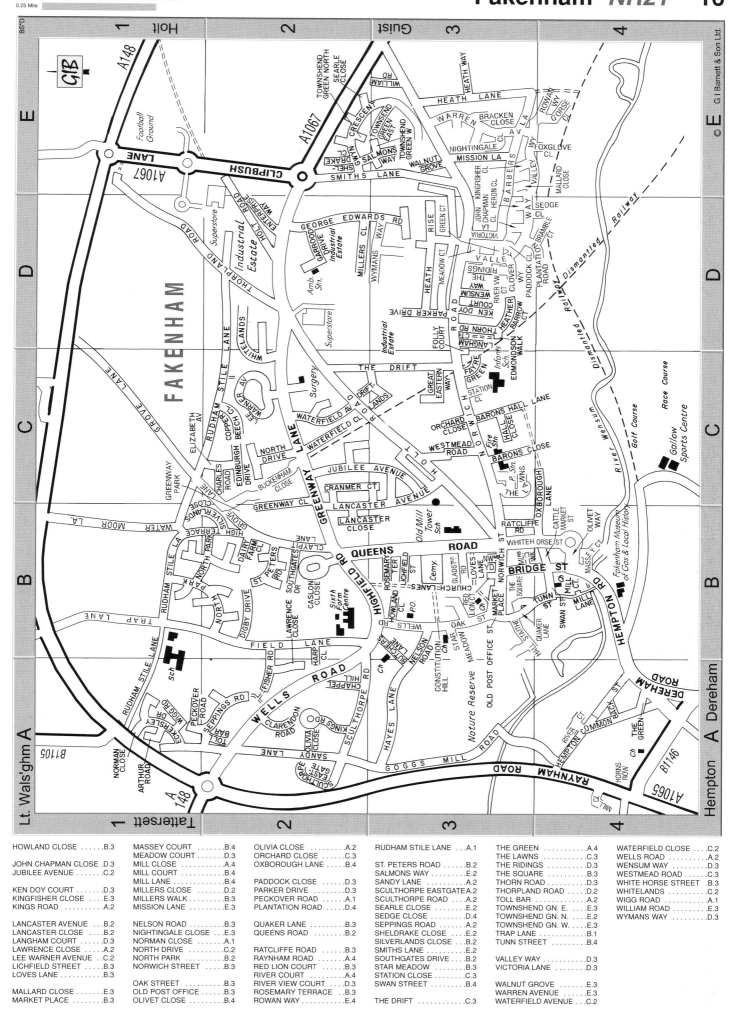

© G I Barnett & Son Ltd.

HOWLAND CLOSE B.3	MASSEY COURT B.4	OLIVIA CLOSE A.2	RUDHAM STILE LANE . . .A.1
	MEADOW COURT D.3	ORCHARD CLOSE C.3	
JOHN CHAPMAN CLOSE .D.3	MILL CLOSE A.4	OXBOROUGH LANE B.4	ST. PETERS ROAD B.2
JUBILEE AVENUE C.2	MILL COURT B.4		SALMONS WAY E.2
	MILL LANE B.4	PADDOCK CLOSE D.3	SANDY LANE A.2
KEN DOY COURT D.3	MILLERS CLOSE D.2	PARKER DRIVE D.3	SCULTHORPE EASTGATE A.2
KINGFISHER CLOSE E.3	MILLERS WALK B.3	PECKOVER ROAD A.1	SCULTHORPE ROAD A.2
KINGS ROAD A.2	MISSION LANE E.3	PLANTATION ROAD D.4	SEARLE CLOSE E.2
			SEDGE CLOSE D.4
LANCASTER AVENUE . .B.2	NELSON ROAD B.3	QUAKER LANE B.3	SEPPINGS ROAD A.2
LANCASTER CLOSE B.2	NIGHTINGALE CLOSE E.3	QUEENS ROAD B.2	SHELDRAKE CLOSE E.2
LANGHAM COURT D.3	NORMAN CLOSE A.1		SILVERLANDS CLOSE B.2
LAWRENCE CLOSE A.2	NORTH DRIVE C.2	RATCLIFFE ROAD B.3	SMITHS LANE E.2
LEE WARNER AVENUE . .C.2	NORTH PARK B.2	RAYNHAM ROAD A.4	SOUTHGATES DRIVE B.2
LICHFIELD STREET B.3	NORWICH STREET B.3	RED LION COURT B.3	STAR MEADOW B.3
LOVES LANE B.3		RIVER COURT A.4	STATION CLOSE C.3
	OAK STREET B.3	RIVER VIEW COURT D.3	SWAN STREET B.4
MALLARD CLOSE E.3	OLD POST OFFICE B.3	ROSEMARY TERRACE B.3	
MARKET PLACE B.3	OLIVET CLOSE B.4	ROWAN WAY E.4	THE DRIFT C.3

THE GREEN A.4	WATERFIELD CLOSE C.2
THE LAWNS C.3	WELLS ROAD A.2
THE RIDINGS D.3	WENSUM WAY D.3
THE SQUARE B.3	WESTMEAD ROAD C.3
THORN ROAD D.3	WHITE HORSE STREET .B.3
THORPLAND ROAD D.2	WHITELANDS C.2
TOLL BAR A.2	WIGG ROAD A.1
TOWNSHEND GN. E. E.3	WILLIAM ROAD E.3
TOWNSHEND GN. N. E.2	WYMANS WAY D.3
TOWNSHEND GN. W. E.2	
TRAP LANE B.1	
TUNN STREET B.4	
VALLEY WAY D.3	
VICTORIA LANE D.3	
WALNUT GROVE E.3	
WARREN AVENUE E.3	
WATERFIELD AVENUE . . .C.2	

17 Blakeney *NR25*

0.5 Km
0.25 Mile

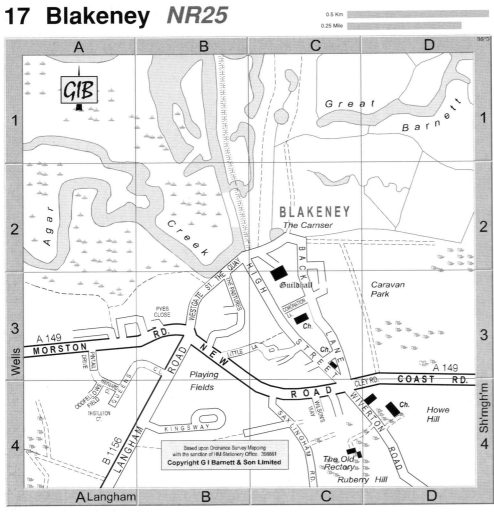

Cley next the Sea *NR25*

0.5 Km
0.25 Mile

0.5 Km
0.25 Mile

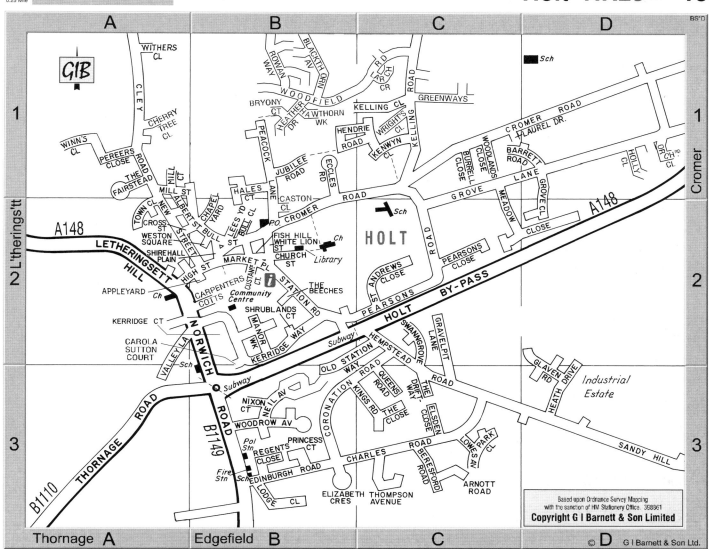

ALBERT STREET A.2
APPLEYARD B.2
ARNOTT ROAD C.3

BARRETT ROAD D.1
BERESFORD ROAD C.3
BLACKTHORN AVENUE B.1
BRYONY COURT B.1
BULL CLOSE B.2
BULL STREET B.2
BURRELL CLOSE C.1

CAROLA SUTTON COURT B.2
CARPENTERS COTTAGES B.2
CASTON CLOSE B.2
CHAPEL YARD B.2
CHARLES ROAD C.3
CHERRY TREE CLOSE A.1
CHURCH STREET B.2
CLEY ROAD A.1
CORONATION ROAD B.3
CROMER ROAD B.2
CROSS STREET A.2

CUSTANCE COURT B.2

ECCLES ROAD B.1
EDINBURGH ROAD B.3
ELIZABETH CRESCENT B.3
ELSDEN CLOSE C.3
FISH HILL B.2

GLAVEN ROAD D.3
GRAVELPIT LANE C.2
GREENWAYS C.1
GROVE CLOSE D.1
GROVE LANE C.1

HALES COURT B.1
HAWTHORN WALK B.1
HEATH DRIVE D.3
HEATHER DRIVE B.1
HEMPSTEAD ROAD C.2
HENDRIE ROAD B.1
HIGH STREET B.2
HOLLY CLOSE D.1
HOLT BY-PASS C.2

JUBILEE ROAD B.1

KELLING CLOSE C.1
KELLING ROAD C.1
KENWYN CLOSE C.1
KERRIDGE COURT B.2
KERRIDGE WAY B.2
KINGS ROAD C.3

LARCH CRESCENT C.1
LAUREL DRIVE C.1
LEES YARD B.2
LETHERINGSETT HILL A.2
LODGE CLOSE B.3
LOWES AVENUE C.3

MANOR WALK B.2
MARKET PLACE B.2
MEADOW CLOSE C.2
MILL COURT A.1
MILL STREET A.1

NEIL AVENUE B.3

NEW STREET A.2
NIXON COURT B.3
NORWICH ROAD B.2

OLD STATION WAY C.2
ORCHARD CLOSE D.1

PARK CLOSE C.3
PEACOCKS LANE B.1
PEARSONS CLOSE C.2
PEARSONS ROAD C.2
PEREERS CLOSE A.1
PRINCESS COURT B.3

QUEENS ROAD C.3

REGENTS CLOSE B.3
ROWAN WAY B.1

SANDY HILL D.3
SHIREHALL PLAIN B.2
SHRUBLANDS COURT B.2
ST. ANDREWS CLOSE C.2

STATION ROAD B.2
SWANNGROVE C.2

THE BEECHES B.2
THE CLOSE C.3
THE DRIFTWAY C.3
THE FAIRSTEAD A.1
THOMPSON AVENUE C.3
THORNAGE ROAD A.3
TOWN CLOSE A.2

VALLEY LANE A.2

WESTON SQUARE B.2
WHITE LION STREET B.2
WINN'S CLOSE A.1
WITHERS CLOSE A.1
WOODFIELD ROAD B.1
WOODFLANDS CLOSE C.1
WOODROW AVENUE B.3
WRIGHT'S CLOSE C.1

0.5 Km
0.5 Mile

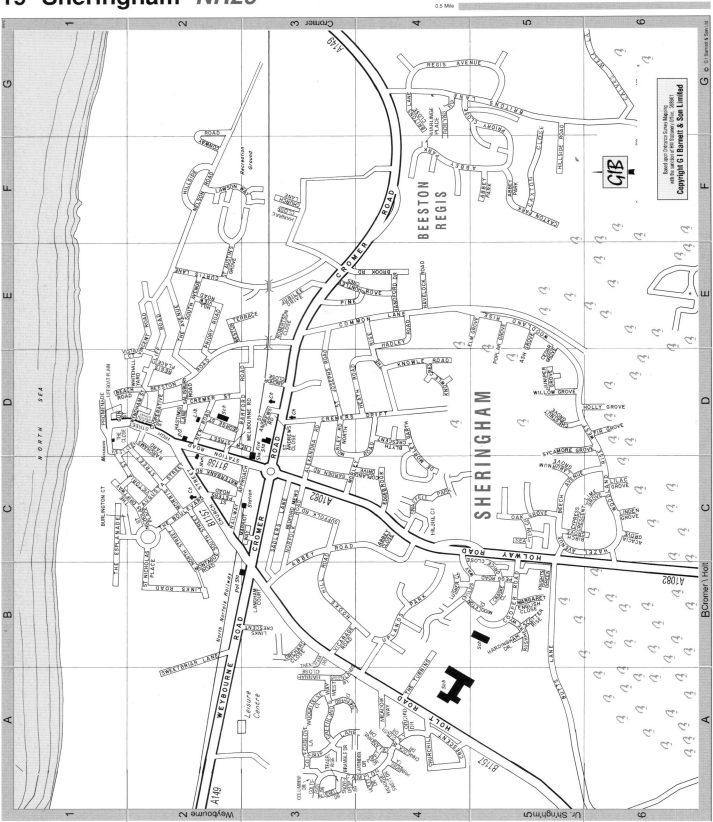

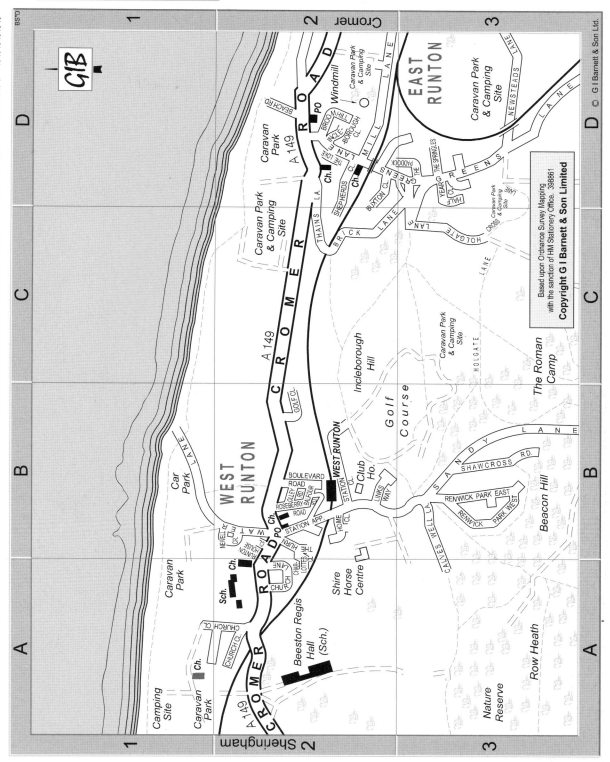

Sheringham...*map on facing page*

1 Km
0.5 Mile

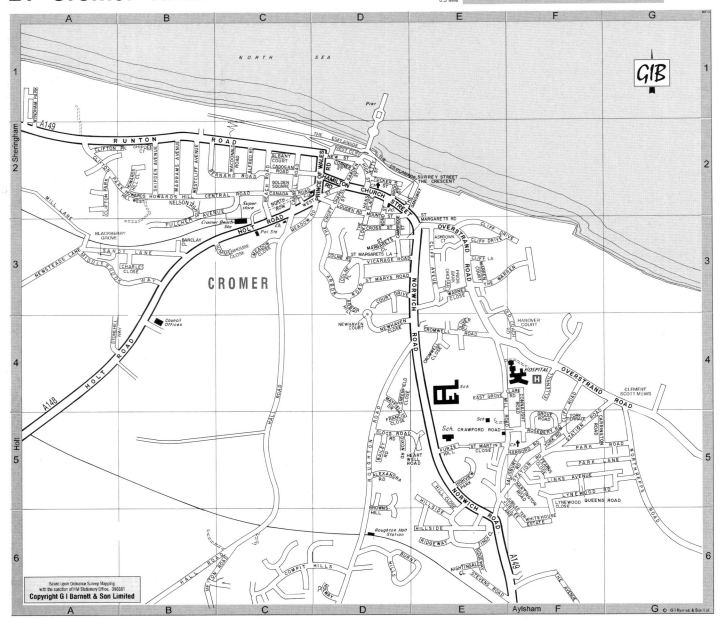

ALBANY COURT C.2
ALEXANDRA ROAD D.5
ALFRED ROAD C.2
ARBOR HILL D.3
ARBOR ROAD D.3
ASHDOWN COURT E.3

BAILEY ROAD D.5
BARCLAY CLOSE B.3
BEACH ROAD C.2
BERNARD ROAD B.2
BLACKBERRY GROVE A.3
BLOGG ROAD D.5
BOND STREET D.3
BROOK STREET D.2
BROWNSHILL D.5
BURNT HILLS D.6

CABBELL ROAD C.2
CADOGAN ROAD C.2
CAMBRIDGE STREET D.3
CANADA ROAD C.2
CARRINGTON ROAD F.5
CENTRAL ROAD B.2
CHAPEL STREET D.2
CHARLES CLOSE B.3
CHURCH STREET D.2
CLARE ROAD F.4
CLEMENT SCOTT MEWS G.4
CLIFF AVENUE E.3
CLIFF DRIVE E.3
CLIFF LANE E.3
CLIFF ROAD F.4

CLIFTON PARK A.2
COLNE PLACE D.3
COLNE ROAD D.3
COMPIT HILLS C.6
CONNAUGHT ROAD F.4
CORNER STREET D.2
COURT DRIVE D.3
CRAWFORD ROAD F.5
CROMWELL CLOSE E.4
CROMWELL ROAD E.4
CROSS STREET D.3

DIXON ROAD D.5

EAST GROVE E.4
ELLENHILL F.4
ESPLANADE D.2

FEARNS CLOSE F.5
FINCH CLOSE E.6
FRANCIS CLOSE D.5
FURZE HILL E.5

GARDEN STREET D.2
GOLDEN SQUARE C.2
GREENFIELD CLOSE D.4
GROVE ROAD F.5

HALL ROAD C.5
HAMILTON ROAD D.2
HANOVER COURT F.4
HANS PLACE D.2
HARBORD ROAD F.5

HARTINGTON ROAD F.5
HEART WELL ROAD E.5
HIGH STREET D.2
HIGHVIEW PARK E.5
HILL CLOSE E.5
HILLSIDE E.6
HOLT ROAD C.3
HOLWAY CLOSE D.6
HOWARDS HILL B.2
HOWARDS HILL CLOSE B.2
HOWARDS HILL WEST B.2

JETTY STREET D.2
JUBILEE LANE E.5
JUBILEE TERRACE F.6

LINKS AVENUE F.5
LOUDEN ROAD D.2
LYNEWOOD CLOSE F.5
LYNEWOOD ROAD F.5

MACDONALD ROAD C.2
MARRRAMS AVENUE B.2
MAYFIELD DRIVE D.4
MEADOW CLOSE C.3
MEADOW ROAD C.3
METTON ROAD B.6
MIDDLEBROOK WAY A.3
MILL LANE A.2
MILL ROAD E.4
MOUNT STREET D.2

NEW STREET D.2

NEWHAVEN CLOSE D.4
NEWHAVEN COURT D.4
NEWSTEADS LANE A.3
NIGHTINGALE CLOSE E.6
NORTH ROW C.2
NORTHREPPS ROAD G.5
NORWICH ROAD E.3

OLD COACH ROAD F.4
OLIVER COURT E.4
OVERSTRAND ROAD E.3

PARK LANE F.5
PARK ROAD F.5
PRINCE OF WALES ROAD ...D.2
PRIOR BANK ORCHARD E.3

QUEENS ROAD F.5

RIDGEWAY E.6
ROSEBERY ROAD F.5
ROUGHTON ROAD D.5
RUNTON ROAD B.2

ST. MARGARETS CLOSE D.3
ST. MARGARETS LANE D.3
ST. MARGARETS ROAD E.2
ST. MARTIN'S CLOSE E.5
ST. MARYS ROAD D.3
SALISBURY ROAD F.5
SANDY LANE A.3
SHIPDEN AVENUE B.2
SHIPDEN COURT B.2

STATION ROAD F.5
STEVENS ROAD E.6
STONEHILL WAY A.4
SUMMERHOUSE CLOSE C.3
SURREY STREET D.2

THE AVENUE F.6
THE CRESCENT E.2
THE CROFT D.2
THE GANGWAY D.2
THE LOKE D.3
THE WARREN E.3
TUCKER STREET D.2

VICARAGE ROAD D.3

WARNES CLOSE E.3
WARREN COURT E.3
WEST CLIFF D.2
WEST STREET C.2
WESTCLIFF AVENUE B.2
WHITEHOUSE ESTATE F.6
WYNDHAM PARK A.1

YORK ROAD F.5
YORK TERRACE F.5

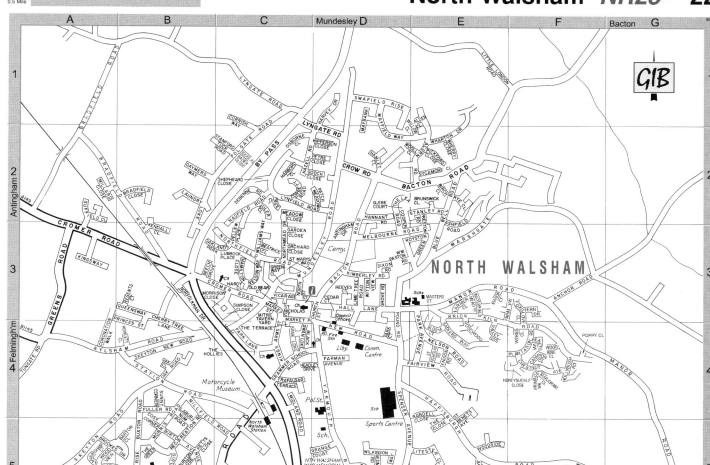

ACORN ROAD D.2	COSY CORNER B.5	HARBORD CLOSE C.2	MAYBANK D.1	PLUMBLY CLOSE D.6	SWAFIELD RISE D.1
ALDER CLOSE E.1	CRADLEWOOD ROAD ..E.5	HARDY CLOSE C.3	MAYFIELD WAY D.1	POPPY CLOSE F.4	SYCAMORE CLOSE E.2
ANCHOR ROAD F.3	CROMER ROAD A.3	HARMER CLOSE E.3	MEADOW CLOSE C.2	POUND ROAD D.3	
ANTINGHAM DRIVE ...D.3	CROW ROAD D.2	HARVEY DRIVE D.1	MELBOURNE ROAD ...D.3	PRESTON ROAD E.2	TENNISON ROAD E.4
ASHFIELD ROAD E.2		HAZELL ROAD C.2	MIDLAND ROAD C.4	PRIMROSE WALK F.4	THE CLOSE E.5
AYLSHAM ROAD A.4	DEBENNE ROAD C.2	HEADLEY DRIVE C.4	MILLARD CLOSE A.2	PRINCES STREET B.4	THE GREEN B.5
	DIXON ROAD D.3	HIPPERSON CLOSE ...D.2	MILLFIELD ROAD B.4		THE LEA D.2
BACTON ROAD E.2	DOUGLAS BADER CLOSE C.2	HOLLYBUSH ROAD F.4	MITRE TAVERN YARD ...C.3	QUEENSWAY B.3	THE TERRACE C.4
BAKER CLOSE E.5		HONEYSUCKLE CLOSE ..F.4	MORRIS ROAD B.5		THIRLBY ROAD D.5
BANK LOKE C.4	ELLINOR ROAD D.6	HOWLETT CLOSE B.4	MORRISON CLOSE ...C.3	RANDELL CLOSE E.4	TRAFALGAR TERRACE ..C.4
BANNINGHAM COURT ..A.5			MUNDERSLEY ROAD ..C.3	RECREATION ROAD B.5	TUNGATE ROAD A.4
BARTON CLOSE B.5	FAIRSTEAD CLOSE A.5	JULER CLOSE C.2		REDMAN ROAD D.5	
BEATRICE CLOSE C.3	FAIRVIEW ROAD E.4		NELSON ROAD E.4	REEVES COURT D.3	VALLEY GARDENS E.4
BEECH DRIVE B.3	FARM VIEW F.3	KENDAL CLOSE B.3	NELSON WAY C.3	REGENTS COURT B.3	VICARAGE STREET ...C.3
BENETS VIEW F.4	FARMAN AVENUE D.4	KETTS CLOSE B.5	NEW ROAD D.4	ROSEWOOD E.4	
BIRCH CLOSE E.2	FERN DRIVE F.4	KIMBERLEY ROAD D.3	NORFOLKMAN DRIVE ..B.3	ROYSTON GREEN E.3	W M PASTON ROAD ...D.3
BIRDS ROAD B.5	FIELD LANE E.6	KINGS ARMS STREET ..C.4	NORTH STREET C.3	RYE CLOSE E.2	WATERFIELD MEADOWS E.3
BLACK SWAN LOKE C.4	FOLGATE ROAD C.2	KINGSWAY A.3	NORTHFIELD ROAD ...C.3		WEAVERS' WAY E.6
BLOOM COURT E.4	FOXGLOVE CLOSE F.4		NORTHMEAD DRIVE ..C.3	SADLERS WAY E.4	WEBBS CLOSE F.4
BLUE BELL ROAD E.3	FULLER ROAD B.4	LABURNUM ROAD B.4	NORWICH ROAD B.6	ST. BENETS AVENUE ..E.4	WELLS AVENUE A.5
BRADFIELD CLOSE ...B.2	FURZE HILL DRIVE E.5	LAUNDRY LOKE B.2	NURSERY DRIVE C.5	ST. MARYS WAY C.3	WESTWICK DRIVE A.5
BRADFIELD ROAD A.2		LE GRICE CRESCENT ..D.6		ST. NICHOLAS COURT ..C.3	WHARTON DRIVE E.2
BRICK KILN ROAD E.3	GARDEN CLOSE C.3	LIME TREE ROAD D.3	OAK CLOSE B.4	ST. NICHOLAS ROAD ..E.4	WHERRY CLOSE E.2
BROOKES DRIVE A.5	GAYMERS WAY B.2	LITESTER CLOSE E.5	OAK ROAD B.4	SAMPSON ROAD D.5	WHITE HORSE COMMON F.5
BRUNSWICK CLOSE ...E.2	GLEBE COURT D.2	LITTLE LONDON ROAD ..E.1	OAKLANDS PARK B.3	SENDALL ROAD B.5	WILKINSON WAY C.3
BURTON AVENUE B.5	GOOCH CLOSE C.2	LONG BARROW DRIVE ..D.6	OLD BEAR COURT C.3	SHEPHEARD CLOSE ...C.2	WILLIAMS WAY C.3
BURTON CLOSE B.5	GRAMMAR SCHOOL RD ..C.4	LUBBOCK PLACE C.3	ORCHARD CLOSE C.3	SIMPSON CLOSE C.3	WILLOW CLOSE E.2
BUXTON ROAD B.5	GRANGE COURT D.5	LYNFIELD ROAD C.2	OSBORNE CLOSE C.2	SKEYTON NEW ROAD ..B.4	WITTON VIEW D.3
	GREENS ROAD A.3	LYNGATE ROAD C.1		SKEYTON ROAD A.5	WOOD VIEW A.5
CAMPION CLOSE F.4	GREENWAY CLOSE ...C.3		PAGE CLOSE C.2	SKEYTON VIEW B.5	WOODBINE CLOSE G.4
CEDAR COURT D.3	GROVE ROAD D.3	MAJORAM CLOSE F.4	PARK AVENUE E.4	SOUTH RISE B.5	WOODSIDE E.5
CHERRY TREE LANE ...B.3		MANOR COURT E.3	PARK COURT D.4	SPENSER AVENUE D.4	WOOLL CLOSE E.2
CHESTNUT AVENUE ...F.4	HADFIELD ROAD C.2	MANOR ROAD E.3	PARK LANE C.4	SPURDENS CRESCENT ..E.5	
CHURCH STREET C.3	HALL LANE D.3	MARJORAM CLOSE ...F.4	PATCH MEADOW D.2	STANFORD TUCK ROAD ..C.2	YARMOUTH ROAD D.4
COOPER ROAD D.2	HAMILTON CLOSE C.3	MARKET PLACE C.3	PELLEW PLACE C.3	STANLEY ROAD E.2	YOUNGMANS CLOSE ..D.5
CORBET ROAD C.2	HAMLET CLOSE D.2	MARKET STREET C.3	PETRE CLOSE D.2	STATION ROAD B.4	
CORNISH WAY C.1	HANNANT ROAD D.2	MARSHGATE E.3	PICKFORD CLOSE E.2	SUFFIELD CLOSE A.2	
CORONATION WALK ...A.4	HAPPISBURGH ROAD ..E.4	MASTERS COURT E.3	PLANTATION ROAD ...F.4	SUNNY CORNER B.4	

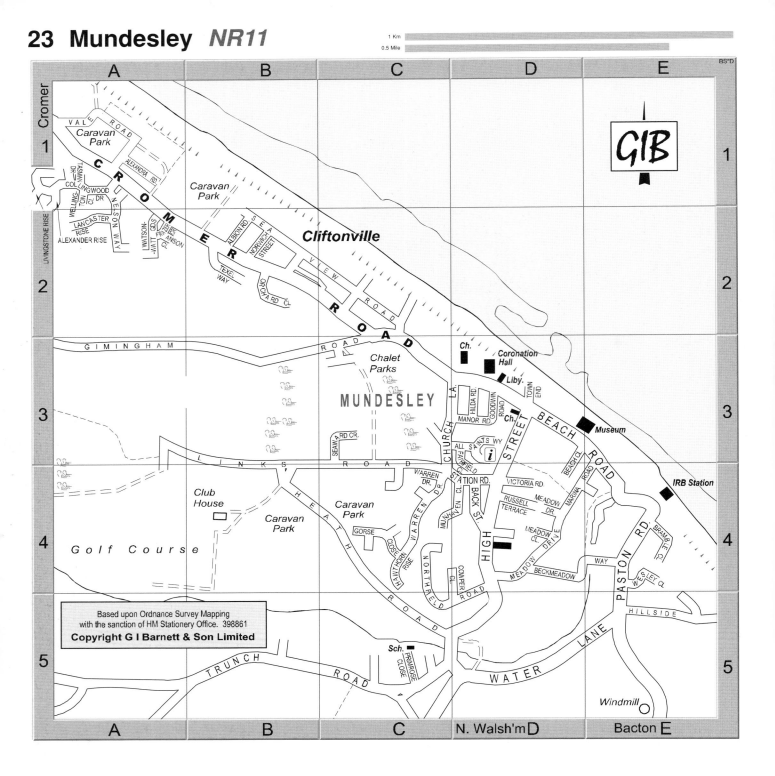

ALBION ROAD B2	FAIRFIELD CLOSE D3	MANOR ROAD D3	SEA VIEW ROAD B2
ALEXANDRA RISE A1	FRAZER CRESCENT A2	MARINA ROAD D4	SEAWARD CRESCENT C3
ALEXANDRA ROAD A1		MEADOW CLOSE D4	STATION ROAD D4
ALL SAINTS WAY D3	GIMNGHAM ROAD A3	MEADOW DRIVE D4	TASMAN DRIVE A1
ANSON CLOSE A2	GOODWIN ROAD D3	MUNHAVEN CLOSE C4	TEXEL WAY B2
	GORSE CLOSE C4		TOWN END D3
BACK STREET D4		NELSON WAY A1	TRUNCH ROAD B.5
BEACH CLOSE D4	HAWTHORN RISE C4	NORTHFIELD ROAD C4	
BEACH ROAD D3	HEATH ROAD B4-C5	NORWICH STREET B.2	VALE ROAD A1
BECKMEADOW WAY D4	HIGH STREET D4		VICTORIA ROAD D4
BRAMBLE CLOSE E.4	HILDA ROAD D3	ORCHARD CLOSE B.2	
	HILLSIDE E5		WARREN DRIVE C4
CHURCH LANE C3		PASTON ROAD E4	WATER LANE D5
COLLINGWOOD DRIVE A1	LANCASTER RISE A2	PRIMROSE CLOSE C.5	WATSON-WATT GARDENS A2
COWPER CLOSE D4	LINKS ROAD B3		WELLINGTON CLOSE A1
CROMER ROAD A1-C2	LIVINGSTONE RISE A.1	RUSSELL TERRACE D4	WESLEY CLOSE E.4

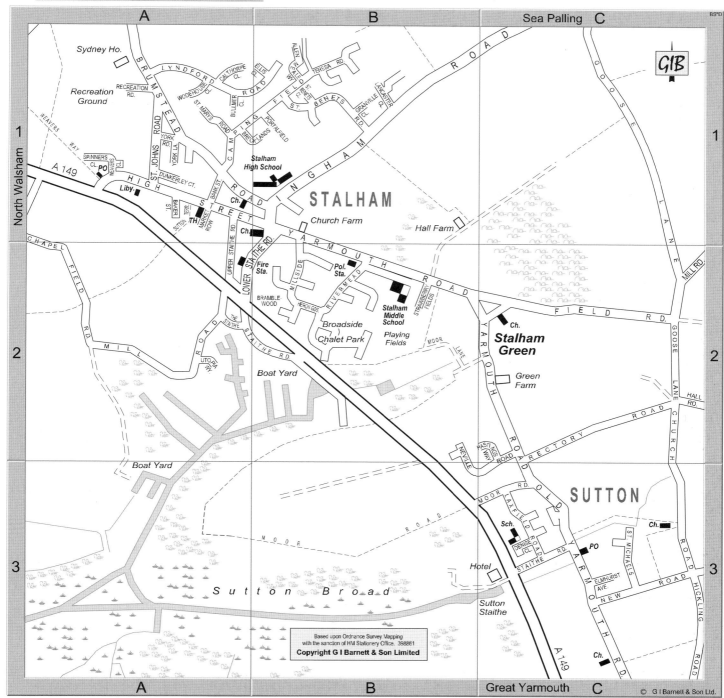

ALLEN MEALE WAY B.1

BAKER STREET A.1
BANK STREET A.1
BRAMBLEWOOD B.2
BRECKLANDS A.1
BRUMSTEAD ROAD A.1
BULLMER CLOSE A.1

CALTHORPE CLOSE A.1
CAMPING FIELDS ....
CHAPEL FIELDS ROAD A.2
CHURCH ROAD C.2

DENISE CLOSE C.3
DUNKERLEY COURT A.1

ELLIS COURT B.1
ELMHURST AVENUE C.3

FIELD ROAD C.2
GOOSE LANE C.1-C.2
GRANVILLE CLOSE B.1

HALL ROAD C.2
HASTINGS WAY C.2
HERON GARDENS B.2
HICKLING ROAD C.3
HIGH STREET A.1

INGHAM ROAD B.1

LANCASTER CLOSE B.1
LAXFIELD ROAD C.3

LOWER STAITHE ROAD A.2
LYNDFORD ROAD A.1
MARKET ROW A.1
MILL ROAD (STALHAM) A.2
MILL ROAD (SUTTON) C.2
MILLSIDE B.2
MOOR LANE (PATH) B.2
MOOR ROAD C.3

NEVILLE ROAD B.2
NEW ROAD C.3

OLD YARMOUTH ROAD C.3

PORTAFIELD B.1

RECREATION ROAD A.1

RECTORY ROAD C.2
RIVERMEAD B.2

SPINNERS CLOSE A.1
ST MICHAELS C.3
ST. BENETS CLOSE B.1
ST. BENETS ROAD B.1
ST. JOHNS ROAD A.1
ST. MARYS ROAD A.1
STAITHE ROAD (STALHAM) A.2
STAITHE ROAD (SUTTON) C.3
STALHAM B.1
STRAWBERRY FIELDS B.2
SUTTON C.3
SUTTON TERRACE A.1

TERESA ROAD B.1

THE STAITHE A.2

UPPER STAITHE ROAD A.2
UTOPIA WAY A.2
WEAVERS CLOSE A.1
WEAVERS WAY (PATH) A.1
WODEHOUSE CLOSE A.1

YARMOUTH ROAD B.1-C.2
YORK LANE A.1
YORK ROAD A.1

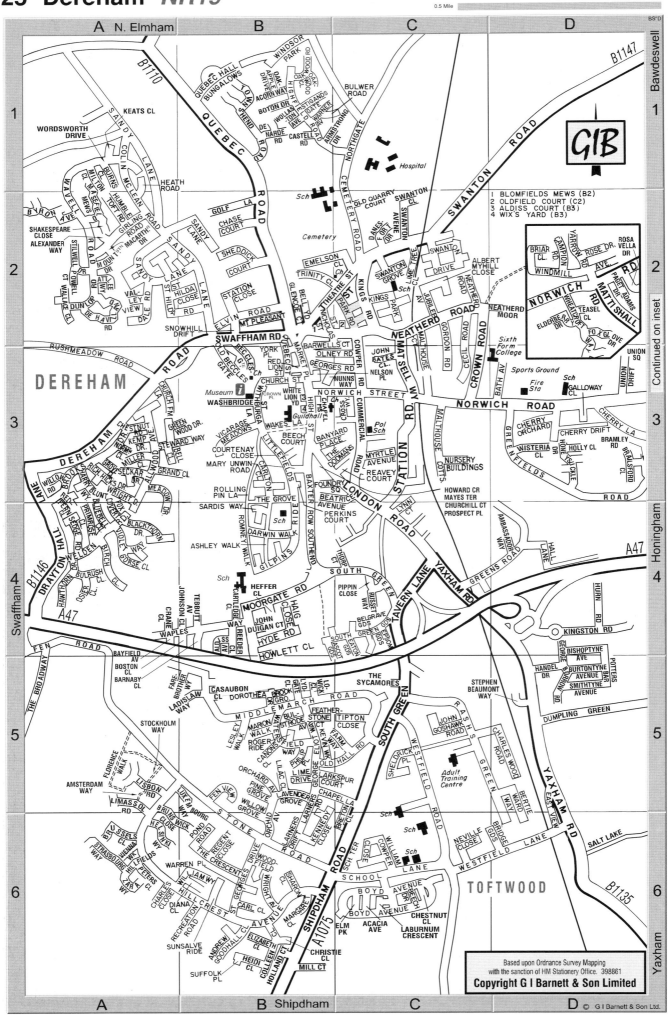

ACACIA AVENUE C.6
ACORN WAY B.1
ALBERT MYHILL CL. C.2
ALDISS AVENUE B.4
ALLWOOD AVENUE A.3
AMBASSADOR WAY D.4
AMSTERDAM WAY A.5
ANDREW GODALL CL. ..B.6
ARMSTRONG DRIVE C.1
ASCOT GARDENS B.4
ASHLEY WALK B.4
ATTLEE WAY A.2

BANYARD PLACE B.3
BARNABY CLOSE B.4
BARWELLS COURT B.3
BATH AVENUE D.3
BAXTER ROW B.3
BAYFIELD AVENUE A.4
BEATRICE AVENUE B.3
BECCLESGATE B.2
BEECH COURT B.3
BEECH DRIVE C.6
BELGRAVE GARDENS ..C.4
BELL CLOSE A.3
BELL YARD B.2
BERTIE WARD WAY ...D.5
BISHOPTYNE AVENUE .D.4
BLOMFIELDS MEWS (1) .B.2
BOSTON CLOSE B.4
BOSTON DRIVE B.1
BOYD AVENUE C.6
BRAILSFORD CLOSE ...D.3
BRAMLEY ROAD D.3
BRETON CLOSE C.6
BRIDGE GARDENS D.6
BROOK GROVE B.5
BROOKS DRIVE A.3
BRUNSWICK CLOSE ...A.5
BRUSSELS CLOSE A.6
BULSTRODE AVENUE ..B.5
BULWER ROAD C.1
BURNS CLOSE A.1
BURTONTYNE AVENUE .D.5
BYRON AVE. A.2

CANONS CLOSE B.5
CARL CLOSE B.6
CARLTON CLOSE B.3
CARTLEDGE CLOSE ...B.4
CASAUBON CLOSE B.5
CASTELL ROAD B.1
CECIL ROAD C.3
CEMETERY ROAD C.2
CHAPEL LANE B.5
CHAPEL MEWS B.3
CHARLES CLOSE A.6

CHARLES WOOD RD ..D.5
CHASE COURT B.2
CHERRY DRIFT D.3
CHERRY LANE D.3
CHERRY ORCHARD ...D.3
CHESTNUT CLOSE C.6
CHESTNUT ROAD A.3
CHRISTIE CLOSE B.6
CHURCH STREET B.3
CHURCHILL COURT ...C.3
COLIN MCLEAN ROAD .A.1
COLLEAN CLOSE A.1
COMMERCIAL ROAD ..C.3
COURTENAY CLOSE ...B.3
COWPER ROAD C.3
CRANE CLOSE A.4
CROSS WAY C.3
CROWN ROAD C.3

DALE ROAD A.2
DANESFORT DRIVE ...C.2
DARWIN WALK B.4
DE HAVILLAND ROAD .A.2
DE NARDE ROAD B.1
DEREHAM ROAD A.3
DIANA CLOSE B.6
DOROTHEA DRIVE ...B.5
DRAYTON HALL LANE .A.4
DUMPLING GREEN D.5
DUNLOP ROAD B.3

EAST VIEW D.5
EATON GARDENS C.4
ELDERBERRY DRIVE .INSET
ELIZABETH CLOSE B.6
ELM PARK B.6
ELVIN ROAD B.2
EMELSON CLOSE B.2
EPSOM GARDENS C.4

FAREBROTHER WAY ...B.5
FARM WAY B.5
FEATHERSTONE CT ...B.5
FEN ROAD A.4
FEN VIEW B.5
FLORENCE WALK A.5
FOUNDRY SQUARE ...B.3
FOXGLOVE DRIVE ...INSET

GALLOWAY CLOSE D.3
GEORGE BORROW RD .D.4
GEORGE ELIOT WAY ..B.4
GEORGES ROAD B.3
GILPINS RIDE B.4
GIRLING ROAD A.2
GLENCOE COURT B.2
GOLF LANE B.2

GORDON ROAD C.2
GRAND CLOSE A.3
GREENFIELDS ROAD ..D.3
GREENS ROAD C.4
GREENWOOD DRIVE ..A.3
GROVE CLOSE A.3

HAIG CLOSE B.4
HALL LANE D.4
HANDEL DRIVE D.5
HEATH ROAD A.1
HEFFER CLOSE B.4
HEIDI CLOSE B.6
HELSINKI WAY A.6
HIGH STREET B.3
HIGHFIELD ROAD B.1
HILL FIELDS A.6
HILLCREST AVENUE ..A.6
HOLLAND COURT B.6
HOLLY CLOSE D.3
HONEYSUCKLE DRIVE .D.3
HOWARD CRESCENT ..B.3
HOWLETT CLOSE B.4
HUMBLE TOFT ROAD .A.2
HURN ROAD D.4
HYDE ROAD B.4

JOHN BATES CLOSE ..C.3
JOHN DUIGAN COURT .B.4
JOHN GOSHAWK ROAD .C.5
JOHNSON CLOSE B.4
JUBILEE AVENUE C.2

KEATS CLOSE A.1
KEMP DRIVE A.3
KENNEDY CLOSE B.6
KEVIN WALK B.5
KINGSTON ROAD D.4
KINGS PARK C.2
KINGS ROAD C.2

LABURNUM CR. C.6
LADISLAW WAY B.5
LARKSPUR COURT B.5
LARNERS DRIFT B.6
LARNERS ROAD B.6
LAVENDER GROVE ...B.5
LESLEY WALK B.5
LILAC CLOSE B.5
LIMASSOL ROAD A.5
LIME DRIVE B.5
LIME TREE CLOSE C.2
LISBON ROAD A.5
LITTLEFIELDS B.3
LONDON ROAD C.4
LOWICK CLOSE B.4
LUXEMBOURG WAY ...B.5

GORDON ROAD C.2
LYDGATE CLOSE B.5
LYNN COURT C.4

MACARTHUR DRIVE ...A.2
MALTHOUSE COURT ..C.2
MARGARET CLOSE ...B.6
MARION WALK B.5
MARKET PLACE B.3
MARY UNWIN ROAD ..B.3
MATSELL WAY C.3
MASEFIELD MEWS A.1
MAYES TERRACE B.3
MEADOW DRIVE A.4
MIDDLEMARCH RD ...B.5
MILL COURT B.6
MILLER CLOSE A.3
MILTON CLOSE A.1
MOORGATE ROAD ...B.4
MT. PLEASANT B.3
MYRTLE AVENUE C.3

NEATHERD MOOR D.2
NEATHERD ROAD C.2
NELSON PLACE C.2
NEVILLE CLOSE C.6
NORMAN CLOSE A.3
NORTHGATE C.1
NORWICH ROAD B.3
NORWICH STREET ...B.3
NUNNS WAY B.2

OAKAPPLE DRIVE B.1
OAKWOOD CLOSE ...B.1
OAKWOOD ROAD B.1
OLD BECCLES GATE ..B.3
OLD HALL ROAD B.5
OLD QUARRY COURT .C.2
OLDFIELD COURT (2) .C.2
OLNEY ROAD B.3
ORCHARD AVENUE ...B.6
ORCHID AVENUE B.5

PARK ROAD C.2
PERKINS COURT B.3
PETERS CLOSE A.6
PHILIP PLACE B.5
PINE GROVE B.5
PIPPIN CLOSE C.4
POND ROAD B.6
POTTERS BAR D.4
POWELL COURT A.2
PROSPECT PLACE B.3

QUEBEC HALL BNGLWS. B.1
QUEBEC ROAD B.1
QUEBEC STREET B.3

RASHS GREEN C.5
REAVEY COURT B.3
RECREATION ROAD ..B.6
RED LION STREET ...B.3
REEDER CLOSE B.4
REGENTS CLOSE B.5
RICHARD HICKS DRIVE .A.4
ROGER RIDE B.5
ROLLING PIN LANE ...B.3
ROMNEY WALK B.4
ROSE VELLA DRIVE ..INSET
RUSHMEADOW ROAD ..A.3
RUSSET WAY C.4

ST. GEORGES DRIVE ..B.6
ST. HILDA CLOSE B.2
ST. HILDA ROAD A.2
ST. NICHOLAS ST. B.2
ST. WITHBURGA LA. ..B.3
SALT LANE D.6
SANDY LANE A.1
SARDIS WAY B.4
SCHOOL LANE C.6
SCHOOL TERRACE ...C.6
SECKAR DRIVE A.3
SHARON CLOSE B.6
SHAKESPEARE CL. ...A.2
SHEDDICK COURT B.2
SHELDRICK PLACE ...C.5
SHIPDHAM ROAD B.6
SMITHTYNE AVENUE .D.5
SNOWHILL DRIFT B.2
SOUTHEND B.4
SOUTH GREEN C.5
SOUTH GREEN C.5
SOUTH GREEN GDS ..C.4
STATION CLOSE B.2
STATION ROAD C.3
STPHN. BEAUMONT WY .D.5
STONE ROAD B.6
STRASBOURG WAY ...A.6
SUFFOLK PLACE B.6
SUNSALVE RIDE B.6
SWAFFHAM ROAD ...B.2
SWANTON AVENUE ..C.2
SWANTON CLOSE ...C.2
SWANTON DRIVE C.2
SWANTON GROVE ...C.2
SWANTON ROAD C.2

TAVERN LANE C.4
TEASEL CLOSE .....INSET
TEBBUTT AVENUE ...B.4
THE BROADWAY A.5
THE CRESCENT B.6
THE DODMANS B.3
THE GROVE B.3

THE SYCAMORES C.5
THEATRE STREET B.2
THORP COURT B.4
TIPTON CLOSE C.5
TOWNSHEND ROAD ..B.1
TOFTWOOD C.6
TRINITY CLOSE B.2

UNION DRIFT D.3
UNION SQUARE D.3

VALLEY VIEW A.2
VICARAGE MEADOWS .B.3
VIENNA WALK A.6

WAKES LANE B.3
WALLACE COURT B.2
WAPLES WAY A.4
WARNER AVENUE ...B.1
WARREN PLACE B.6
WASHBRIDGE B.3
WATERSFIELD WAY ..B.5
WAVELL ROAD A.1
WELLINGTON ROAD ..C.3
WESTFIELD LANE ...C.6
WESTFIELD ROAD ...C.5
WHEATCROFT WAY ..INSET
WHITE LION YARD ...B.3
WILLIAM COWPER CL. .C.6
WILLIAM WAY B.6
WILLOW GROVE B.5
WINDSOR PARK B.1
WISTERIA CLOSE D.3
WIX'S YARD (4) B.3
WOLLASTON AVENUE .B.1
WOODFIELD B.6
WORDSWORTH DRIVE .A.1
WRIGHT AVENUE B.6
WRIGHT DRIVE A.4

YAXHAM ROAD C.4
YORK PLACE B.3

ZARA WAY A.6

BACK STREET A2
BARTLE COURT A1
BIRCHAM RD. B2
BROOMHILL LA. A2

CAWSTON RD. B1
CHAPEL CL. A2
CHURCH HILL A2
CHURCH STREET ...A2
COLES WAY A1
COLLERS WAY B1
CROWN MEADOW ..B1

DEREHAM RD A2

ELIZABETH CL. A2
EWING CL. A2

FURZE LA. B2

IRWIN CL. B1

KERDISTON RD. ...A1

LABURNUM GROVE ..B1

MALTHOUSE YARD ..A2
MARKET PLACE A2
MILL RD. A2
MOORHOUSE CL. ..B1

NEW RD. B1
NORWICH RD. B2

OLD BREWERY LA. ..A2
OLLANDS RD. A2
ORCHARD LA. B1

PARK LA. A2
PIGHTLE WAY A1

RICHMOND RISE ...B1
ROBINS LA. A2
RUDDS LA. A2

SCHOOL RD. A2
SILVER END A1
SMUGGLER'S LA. ...A2
STATION RD. A2-A1
STEWARDS CL. A2
STONY LA. A1
SUN BARN RD. A2
SUNBARN CL. A2

THE MOOR B2
THE STREET A2

WHITWELL RD. A2
WHITWELL ST. A2
WOOD DALLING RD. .B1

Reepham *NR10*

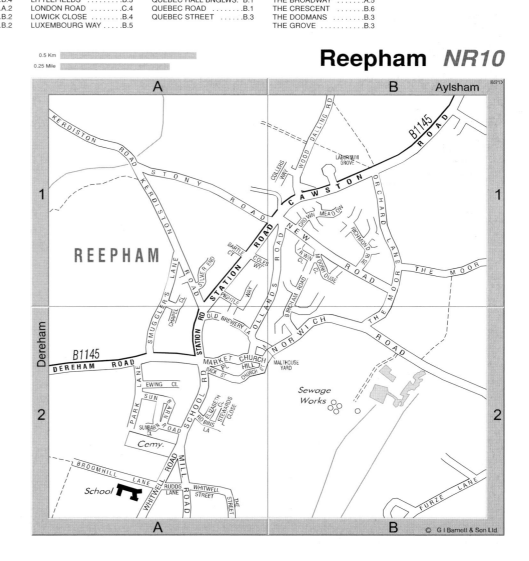

© G I Barnett & Son Ltd.

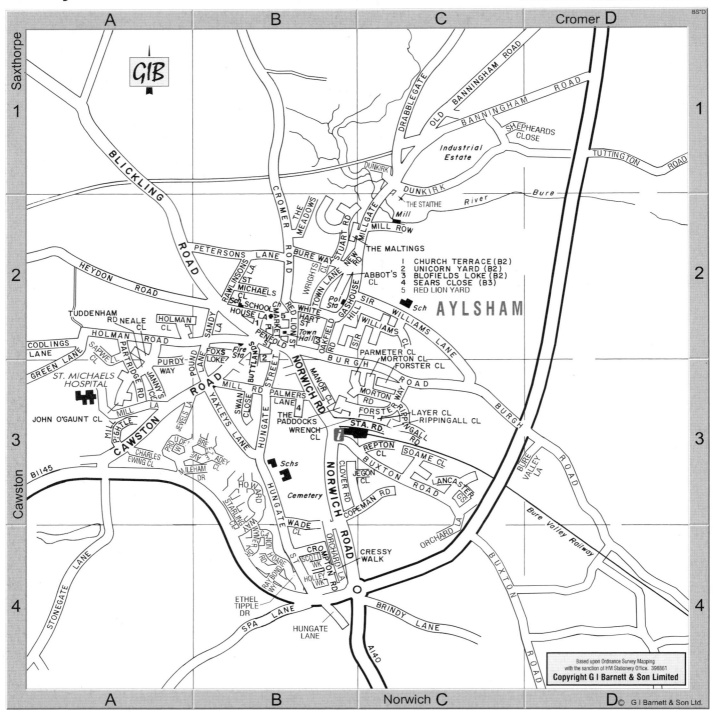

Saxthorpe

0.5 Km
0.5 Mile

BS"D

A   B   C   Cromer D

GIB

1   1

BLICKLING ROAD

OLD BANNINGHAM ROAD
BANNINGHAM ROAD
SHEPHEARDS CLOSE
TUTTINGTON ROAD

Industrial Estate

DRABBLEGATE
DUNKIRK
DUNKIRK
THE STAITHE
River   Bure
Mill
MILL ROW

HEYDON ROAD
CROMER ROAD
PETERSONS LANE
THE MEADOWS
BURE WAY
STUART RD
NEW RD
MILLGATE
THE MALTINGS

2   2

RAWLINSONS LA
ST MICHAELS CL
SCHOOL
HOUSE LA
WRIGHTS CL
TOWN LANE
RED LION ST
WHITE HART ST
ABBOT'S CL
Pol Sta
GASHOUSE HILL
SIR WILLIAMS LANE
Sch

1 CHURCH TERRACE (B2)
2 UNICORN YARD (B2)
3 BLOFIELDS LOKE (B2)
4 SEARS CLOSE (B3)
5 RED LION YARD

AYLSHAM

TUDDENHAM RD
NEALE CL
HOLMAN CL
HOLMAN ROAD
MARKET PLACE
Town Hall
OAKFIELD
SIR WILLIAMS CL
PARMETER CL
MORTON CL
FORSTER CL

CODLINGS LANE
GREEN LANE
SAPWELL CL
PARTRIDGE RD
JANNY'S CL
PURDY WAY
POUND LANE
FOXS LOKE
PENFOLD STREET
Fire Sta
BUTTLANDS
BURGH ROAD
MORTON RD
FORSTER

ST. MICHAELS HOSPITAL
MILL RD
SWAN CLOSE
PALMERS LANE
NORWICH RD
LAYER CL
RIPPINGALL CL
RIPPINGALL RD
BURGH ROAD

JOHN O'GAUNT CL
MILL PIGTLE
JEWELS LA
YAXLEYS LANE
HUNGATE
THE PADDOCKS
WRENCH CL
STA. RD
MANOR CL
REPTON CL
SOAME CL
BURE VALLEY LA

3   3

CAWSTON
B1145
CHARLES EWING CL
PRO UDF WK
BRE AVE
ADEY CL
MILEHAM DR
HOWARD WAY
STARLING CLO
Schs
Cemetery
NORWICH ROAD
CLOVER RD
JEGON CL
COPEMAN RD
BUXTON ROAD
LANCASTER GDS
SOAME CL
CRESSY WALK
ORCHARD LA
BUXTON ROAD

Bure Valley Railway

STONEGATE LANE
WYMER AVE
CA TON HOARE RD
RAY BOND WY
HOLLEY WK
SCOTT WK
CROMPTON RD
WADE CL
ORCHARD RD
BRINDY LANE

ETHEL TIPPLE DR
SPA LANE
HUNGATE LANE
A140

4   4

A   B   Norwich C   D © G I Barnett & Son Ltd.

ABBOTT'S CLOSE B.2
ADEY CLOSE B.3

BANNINGHAM ROAD C.1
BLICKLING ROAD A.1
BLOFIELDS LOKE (3) B.2
BREEZE AVENUE B.3
BRINDY LANE C.4
BURE VALLEY LANE D.3
BURE WAY B.2
BURGH ROAD C.3
BUTTLANDS B.3
BUXTON ROAD C.3

CANON HOARE ROAD B.3
CAWSTON ROAD A.3
CHARLES EWING CLOSE ...A.3
CHURCH TERRACE (1) B.2
CLOVER ROAD B.3
CODLINGS LANE A.2
COPEMAN ROAD B.3
CRESSY WALK B.4
CROMER ROAD B.2
CROMPTON ROAD B.4
DRABBLEGATE C.1
DUNKIRK C.1

ETHEL TIPPLE DRIVE B.4

FORSTER CLOSE C.3
FORSTER WAY C.3
FOXS LOKE B.2

GASHOUSE HILL B.2
GREEN LANE A.3

HEYDON ROAD A.2
HOLLEY WALK B.4
HOLMAN CLOSE A.2
HOLMAN ROAD A.2
HOWARD WAY B.3
HUNTGATE LANE B.4
HUNGATE STREET B.3

JANNY'S CLOSE B.3
JEGON CLOSE C.3
JEWELS LANE A.3
JOHN O'GAUNT CLOSE ...A.3
LANCASTER GARDENS ...C.3
LAYER CLOSE C.3

MANOR CLOSE B.3
MARKET PLACE B.2
MILEHAM DRIVE A.3

MILL LANE A.3
MILL PIGHTLE A.3
MILL ROAD B.3
MILL ROW C.2
MILLGATE C.2
MORTON CLOSE C.3
MORTON ROAD C.3

NEALE CLOSE A.2
NEW ROAD B.2
NORWICH ROAD B.3

OAKFIELD ROAD B.2
OLD BANNINGHAM ROAD ..C.1
ORCHARD LANE C.4

PALMERS LANE B.3
PARMETER CLOSE B.3
PARTRIDGE ROAD A.3
PENFOLD STREET B.2
PETERSONS LANE B.2
POUND LANE A.3
PROUDFOOT WAY A.3
PURDY WAY A.3

RAWLINSONS LANE B.2
RAY BOND WAY B.4

RED LION STREET B.2
RED LION YARD (5) B.2
REPTON CLOSE C.3
RIPPINGALL CLOSE C.3
RIPPINGALL ROAD C.3

ST. MICHAELS CLOSE B.2
SANDY LANE B.2
SAPWELL CLOSE A.2
SCHOOL HOUSE LANE ...B.2
SCOTT WALK B.4
SEAR CLOSE (4) B.3
SHEPHEARDS CLOSE C.1
SIR WILLIAMS CLOSE ...C.2
SIR WILLIAMS LANE C.2
SOAME CLOSE C.3
SPA LANE B.4
STARLING CLOSE B.3
STATION ROAD B.3
STONEGATE LANE A.4
STUART ROAD B.2
SWAN CLOSE B.3

THE MALTINGS B.2
THE MEADOWS B.2
THE PADDOCKS B.3
THE STAITHE C.2

TOWN LANE B.2
TUDDENHAM ROAD A.3
TUTTINGTON ROAD D.1

UNICORN YARD (2) B.2

WADE CLOSE B.3
WHITE HART STREET ...B.2
WRENCH CLOSE B.3
WRIGHTS CLOSE B.2
WYMER DRIVE B.3

YAXLEYS LANE B.3

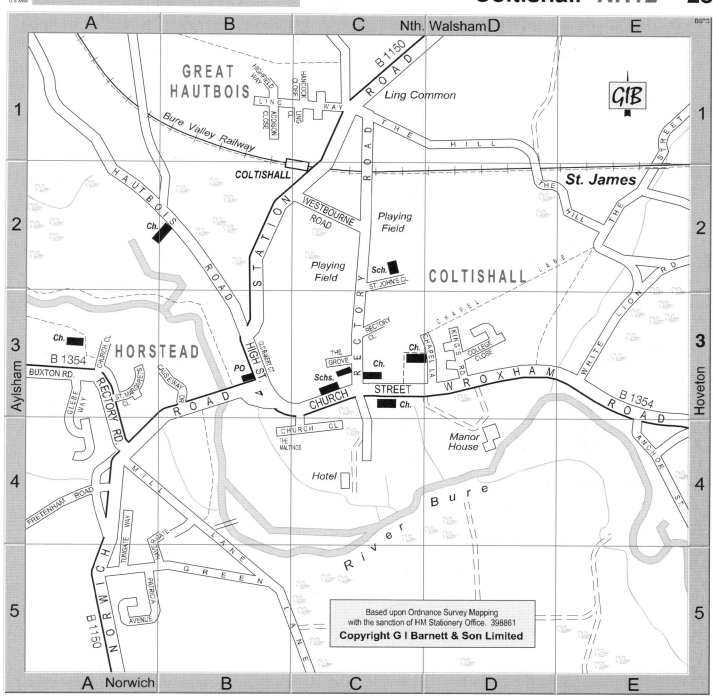

ADDISON CLOSE B.1
ANCHOR STREET E.4

BUXTON ROAD A.3

CAUSEWAY DRIVE B.3
CHAPEL LANE D.3
CHURCH CLOSE (COLTISHALL) B.4
CHURCH CLOSE (HORSTEAD) .A.3
CHURCH STREET C.3
COLLEGE CLOSE D.3
COLTISHALL; D.2

FRETENHAM ROAD A.4

GLEBE WAY A.3
GREEN LANE B.5

HANCOCK CLOSE C.1
HAUTBOIS ROAD A.2

HAVERGATE A.5
HIGH STREET B.3
HIGHFIELD WAY B.1
HORSTEAD; A.3

KING'S ROAD D.3

LING CLOSE C.1
LING WAY B.1

MILL LANE A.4

NORWICH ROAD A.5

OLD BAKERY COURT B.3

PATRICIA AVENUE A.5

RECTORY CLOSE C.3
RECTORY ROAD (COLTISHALL) C.3

RECTORY ROAD (HORSTEAD) .A.3

ST. JAMES E.2
ST. JOHN.S CLOSE C.2
ST. MARGARETS CLOSE A.3
STATION ROAD B.2

THE GROVE C.3
THE HILL C.1
THE MALTINGS B.4
THE STREET E.2
TUNGATE WAY A.5

WESTBOURNE ROAD C.2
WHITE LION ROAD E.3
WROXHAM ROAD D.3

0.5 Km
0.25 Mile

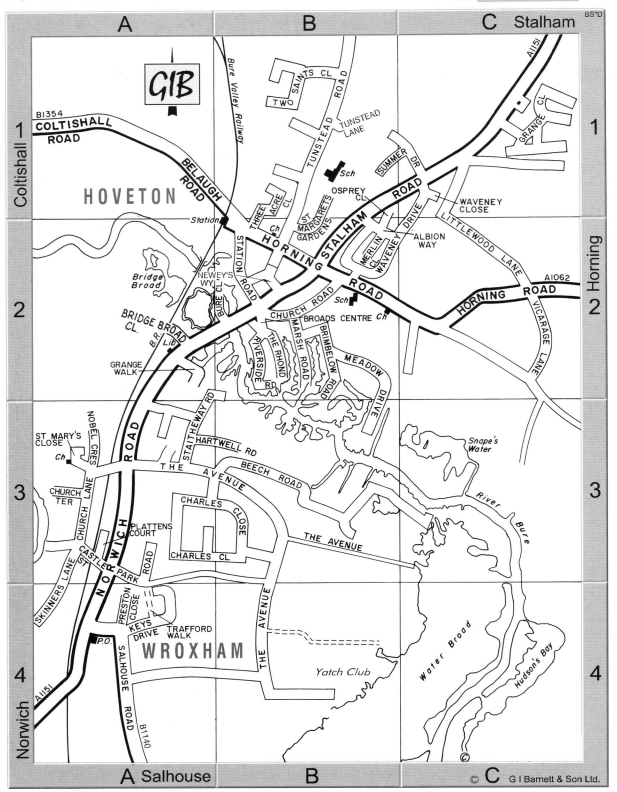

ALBION WAY B.2	MARSH ROAD B.2	THE AVENUE A.3
	MEADOW DRIVE B.2	THE RHOND B.2
BEECH ROAD B.3	MERLIN CLOSE B.2	THREE ACRE CLOSE B.2
BELAUGH ROAD A.1		TRAFFORD WALK A.4
BRIDGE BROAD CLOSE A.2	NEWEY'S WAY B.2	TUNSTEAD ROAD B.1
BRIMBELOW ROAD B.2	NOBEL CRESCENT A.3	TWO SAINTS CLOSE B.1
BROADS CENTRE B.2	NORWICH ROAD A.3	
BURE CLOSE B.2		VICARAGE LANE C.2
	OSPREY CLOSE B.1	
CASTLE STREET A.3		WAVENEY CLOSE C.1
CHARLES CLOSE A.3	PARK ROAD A.3	WAVENEY DRIVE B.2
CHURCH LANE A.3	PLATTENS COURT A.3	
CHURCH ROAD B.2	PRESTON CLOSE A.4	
CHURCH TERRACE A.3		
COLTISHALL ROAD A.1	RIVERSIDE ROAD B.2	
GRANGE CLOSE C.1	ST MARGARETS GARDENS . . .B.2	
GRANGE WALK A.2	ST MARY'S CLOSE A.3	
	SALHOUSE ROAD A.4	
HARTWELL ROAD A.3	SKINNERS LANE A.4	
HORNING ROAD B.2	STAITHEWAY ROAD A.3	
KEYS DRIVE A.4	STALHAM ROAD B.2	
	STATION ROAD B.2	
LITTLEWOOD LANE C.2	SUMMER DRIVE C.1	

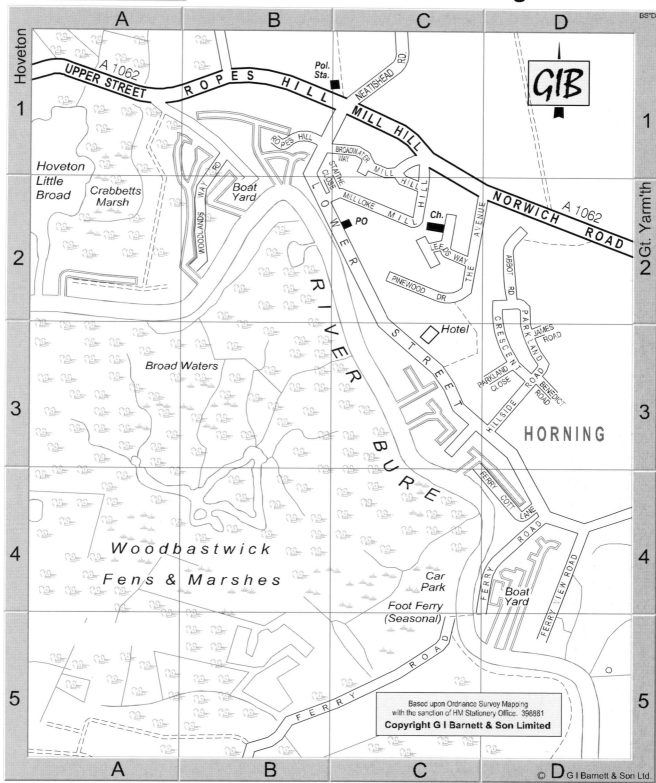

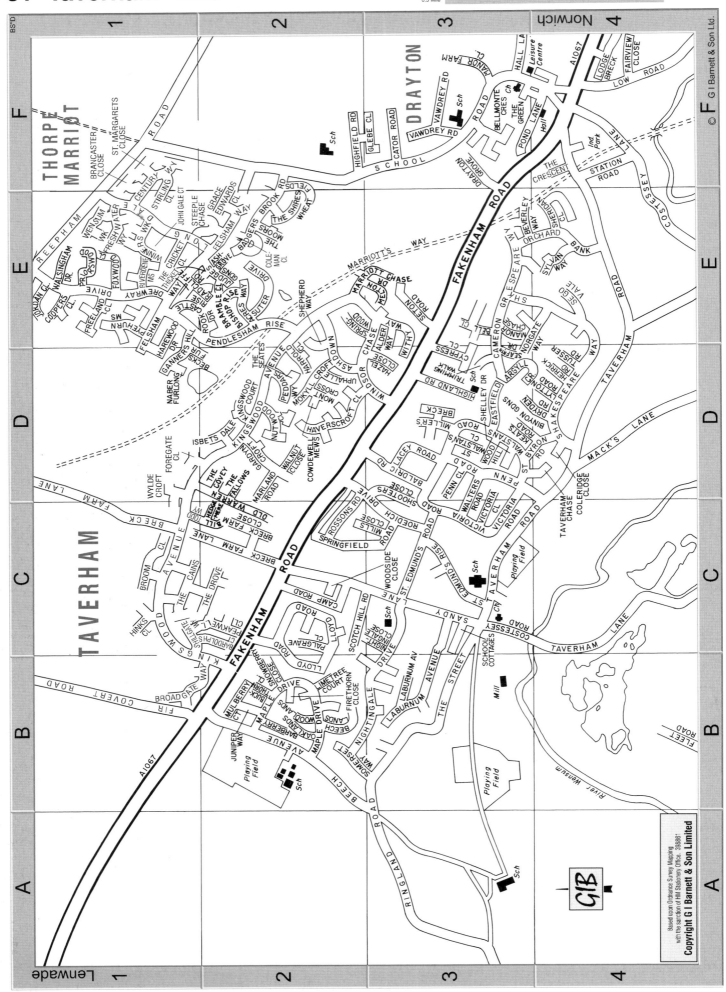

Based upon Ordnance Survey Mapping with the sanction of HM Stationery Office. 393861
Copyright G I Barnett & Son Limited

ACRES WAY E.2
ALDER WAY E.3
ARGYLL CRESCENT D.3
ASHDOWN D.2

BADGERS BROOK ROAD E.2
BALDRIC ROAD D.3
BARBERRY B.2
BARDOLPHS COURT C.2
BECKS FUR D.1
BEECH AVENUE B.2
BEECH LANDS B.2
BELL CLOSE E.3
BELLMONTE CRESCENT F.3
BEVERLEY WAY E.3
BILL TODD WAY C.2
BINYON GARDENS D.3
BISHOP RISE E.2
BRAMBLE CLOSE E.2
BRANCASTER CLOSE F.1
BRECK FARM CLOSE C.2
BRECK FARM LANE C.2
BROADGATE B.1
BROOM CLOSE C.1
BUCKTHORN CLOSE B.2
BYRON ROAD D.4

CAMERON GREEN E.3
CAMP ROAD C.2
CASTLE RISE E.1
CATOR ROAD F.3
CENTURY WAY E.1
COLEMAN CLOSE E.2
COLERIDGE CLOSE D.4
COOPERS CLOSE E.1
COSTESSEY LANE E.4
COSTESSEY ROAD C.3
COWDEWELL MEWS D.2
CRICKET CLOSE E.1
CYPRESS CLOSE D.3

DRAYTON F.3
DRAYTON GROVE F.3
DREWRAY DRIVE E.1
DRYDEN ROAD D.4

EASTFIELD D.3

FAIRVIEW CLOSE F.4
FAKENHAM ROAD C.2
FELSHAM WAY E.1
FIR COVERT ROAD B.1
FIRETHORN CLOSE B.2
FLEET ROAD B.4
FOREGATE CLOSE D.1
FOXWOOD CLOSE E.1
FREELAND CLOSE E.1
FRESHWATER WAY E.1

GRACE EDWARDS CLOSE E.2
GRANNERS HILL D.1
GARDYN CROFT D.2
GLEBE CLOSE F.3

HALL LANE F.3
HAREWOOD DRIVE E.1
HARROLD CLOSE D.2
HAVERSCROFT CLOSE D.2
HAZEL CLOSE D.3
HEDGEMERE C.2
HERRICK ROAD D.4
HIGHFIELD ROAD F.2
HIGHLAND ROAD D.3
HINKS CLOSE C.1

ISBETS DALE D.2

JOHN GALE COURT E.1
JORDAN CLOSE E.1
JUDGES GARDENS E.2
JUNIPER WAY B.2

KEATS ROAD D.3
KINGSWOOD AVENUE D.2
KINGSWOOD COURT D.2

LABURNUM AVENUE B.3
LACEY ROAD D.3
LIMETREE COURT B.2
LLOYD ROAD C.2
LODGE BRECK F.4
LONG DALE E.2
LOW ROAD F.4
LYTTON ROAD D.4

MACK'S LANE D.4
MANOR CHASE E.3
MANOR FARM CLOSE F.3
MAPLE DRIVE B.2
MARLAND ROAD D.2
MARRIOTT CHASE E.2
MELTON DRIVE E.3
MILLER'S BRECK D.3
MILLS CLOSE C.3
MOKYLL CROFT D.2
MONT CROSS D.2
MULBERRY COURT B.2

NABER FURLONG D.1
NIGHTINGALE CLOSE C.3
NIGHTINGALE DRIVE B.3
NORGATE WAY E.4
NUTWOOD CLOSE D.2

OAKLANDS B.2
OLD WARREN C.2
ORCHARD BANK E.3

PALGRAVE CLOSE C.2
PEAKWELL CLOSE C.2
PEDDARS WAY D.2
PENDLESHAM RISE E.2

PENN CLOSE D.3
PENN ROAD D.3
POND LANE F.3
PRIORSWOOD E.1
PYEHURN MEWS E.1

RADCLIFFE ROAD E.1
REEPHAM ROAD E.1
RINGLAND ROAD A.3
RIVERDENE MEWS E.1
ROEDICH DRIVE C.3
ROOK DRIVE E.2
ROSSONS ROAD C.2

ST. EDMUND'S RISE C.3
ST. EDMUND'S ROAD C.3
ST. MARGARETS CLOSE F.1
ST. WALSTANS CLOSE D.3
ST. WALSTANS ROAD D.3
SANDY LANE C.3
SCHOOL COTTAGES C.3
SCHOOL ROAD F.3
SCOTCH HILL ROAD C.2
SEAFORTH DRIVE D.3
SEGO VALE E.4
SETON ROAD E.3
SHAKESPEARE WAY D.4
SHAKESPEARE WAY E.3
SHELLEY DRIVE D.3
SHEPHERD WAY E.2
SHERIDAN CLOSE E.4
SHILLGATE WAY C.1
SHOOTERS CLOSE D.3
SNOWBERRY CLOSE B.2
SOMERSET WAY B.2
SPRINGFIELD ROAD C.2
SPRINGWOOD E.2
STATION ROAD F.4
STEEPLE CHASE E.2
STIRLING CLOSE E.1

SUTER DRIVE E.2
SYLVAN WAY E.4

TAVERHAM CHASE D.4
TAVERHAM LANE C.4
TAVERHAM ROAD C.3
THE CAINS C.1
THE COVEY D.2
THE CRESCENT F.4
THE DROVE D.2
THE FALLOWS D.2
THE GREEN F.3
THE MOORS E.2
THE SEATES E.2
THE SHIRES E.2
THE STREET B.3
THORPE MARRIOT F.1
TRIMMING WALK E.1
TUSSER ROAD D.4

UPHALLE D.2

VAWDREY ROAD F.3
VICTORIA CLOSE C.3
VICTORIA ROAD C.3

WALNUT CLOSE D.2
WALSINGHAM DRIVE E.1
WALTERS ROAD C.3
WENSUM WALK E.1
WHEAT FIELDS F.2
WINDSOR CHASE D.3
WINNERS WALK E.1
WITHY WAY E.3
WOOD HILL D.3
WOODLANDS B.2
WOODSIDE CLOSE C.2
WYLDE CROFT D.1

Norwich....*maps on pages 37 to 46*

ABBEY LANE F.9 45
ABBOT ROAD G.8 44
ABBOTT ROAD G.8 44
ABERDARE CLOSE D.10 40
ABINGER WAY H.6 43
ACACIA ROAD D.13 41
ACLAND MEWS A.7 39
ADAMS CLOSE A.10 40
ADDEY CLOSE A.9 40
ADELAIDE STREET D.7 39
AERODROME CRESCENT ..D.11 40
AERODROME ROAD D.11 40
AIREDALE CLOSE C.7 39
ALAN ROAD F.9 45
ALBANY ROAD C.8 39
ALBERT PLACE E.10 40
ALBERT TERRACE F.7 44
ALBION DRIVE B.10 40
ALBION WAY E.9 40
ALBURY WALK H.5 43
ALDRYCHE ROAD D.10 40
ALEXANDRA ROAD E.7 39
ALFORD GROVE B.10 40
ALFRED NICHOLLS COURT ..B.8 39
ALL SAINTS GREEN F.8 44
ALLANDALE ROAD H.7 44
ALLEN'S AVENUE A.10 40
ALLENS LANE F.7 44
ALLEN'S LA., OLD CATTON ..A.9 40
ALLERTON CLOSE B.10 40
ALLERTON ROAD B.10 40
ALMA TERRACE D.8 39
ALNWICK COURT D.2 37
ALSTON ROAD B.5 38
ALTONGATE B.14 41
AMBLESIDE CLOSE E.3 37
AMBROSE CLOSE D.2 37
AMDERLEY DRIVE H.5 43
AMHURST CLOSE C.9 40
AMPTHILL STREET E.7 39
AMSTERDAM WAY M.6 46
ANCHOR CLOSE D.9 40
ANCHOR STREET D.9 40
ANDERSONS MEADOW C.7 39
ANGEL ROAD C.8 39
ANGLIA SQUARE D.8 39
ANMER CLOSE B.9 40
ANNE CLOSE D.13 41
ANNE'S WALK D.8 39
ANSON ROAD N.7 46
ANTHONY DRIVE B.9 40
ANTINGHAM ROAD C.12 41
APPLEACRES N.8 46
APPLEYARD CRESCENT B.6 38
APSLEY COURT E.5 38
ARDEN GROVE M.5 46
ARDERON COURT D.7 39
ARDNEY RISE B.8 39
ARGYLE STREET F.9 45
ARLINGTON LANE F.7 44
ARMES CRESCENT D.6 38
ARMES STREET D.6 38
ARMINGHALL CLOSE B.7 39
ARMINGHALL LANE J.10 45
ARMITAGE CLOSE J.3 42
ARMS PARK ROAD N.7 46
ARMSTRONG ROAD C.13 41
ARNFIELD LANE C.3 37
ARNOLD MILLER CLOSE G.9 45
ARNOLD MILLER ROAD H.9 45
ASH GROVE C.8 39
ASHBOURNE TOWER C.12 41
ASHBY STREET F.8 44
ASHTREE ROAD B.3 37
ASHWELL COURT D.1 37
ASPEN WAY J.4 43
ASPLAND ROAD E.9 40
ASSOCIATION WAY D.14 41
ASTELL ROAD J.8 44

ASTLEY ROAD D.1 37
ATKINSON CLOSE C.1 37
ATMERE CLOSE H.5 43
ATTELSEY WAY D.1 37
ATTHILL ROAD D.6 38
AUDAX ROAD N.7 46
AUGUSTUS HARE DRIVE E.3 37
AURANIA AVENUE G.8 44
AUSTER CLOSE A.7 39
AUTUMN DRIVE C.3 37
AVEBURY ROAD H.7 44
AVENUE ROAD E.6 38
AVIAN WAY B.11 40
AVONMOUTH ROAD C.7 39
AYLESBURY CLOSE B.8 39
AYLMER TOWER B.6 38
AYLSHAM CRESCENT B.7 39
AYLSHAM ROAD B.7 39
AYLSHAM WAY B.7 39

BACON ROAD E.5 38
BACTON ROAD B.6 38
BAINES WAY C.1 37
BAKERS ROAD D.8 39
BALFOUR STREET D.9 40
BANK PLAIN E.8 39
BANK STREET E.8 39
BARBER PLACE E.12 41
BARCLAY GREEN C.12 41
BARCLAY ROAD C.12 41
BARGATE COURT D.9 40
BARKER STREET D.7 39
BARKER WAY B.14 41
BARLEY COURT C.1 37
BARN MEADOW H.10 45
BARN ROAD E.7 39
BARNARD ROAD C.1 37
BARNEBEE ROAD E.2 37
BARNES CLOSE C.11 40
BARNES ROAD A.10 40
BARNES YARD D.8 39
BARNESDALE ROAD J.7 44
BARNHAM CLOSE D.1 37
BARRACK ROAD D.10 40
BARRACK STREET D.9 40
BARRETT ROAD H.8 44
BARROW CLOSE C.5 38
BARTON WAY F.10 45
BASSINGHAM ROAD B.6 38
BATELEY COURT E.6 38
BATEMAN CLOSE D.2 37
BATES GREEN C.4 38
BATHURST ROAD E.7 39
BAXTER COURT B.7 39
BEACONSFIELD ROAD E.10 40
BEATRICE ROAD E.10 40
BEATTY ROAD H.7 44
BEAUFORT CLOSE N.8 46
BEAUMONT PLACE F.7 44
BEAUMONT ROAD C.3 37
BEDDING LANE D.9 40
BEDFORD STREET E.8 39
BEECH BANK COURT F.6 43
BEECH DRIVE, NR1 .....D.10 40
BEECH DRIVE, NR2 .....F.6 43
BEECH DR., OLD CATTON ..A.7 39
BEECHBANK F.6 43
BEECHBANK DRIVE B.14 41
BEECHCROFT, NW. CSTSSY. ..C.2 37
BEECHCROFT, NR3 .....B.9 40
BEECHENO ROAD D.3 37
BEECHES CLOSE A.9 40
BEECHING CLOSE H.8 44
BEECHING ROAD H.8 44
BEECHWOOD DRIVE C.12 41
BEECHWOODS N.8 46
BEK CLOSE G.5 43
BELL CLOSE N.5 46
BELL ROAD C.9 40

BELLVILLE CRESCENT F.9 45
BELMORE CLOSE C.12 41
BELMORE ROAD C.12 41
BELOE AVENUE D.2 37
BELSIZE ROAD D.10 40
BELVEDERE PLACE G.6 43
BELVOIR STREET E.7 39
BENDISH WAY D.1 37
BENSLEY ROAD F.6 43
BENTLEY WAY A.7 39
BER STREET E.8 39
BERKLEY CLOSE N.6 46
BERNERS CLOSE C.7 39
BERNERS COURT C.7 39
BERNERS STREET C.7 39
BERNHAM ROAD N.5 46
BERRINGTON ROAD N.5 46
BERTIE ROAD C.7 39
BESSEMER ROAD H.8 44
BETHAL STREET E.8 39
BEVAN CLOSE E.3 37
BEVERLEY CLOSE E.5 38
BEVERLEY ROAD E.4 38
BEWFELD ROAD D.1 37
BEWIT ROAD A.11 40
BIGNOLD ROAD B.6 38
BIRCH COURT A.12 41
BIRCH TREE AVENUE C.10 40
BIRCHWOOD E.13 41
BIRKBECK CLOSE G.8 44
BIRKBECK ROAD G.8 44
BIRKBECK WAY D.13 41
BIRKDALE G.6 43
BISHOPS CLOSE E.12 41
BISHOPSBRIDGE ROAD E.9 40
BISHOPSGATE E.9 40
BISHY BARNEBEE WAY E.2 37
BIXLEY CLOSE E.4 38
BLACK HORSE LANE B.9 40
BLACKBERRY COURT B.5 38
BLACKBURN ROAD N.7 46
BLACKFRIARS STREET D.8 39
BLACKHORSE LANE B.9 40
BLACKHORSE OPENING B.9 40
BLACKHORSE STREET D.7 39
BLACKS AVENUE H.10 45
BLACKSMITHS WAY N.9 46
BLACKTHORN CLOSE A.8 39
BLACKWELL AVENUE B.10 40
BLADEWATER ROAD E.2 37
BLAKENEY CLOSE G.5 43
BLAKES COURT B.9 40
BLAKES LOKE B.9 40
BLAKESTONE DRIVE D.12 41
BLAND ROAD E.3 37
BLENHEIM CLOSE A.11 40
BLENHEIM ROAD A.10 40
BLICKLING ROAD N.8 46
BLITHEMEADOW COURT B.11 40
BLITHEMEADOW DRIVE B.11 40
BLITHEWOOD GARDENS B.11 40
BLOMFIELD ROAD B.7 39
BLUE BOAR LANE A.11 40
BLUEBELL CRESCENT G.4 43
BLUEBELL ROAD F.4 43
BLYTH ROAD B.8 39
BOARDMAN CLOSE B.8 39
BOILEAU CLOSE H.7 44
BOLINGBROKE ROAD B.7 39
BOND STREET D.6 38
BONIFACE CLOSE H.7 44
BOOTY ROAD C.13 41
BORROWDALE DRIVE D.10 40
BOSTON STREET B.8 39
BOSWELLS YARD D.8 39
BOTOLPH STREET D.8 39
BOTOLPH WAY D.8 39
BOTTOM BRECK CLOSE B.1 37
BOULDERSIDE CLOSE D.12 41

BOULTON CLOSE E.11 40
BOULTON STREET E.9 40
BOUNDARY AVENUE A.6 38
BOUNDARY LANE E.14 41
BOUNDARY ROAD B.6 38
BOWERS AVENUE B.6 38
BOWERS CLOSE B.6 38
BOWMAN ROAD J.7 44
BOWTHORPE D.2 37
BOWTHORPE HALL ROAD D.1 37
BOWTHORPE ROAD E.4 38
BRABAZON ROAD B.8 39
BRACEY AVENUE A.9 40
BRACKEN AVENUE A.6 38
BRACONDALE F.9 45
BRACONDALE COURT G.9 45
BRACONDALE GREEN F.9 45
BRACONDALE GROVE F.9 45
BRACONDALE MILLGATE G.10 45
BRADE CROFT D.3 37
BRADEHAM WAY H.6 43
BRADEFORD CLOSE C.5 38
BRAITH WAIT CLOSE D.2 37
BRAKENDON CLOSE F.9 45
BRAMBLE AVENUE A.6 38
BRAMFIELD CLOSE D.6 38
BRAMPTON COURT D.2 37
BRANDON CLOSE A.5 38
BRANFORD ROAD C.9 40
BRANKSOME CLOSE G.6 43
BRANKSOME ROAD G.6 43
BRASIER ROAD B.6 38
BRAZENGATE F.8 44
BRECK ROAD B.12 41
BRECKLAND ROAD C.2 37
BRENDA JAMES CLOSE D.12 41
BRENNEWATER MEWS C.2 37
BRENTWOOD H.5 43
BRERETON CLOSE D.3 37
BRETTINGHAM AVENUE J.3 42
BREWERS COURT D.9 40
BREYDON ROAD A.9 40
BRIAN AVENUE G.8 44
BRIARS COURT D.5 38
BRIDGE FARM LANE E.3 37
BRIGG STREET E.8 39
BRIGHTWELL ROAD A.8 39
BRIGHTYS OPENING D.6 38
BRISTOL TERRACE F.8 44
BRITANNIA COURT C.3 37
BRITANNIA ROAD D.10 40
BROAD VIEW B.14 41
BROADHURST ROAD H.7 44
BROADLAND DRIVE B.14 41
BROADMEAD GREEN B.14 41
BROADSMAN CLOSE F.10 45
BROCKWELL COURT B.9 40
BRONDE CLOSE N.8 46
BROOKE PLACE F.8 44
BROOM AVE., OLD CATTON ..N.6 46
BROOM AV., THRP. ST ANDRW D.12 41
BROWNE STREET D.7 39
BROWNS COURT G.8 44
BRUNSWICK ROAD F.7 44
BRYONG CLOSE N.8 46
BUCK COURTNEY CR. B.8 39
BUCK YARD E.12 41
BUCKINGHAM ROAD F.5 43
BUCKLAND RISE H.5 43
BULL CLOSE D.8 39
BULL CLOSE ROAD D.8 39
BULL LANE F.8 44
BULLACE ROAD B.2 37
BULLARD ROAD B.7 39
BULMER ROAD C.2 37
BUMPSTEDE COURT C.2 37
BUNGALOW LANE E.13 41
BUNNET SQUARE F.5 43
BUNYAN CLOSE D.14 41

BURGES ROAD C.6 38
BURHILL CLOSE H.5 43
BURLEIGH TOWER C.12 41
BURMA CLOSE A.9 40
BURNET ROAD C.6 38
BURTON CLOSE A.7 39
BURTON ROAD A.7 39
BURY STREET F.7 44
BUSH ROAD M.6 46
BUSSEY ROAD A.8 39
BUTTERCUP WAY E.2 37
BUTTERMERE ROAD E.3 37
BUXTON ROAD D.8 39
BYFIELD COURT C.7 39

CADDOW ROAD E.2 37
CADGE CLOSE D.4 38
CADGE ROAD D.4 38
CAERNARVON ROAD E.6 38
CALEDONIAN WAY A.7 39
CALEY CLOSE B.5 38
CALTHORPE ROAD D.3 37
CALVERT STREET D.8 39
CAMBERLEY ROAD G.6 43
CAMBORNE CLOSE C.4 38
CAMBRIDGE STREET F.7 44
CAMP GROVE E.10 40
CAMPBELL COURT D.9 40
CAMPION HOUSE D.2 37
CANARY WAY F.9 45
CANNELL GREEN D.9 40
CANNERBY LANE B.10 40
CANTERBURY PLACE D.7 39
CANTLEY LANE J.3 42
CAPPS ROAD C.8 39
CARDIFF ROAD E.6 38
CARDIGAN PLACE D.7 39
CARLETON CLOSE B.11 40
CARLETON ROAD B.11 40
CARLTON GARDENS F.8 44
CARLYLE ROAD G.9 45
CARNOUSTIE H.6 43
CAROLINE COURT F.5 43
CARROW HILL F.9 45
CARROW ROAD F.9 45
CARROW VALE F.9 45
CARRS HILL CLOSE A.2 37
CARSHALTON ROAD G.9 45
CARTEFORD DRIVE B.8 39
CASTLE MEADOW E.8 39
CASTLE STREET E.8 39
CASTLETON CLOSE D.2 37
CASTON ROAD C.13 41
CATHEDRAL STREET E.9 40
CATHERINE WHEEL OPENING D.8 39
CATTLE MARKET STREET E.8 39
CATTON CHASE N.8 46
CATTON COURT N.8 46
CATTON GROVE ROAD B.8 39
CATTON VIEW COURT B.8 39
CAUSEWAY CLOSE D.7 39
CAVALIER CLOSE D.14 41
CAVALRY RIDE D.9 40
CAVELL ROAD H.8 44
CECIL GOWING COURT A.10 40
CECIL ROAD G.8 44
CEDAR ROAD F.10 45
CENTRAL AVENUE E.14 41
CERE ROAD A.11 40
CHALFONT WALK G.4 43
CHALGROVE FIELD D.14 41
CHALK HILL COURT E.9 40
CHALKHILL ROAD E.9 40
CHAMBERLIN CLOSE B.8 39
CHAMBERLIN ROAD C.8 39
CHAMBERS ROAD B.7 39
CHANCELLORS DRIVE F.3 4
CHANDLERS COURT H.5 3
CHANTRY ROAD E.8 3

CHAPEL BREAK ROAD D.1 37
CHAPEL COURT N.6 46
CHAPEL FIELD EAST E.8 39
CHAPEL FIELD NORTH E.7 39
CHAPEL FIELD ROAD E.7 39
CHAPEL LANE E.12 41
CHAPEL LODGE F.8 39
CHAPEL ROAD B.2 37
CHAPELFIELD GROVE E.8 39
CHARING CROSS E.8 39
CHARLES AVENUE D.13 41
CHARLES JEWSON COURT ..B.7 39
CHARLES SQUARE E.7 39
CHARLES WATLING WAY C.1 37
CHARLTON ROAD H.10 45
CHAROLAIS CLOSE H.10 45
CHARTWELL COURT B.9 40
CHARTWELL ROAD B.8 39
CHASE CLOSE N.8 46
CHATHAM STREET D.8 39
CHERRY CLOSE F.8 44
CHERRY LANE D.8 39
CHESTER PLACE E.7 39
CHESTER STREET F.7 44
CHESTNUT CLOSE B.1 37
CHESTNUT HILL H.5 43
CHEYHAM MOUNT H.5 43
CHIPPERFIELD ROAD C.12 41
CHRISTCHURCH COURT G.6 43
CHRISTCHURCH ROAD E.6 38
CHRISTOPHER CLOSE G.8 44
CHRISTOPHER PLACE D.3 37
CHURCH AVENUE G.6 43
CHURCH AVENUE EAST F.6 43
CHURCH CLOSE D.6 38
CHURCH LANE, EASTON H.5 43
CHURCH LANE, SPROWSTON A.11 40
CHURCH STREET A.9 40
CHURCHFIELD J.4 43
CHURCHFIELD GREEN D.12 41
CHURCHILL ROAD C.8 39
CHURCHMAN ROAD C.11 40
CHURSTON CLOSE G.9 45
CINTRA ROAD E.10 40
CIRRUS WAY B.11 40
CITY ROAD G.9 45
CITY TRADING ESTATE D.7 39
CITY VIEW ROAD A.6 38
CIVIC GARDENS B.6 38
CLABON ROAD B.9 40
CLANCY ROAD C.11 40
CLARE CLOSE E.8 39
CLAREMONT ROAD G.6 43
CLARENCE ROAD F.10 40
CLARENDON ROAD E.7 39
CLARENDON STEPS E.7 39
CLARKE ROAD C.8 39
CLARKSON ROAD D.4 38
CLEVES WAY A.1 37
CLIFTON CLOSE D.7 39
CLIFTON STREET D.7 39
CLINCH LANE A.3 37
CLOVELLY DRIVE B.5 38
CLOVER COURT B.9 40
CLOVER HILL ROAD D.3 37
CLOVER ROAD B.9 40
COACH HOUSE COURT G.6 43
COACHMANS COURT A.9 40
COBHOLM WAY B.11 40
COKE ROAD H.8 44
COLDERSHAW ROAD A.7 39
COLEBURN ROAD J.8 44
COLEGATE E.8 39
COLINDEEP LANE A.10 40
COLKETT DRIVE A.8 39
COLLEGE ROAD E.6 38
COLLINS COURT C.8 39
COLLS ROAD C.12 41
COLLS WALK C.12 41
COLMAN ROAD E.5 38
COLNEY F.2 42
COLNEY DRIVE H.4 43
COLNEY LANE H.3 42
COMMON LANE E.13 41
COMMONWEALTH WAY ...D.14 41
COMPASS TOWER C.12 41
CONCORDE ROAD A.7 39
CONESFORD DRIVE G.9 45
CONISTON CLOSE E.3 37
CONNAUGHT ROAD E.6 38
CONSTABLE ROAD H.6 43
CONSTABLE TERRACE F.3 42
CONSTITUTION HILL C.8 39
CONSTITUTION OPENING ...B.9 40
COOKE CLOSE D.1 37
COOKS BUILDING C.9 40
COOPER LANE J.8 44
COPEMAN STREET E.7 39
COPPICE AVENUE N.5 46
CORBET ROAD B.10 40
CORIE ROAD F.5 43
CORNET CLOSE C.14 41
CORNWALLIS COURT D.2 37
CORONATION CLOSE A.6 38
CORONATION ROAD B.6 38
CORTON ROAD G.9 45
COSLANY STREET E.8 39
COSSGROVE CLOSE B.6 38
COTMAN FIELDS E.9 40
COTMAN ROAD F.10 45
COTTERALL COURT D.2 37
COTTINGHAMS DRIVE N.5 46
COUGHTREY CLOSE A.10 40
COWGATE E.8 39
COZENS-HARDY ROAD A.10 40
CRAFT ROAD F.10 45
CRAIGH RISE H.5 43
CRANCH GARDENS F.8 44
CRANMER EWS C.1 37
CRANWORTH ROAD A.11 40
CRAWFORD LANE F.10 45
CREANCE ROAD D.2 37
CREMER CLOSE N.5 46
CRESCENT CLOSE E.3 37
CRICKET GROUND ROAD G.9 45
CRINGLEFORD J.4 43
CRINGLEFORD BY-PASS H.4 43
CRINGLEFORD CHASE H.3 42
CROCODILE COURT D.7 39
CROFTHOLME WAY D.11 40
CROME ROAD C.9 40
CROMER ROAD A.6 38
CROMWELL ROAD B.10 40
CROOKS PLACE F.8 44
CROSS STREET D.8 39
CROWN ROAD, HELLESDON .C.3 37
CRUMMOCK ROAD E.3 37
CUBITT ROAD D.11 40
CULVERIN CLOSE D.14 41
CULVEDON CLOSE H.5 43
CUNNINGHAM ROAD E.4 38
CURTIS ROAD A.7 39
CUSTANCE COURT G.5 43
CUTHBERT CLOSE A.10 40
CUTLER WAY C.1 37
CYPRUS STREET G.8 44
CYRIL ROAD D.13 41

DACRE CLOSE H.5 43
DAKIN ROAD C.8 39
DALBIER CLOSE D.14 41
DALES LOKE E.12 41
DALRYMPLE WAY A.7 39
DAMOCLES COURT E.7 39
DANBY CLOSE H.7 44
DANIEL JOHN COURT C.8 39
DANIELS ROAD G.7 44
DARREL PLACE D.4 38
DAVEY PLACE E.8 39
DAVIDSON CLOSE D.13 41
DAVIDSON ROAD D.13 41
DAWSON COURT F.8 44
DE HAGUE ROAD F.5 43
DECAUX ROAD C.8 39
DELFT WAY N.6 46
DELL CRESCENT D.4 38
DELL LOKE H.10 45
DELONEY ROAD C.11 40
DELTA CLOSE A.7 39
DENBIGH ROAD E.6 38
DENMARK OPENING C.9 40
DENMARK ROAD C.8 39
DENMEAD CLOSE H.6 43
DENNIS ROAD M.6 46
DENTON ROAD B.9 40
DERBY STREET D.7 39
DEREHAM ROAD C.3 37
DERSLEY COURT D.1 37
DESBOROUGH WAY D.14 41
DEVON AVENUE N.5 46
DEVON WAY H.10 45
DEVONSHIRE STREET D.7 39
DIAMOND ROAD A.7 39
DIBDEN ROAD C.9 40
DISTILLERY SQUARE E.7 39
DIXON ROAD A.10 40
DIXON'S FOLD A.9 40
DIXONS COURT E.8 39
DODDERMAN WAY E.2 37
DOGWOOD ROAD A.8 39
DOLPHIN GROVE D.7 39
DOLPHIN PATH C.7 39
DOMAN ROAD F.9 45
DONCHURCH CLOSE D.2 37
DONKEY LANE H.5 43
DORIS ROAD E.7 39
DOUGLAS CLOSE M.8 46
DOUGLAS HAIG ROAD E.4 38
DOURO PLACE E.7 39
DOVE STREET E.8 39
DOVEDALES A.9 40
DOVEDALES COURT A.9 40
DOVER STREET F.6 43
DOWDING ROAD N.8 46
DOWNING MEWS C.1 37
DOWSING COURT C.14 41
DOWSON ROAD C.6 38
DRAGOON CLOSE D.14 41
DRAGOON STREET D.9 40
DRAPER WAY C.7 39
DRAYTON HIGH ROAD N.4 46
DRAYTON ROAD B.6 38
DRAYTON WOOD ROAD N.4 46
DRURY CLOSE D.3 37
DUCKETT CLOSE H.8 44
DUFF ROAD C.8 39
DUGARD AVENUE D.10 40
DUKE STREET E.8 39
DURHAM STREET F.7 44
DUSSINDALE DRIVE C.14 41
DUVERLIN CLOSE H.6 43
DYERS YARD E.8 39

EADE ROAD C.8 39
EAGLE WALK F.7 44
EARLHAM GREEN LANE ...D.2 37
EARLHAM GREEN LANE ...D.3 37
EARLHAM GROVE D.4 38
EARLHAM LODGE E.3 37
EARLHAM ROAD E.4 38
EARLHAM WEST CENTRE ..E.4 38
EAST HILLS ROAD C.1 37
EASTERN AVENUE D.14 41
EASTERN CLOSE D.14 41
EASTERN CRESCENT D.14 41
EASTERN ROAD E.13 41
EASTWOOD MEWS B.9 40
EATON H.5 43
EATON CHASE G.5 43
EATON HALL G.5 43
EATON STREET H.4 43
EBBISHAM DRIVE H.5 43
EBENEZER PLACE D.8 39
EDEN CLOSE E.11 40
EDENHURST CL. H.5 43
EDGEHILL D.14 41
EDGEWORTH ROAD E.4 38
EDINBURGH ROAD E.6 38
EDMUND BACON COURT ...C.8 39
EDRICH WAY D.1 37
EDWARD GAMBLING CT ...D.7 39
EDWARD STREET D.8 39
EDWARDS COURT A.10 40
EDWARDS ROAD A.10 40
EGYPTIAN ROAD D.9 40
ELEANOR ROAD G.8 44
ELIZABETH AVENUE D.13 41
ELIZABETH FRY ROAD E.5 38
ELLA ROAD E.9 40
ELLCAR RISE H.6 43
ELM CLOSE B.1 37
ELM GROVE LANE B.8 39
ELMDON COURT E.10 40
ELMHILL E.8 39
ELSTEAD CLOSE H.5 43
ELVEDON CLOSE H.5 43
ELVIN WAY C.5 38
ELWYN ROAD H.8 44
ELY STREET D.7 39
EMBREY CRESCENT N.8 46
ENFIELD ROAD D.3 37
ENGLISH ROAD A.9 40
ESDELLE STREET D.8 39
ESSEX STREET F.7 44
ETHEL ROAD E.10 40
EUROPA WAY G.9 45
EUSTACE ROAD B.6 38
EVANS WAY M.8 46
EVERSLEY ROAD A.7 39
EVERSON CLOSE C.3 37
EXCHANGE STREET E.8 39
EXETER STREET D.7 39

FAIRFAX DRIVE C.14 41
FAIRFAX ROAD F.5 43
FAIRFIELD ROAD E.6 38
FAIRHAVEN COURT E.6 38
FAIRMILE CLOSE G.7 44
FAIRSTEAD COURT B.10 40
FAIRSTEAD ROAD B.10 40
FAIRWAYS N.4 46
FALCON MEWS A.11 40
FALCON ROAD EAST B.11 40
FALCON ROAD WEST A.11 40
FALKLAND CLOSE N.4 46
FALLOWFIELD CLOSE D.11 40
FARMER'S AVENUE E.8 39
FARMLAND ROAD B.2 37
FARROW ROAD E.5 38
FASTOLF CLOSE N.5 46
FELLOWES CLOSE E.4 38
FENN CRESCENT C.7 39
FERN HILL F.10 45
FERNDALE CLOSE A.5 38
FERRY ROAD E.9 40
FIDDLE WOOD ROAD A.8 39
FIELDING COURT G.8 44
FIELDVIEW E.5 38
FIENNES ROAD C.14 41
FIFERS LANE N.6 46
FINCH CLOSE C.11 40
FINCHLEY COURT D.6 38
FINDLOW COURT D.10 40
FINKELGATE F.8 44
FIRMAN COURT C.13 41
FIRS ROAD N.6 46
FIRST CLOSE B.9 40
FIRTREE ROAD C.12 41
FIRWOOD CLOSE D.11 40
FISHERGATE D.8 39
FISHERS CLOSE C.1 37
FISHERS LANE E.8 39
FITZGERALD ROAD H.9 45
FITZHENRY MEWS D.3 37
FLEETWOOD DRIVE D.14 41
FLETCHER WAY B.7 39
FLORENCE ROAD E.10 40
FLOWERPOT COURT D.8 39
FOLGATE LANE A.2 37
FOLWELL ROAD C.1 37
FORESTER CLOSE H.7 44
FOSTER ROAD B.8 39
FOULGERS OPENING F.9 45
FOUNTAINS ROAD J.7 44
FOWELL CLOSE D.3 37
FOXBURROW ROAD A.10 40
FOXCOTTE CLOSE M.5 46
FOXLEY CLOSE E.4 38
FRANCIS STONE COURT ..E.14 41
FRANCIS WAY C.1 37
FREEMAN SQUARE D.7 39
FRENSHAM ROAD C.5 38
FRERE ROAD C.11 40
FRESHER MEWS D.2 37
FRESHFIELD CLOSE D.3 37
FRIAR TUCK ROAD H.7 44
FRIARS QUAY E.8 39
FRIENDS ROAD E.6 38
FROGG HALL LANE F.10 45
FROST CLOSE C.13 41
FUGILL GREEN C.12 41
FUGILL ROAD C.12 41
FULFORD CLOSE G.6 43
FULLER MEWS D.1 37
FULTON CLOSE H.6 43
FURZE AVENUE D.12 41
FURZE ROAD C.12 41

GAGE ROAD A.11 40
GAILEY HILL B.6 38
GAMBLING CLOSE M.6 46
GAMEWELL CLOSE G.8 44
GARDEN PLACE D.8 39
GARDEN STREET F.8 44
GARDNERS TERRACE A.9 40
GARGLE HILL D.13 41
GARRETT COURT C.9 40
GARRICK GREEN N.8 46
GAS HILL E.9 40
GATELEY GARDENS B.7 39
GAWDY ROAD C.11 40
GENTLEMAN'S WALK E.8 39
GENTRY PLACE C.4 38
GENTRY ROAD C.3 37
GEOFFREY ROAD G.9 45
GEORGE BORROW ROAD ..E.5 38
GEORGE CARVER COURT ..F.5 43
GEORGE DANCE PLACE ...D.3 37
GEORGE FOX WAY E.3 37
GEORGE HILL A.9 40
GEORGE POPE CLOSE B.7 39
GEORGE POPE ROAD B.7 39
GEORGE WINTER COURT ..B.7 39
GERALD CLOSE D.11 40
GERTRUDE ROAD C.9 40
GILBARD ROAD D.3 37
GILBERT ROAD H.4 43
GILCHRIST CLOSE H.8 44
GILDENCROFT D.8 39
GILMAN ROAD C.9 40
GIPSY CLOSE E.4 38
GIPSY LANE E.4 38
GIRLINGS LANE E.12 41
GIRTON ROAD F.6 43
GLADSTONE STREET E.7 39
GLEBE ROAD F.6 43
GLENALMOND H.6 43
GLENBURN AVENUE B.10 40
GLENBURN COURT B.10 40
GLENDA CLOSE C.3 37
GLENDA CRESCENT B.3 37
GLENDA ROAD C.3 37
GLENDENNING ROAD F.10 45
GLENMORE GARDENS B.7 39
GLOBE LANE E.8 39
GLOBE PLACE F.7 44
GLOUCESTER STREET F.7 44
GODRIC PLACE D.5 38
GOLDEN BALL STREET E.8 39
GOLDENDOG LANE D.8 39
GOLDING PLACE E.7 39
GOLDSMITH STREET D.7 39
GOLDWELL ROAD F.8 44
GOODHALE ROAD D.3 37
GOODMAN SQUARE D.7 39
GORDON AVENUE D.11 40
GORDON SQUARE F.8 44
GORSE AVENUE A.6 38
GORSE ROAD D.12 41
GOSHAWK MEWS A.11 40
GOULBOURN ROAD C.11 40
GOULD ROAD F.5 43
GOVERNORS COURT F.9 45
GOWING CLOSE M.8 46
GOWING COURT B.6 38
GOWING ROAD M.5 46
GRANAGE ROAD H.9 45
GRANGE CLOSE A.9 40
GRANGE ROAD F.6 43
GRANT STREET D.6 38
GRAPES HILL E.7 39
GRASMERE CLOSE E.3 37
GRAVELFIELD CLOSE D.10 40
GRAYS FAIR C.2 37
GREEN CLOSE C.1 37
GREEN HILLS CLOSE A.1 37
GREEN LANE NORTH C.14 41
GREENBOROUGH CLOSE ..B.12 41
GREENBOROUGH ROAD ..B.12 41
GREENCOURT E.12 41
GREENFIELD C.1 37
GREENHILL ROAD D.8 39
GREENWAYS H.5 43
GREENWOOD ROAD H.7 44
GREENWOOD WAY B.13 41
GRESHAM ROAD B.6 38
GREYFRIARS ROAD E.9 40
GREYHOUND OPENING D.7 39
GRIFFIN LANE E.14 41
GRISTOCK PLACE C.4 38
GROSVENOR ROAD E.7 39
GROVE AV., NW. CSTSSY. ..C.2 37
GROVE AVENUE, NR1 ......F.8 44
GROVE PASS E.7 39
GROVE ROAD F.8 44
GROVE WALK G.8 44
GROVEDALE CLOSE C.2 37
GUARDIAN ROAD D.5 38
GUERNSEY ROAD D.8 39
GUNN ROAD B.10 40
GUNNER CLOSE C.14 41
GUNTON LANE B.3 37
GUNTON ROAD E.5 38
GURNEY CLOSE C.3 37
GURNEY COURT C.3 37
GURNEY DRIVE A.12 41
GURNEY LANE G.3 42
GURNEY RD., NW. CSTSSY. .C.2 37
GURNEY ROAD, NR1 ....D.9 40

HADLEY DRIVE E.5 38
HAIG CLOSE D.4 38
HALCOMBE COURT C.8 39
HALDEN AVENUE N.5 46
HALF MOON WAY D.6 38
HALFMILE CLOSE C.7 39
HALFMILE ROAD C.7 39
HALL DRIVE B.1 37
HALL LANE L.4 46
HALL RD, NEW COSTESSEY .B.2 37
HALL RD, NR1,NR4 ...J.7-G.8 44
HALLGATE A.14 41
HAMLIN COURT C.7 39
HAMMOND CLOSE B.12 41
HAMMOND WAY B.12 41
HAMPDEN DRIVE D.14 41
HANBURY CLOSE E.4 38
HANCOCK COURT D.1 37
HANKIN COURT E.3 37
HANLY CLOSE C.11 40
HANOVER ROAD F.7 44
HANSARD CLOSE C.7 39
HANSARD ROAD C.7 39
HANSARD STREET D.8 39
HANSELL ROAD C.13 41
HARBORD ROAD E.5 38
HARBOUR ROAD F.10 45
HARCOURT CLOSE D.9 40
HARDWICK CLOSE H.6 43
HARDY ROAD F.10 45
HARFORD HILL J.7 44
HARFORD MANOR CLOSE ..G.7 44
HARFORD STREET G.8 44
HARLINGTON AVENUE A.6 38
HARMER CLOSE H.4 43
HARMER CRESCENT H.4 43
HARMER RD, CRINGLEFORD .H.4 43
HARMER RD, UPPR HLLSTN. .B.6 38
HARPSFIELD D.1 37
HARRIER WAY M.8 46
HARRIS MEWS D.2 37
HARRISONS DRIVE B.12 41
HARRY BARBER CLOSE D.2 37
HARRY PERRY CLOSE G.7 44
HARSNETT CLOSE C.2 37
HARTBEE ROAD N.7 46
HARTS LANE H.3 42
HARVEY CLOSE D.11 40
HARVEY LANE D.11 40
HARWOOD ROAD H.8 44
HASLIPS CLOSE D.7 39
HASSETT CLOSE D.9 40
HASTINGS AVENUE A.6 38
HATTON ROAD C.7 39
HAUTEYN CLOSE H.5 43
HAVANT CLOSE H.5 43
HAVELOCK ROAD E.6 38
HAVERS ROAD C.7 39
HAWTHORN LANE G.6 43
HAWTHORN ROAD B.3 37
HAWTHORN ROW D.6 38
HAWTHORNE AVENUE N.6 46
HAYDEN COURT F.8 44
HAZEL ROAD B.1 37
HEARNE COURT D.1 37
HEARTSEASE LANE C.11 40
HEATH CLOSE N.6 46
HEATH CRESCENT N.6 46
HEATH ROAD, NR3 ....C.8 39
HEATH RD, THORPE END ..B.14 41
HEATHER AVENUE A.6 38
HEATHERWOOD CLOSE ...B.14 41
HEATHGATE D.9 40
HEATHSIDE ROAD F.10 45
HEIGHAM GROVE E.7 39
HEIGHAM ROAD E.7 39
HEIGHAM STREET D.7 39
HEIGHAM WATERING C.7 39
HELENA ROAD E.6 38
HELFORD STREET A.5 38
HELLESDON ; A.5 38
HELLESDON CLOSE C.4 38
HELLESDON HALL ROAD ...C.5 38
HELLESDON MILL LANE C.4 38
HELLESDON PARK ROAD ...B.5 38
HELLESDON ROAD B.4 38
HEMLIN CLOSE E.4 38
HEMMINGS CLOSE D.2 37
HEMPSTEAD MEWS D.1 37
HEMPSTEAD MEWS B.3 37
HENBY WAY E.11 40
HENDERSON ROAD E.5 38
HENDON CLOSE C.3 37
HENLEY ROAD F.6 43
HERCULES CLOSE A.6 38
HERCULES ROAD A.6 38
HETHERSETT LANE G.1 42
HIGH GREEN E.10 40
HIGHAM CLOSE B.10 40
HIGHFIELD CLOSE E.13 41
HIGHFIELDS C.1 37
HIGHLAND CRESCENT ...H.10 45
HIGHLAND ROAD H.10 45
HIGHLANDS A.2 37
HILLBOROW ROAD C.2 37
HILARY AVENUE D.10 40
HILL CREST B.2 37
HILL CREST ROAD D.12 41
HILL HOUSE ROAD D.12 41
HILL MEAD B.8 39
HILL STREET F.7 44
HILL TOP DRIVE A.2 37
HILLSIDE AVENUE E.12 41
HILLSIDE CLOSE E.12 41
HILLSIDE ROAD E.12 41
HILLVUE CLOSE B.3 37
HILLY PLANTATION E.12 41
HILM FARM CLOSE H.4 43
HINSHALWOOD WAY A.1 37
HOBART LANE F.8 44
HOBART SQUARE F.8 44
HOBROUGH LANE F.9 45
HODGSON ROAD E.5 38
HOLL'S WALK F.8 44
HOLLY BANK B.10 40
HOLLY DRIVE D.6 38
HOLMES CLOSE C.12 41
HOLMWOOD RISE E.11 40
HOLSWORTHY ROAD C.3 37
HOLT ROAD L.5 46
HOME STREET D.7 39
HONEY CLOSE D.10 40
HOOK'S WALK E.9 40
HOOKER ROAD C.12 41
HOOPER LANE B.9 40
HOPTON CLOSE D.14 41
HORNBEAM CLOSE A.12 41
HORNING CLOSE D.4 38
HORNOR CLOSE G.7 44
HORNS LANE F.8 44
HORSE STREET E.8 39
HORSESHOE CLOSE C.1 37
HORSFORD STREET C.7 39
HOSPITAL LANE A.4 38
HOSPITAL LANE G.8 44
HOTBLACK ROAD D.6 38
HOUGHTON CLOSE C.3 37
HOWARD CLOSE D.1 37
HOWARD MEWS C.9 40
HOWARD STREET F.8 44
HOWLETT DRIVE D.2 37
HUDSON WAY D.1 37
HUGHENDEN ROAD D.7 39
HUMBLEYARD D.2 37
HUNTER ROAD B.7 39
HUNTINGFIELD C.1 37
HUNTINGFIELD CLOSE C.1 37

HURD ROAD G.5 43
HURRICANE WAY N.7 46
HUTCHINSON ROAD E.4 38
HUXLEY CLOSE G.9 45
HUXLEY ROAD G.9 45
HYDE COURT C.14 41

ICEHOUSE LANE F.9 45
ILEX COURT A.12 41
INDEPENDENT WAY D.14 41
INDIGO YARD E.8 39
INGLEBY ROAD F.10 45
INGRAM COURT G.8 44
INMAN ROAD A.12 41
INTWOOD ROAD J.4 43
IPSWICH GROVE F.8 44
IPSWICH ROAD H.7 44
IRETON CLOSE D.14 41
IRSTEAD ROAD E.5 38
IRVING ROAD H.7 44
IVES ROAD A.8 39
IVORY ROAD F.4 43

JAMES ALEXANDRA MEWS E.4 38
JAMIESON PLACE D.3 37
JARROLD WAY C.2 37
JASMINE CLOSE E.4 38
JAVELIN ROAD M.7 46
JAY GARDENS C.1 37
JENKINS LANE D.8 39
JERNINGHAM ROAD C.2 37
JESSOPP CLOSE F.5 43
JESSOPP ROAD F.5 43
JEWSON ROAD B.7 39
JEX AVENUE D.4 38
JEX LANE D.4 38
JEX ROAD C.4 38
JOHN STEPHENSON CT C.9 40
JOHNSON PLACE E.7 39
JOLLY GARDENERS CT D.8 39
JORDANS CLOSE D.3 37
JOSEPHINE CLOSE G.8 44
JOYCE WAY C.14 41
JUBILEE ROAD A.10 40
JUBILEE TERRACE G.9 45
JUDGES DRIVE G.5 43
JUDGES WALK G.5 43
JUNCTION ROAD C.7 39
JUPITER ROAD A.7 39

KABIN ROAD B.3 37
KEABLE CLOSE E.4 38
KEDLESTON DRIVE J.3 42
KEELAN CLOSE A.7 39
KEMP CLOSE C.11 40
KENNETT CLOSE F.5 43
KENSINGTON PLACE F.9 45
KERRISON ROAD F.10 45
KERVILLE STREET D.2 37
KESTREL ROAD A.11 40
KESWICK ; K.6 44
KESWICK CLOSE J.4 43
KESWICK RD, CRINGLEFORD J.4 43
KESWICK RD, NW. SPRWSTN. A.9 40
KETTS HILL D.10 40
KEY AND CASTLE YARD D.8 39
KEYES CLOSE G.8 44
KEYES ROAD G.8 44
KILN CLOSE M.9 46
KIMBERLEY STREET E.7 39
KING STREET E.9 40
KINGHORN ROAD F.5 43
KINGS LANE F.8 44
KINGSLEY ROAD F.8 44
KINGSTON SQUARE G.6 43
KINGSWAY D.7 39
KINGSWOOD CLOSE G.6 43
KINGSWOOD DRIVE H.5 43
KINSALE AVE., HELLESDON A.5 38
KINSALE AVE., HELLESDON N.5 46
KINVER CLOSE G.6 43
KIRKLANDS A.1 37
KIRKLEES J.7 44
KIRKPATRICK ROAD B.7 39
KNIGHTS ROAD B.7 39
KNOWLAND GROVE C.3 37
KNOWSLEY ROAD C.8 39
KNOX AVENUE D.10 40
KNOX CLOSE D.10 40
KNOX ROAD D.10 40
KOBLENZ AVENUE F.9 45

LADBROKES CLOSE D.10 40
LADY BETTY ROAD G.8 44
LADY MARY ROAD G.8 44
LADYS LANE E.8 39
LADYSMITH ROAD C.9 40
LAKENFIELDS G.9 45
LAKENHAM ROAD G.7 44
LAMBERT HOUSE D.2 37
LAMBERT ROAD B.10 40
LAMITER ROAD H.8 44
LANCASTER CLOSE N.8 46
LANCASTER COURT D.7 39
LANGHAM PLACE F.8 44
LANGLEY CLOSE J.3 42
LANGLEY STREET D.7 39
LANGLEY WALK D.7 39
LANGTON CLOSE D.3 37
LANSDOWNE ROAD N.7 46
LARCH CLOSE A.11 40
LARKMAN LANE D.3 37
LAUD CLOSE D.14 41
LAUNCESTON TERRACE F.7 44
LAUNDRY CLOSE D.12 41
LAUNDRY LA., SPROWSTON A.12 41
LAUNDRY LA., T. ST ANDRW D.13 41
LAUREL COURT C.12 41
LAUREL ROAD C.12 41
LAVENGRO ROAD C.9 40
LAWN CRESCENT B.14 41
LAWRENCE LANE E.8 39
LAWSON ROAD C.8 39
LAYER CLOSE D.1 37
LAYSON DRIVE C.9 40
LE TUNDER CLOSE D.12 41
LEAS COURT C.4 38

LEEWOOD CRESCENT C.4 38
LEFROY ROAD B.6 38
LEICESTER STREET F.7 44
LENG CRESCENT G.5 43
LENTHALL CLOSE D.14 41
LEONARD STREET D.8 39
LEOPARD COURT D.8 39
LEOPOLD CLOSE G.6 43
LESTRANGE CLOSE E.6 38
LEVEN CLOSE C.14 41
LEVESON ROAD B.11 40
LEYHAM COURT D.2 37
LIBERATOR ROAD M.7 46
LIBRA COURT A.11 40
LILBURNE AVENUE B.8 39
LILIAN CLOSE A.7 39
LILY TERRACE F.9 45
LIME KILN MEWS C.7 39
LIME TREE AVENUE A.1 37
LIME TREE ROAD G.7 44
LIMETREE AVENUE E.11 40
LINACRE AVENUE B.11 40
LINACRE CLOSE A.11 40
LINCOLN STREET F.6 43
LINDEN ROAD C.3 37
LINDFORD DRIVE H.5 43
LINDLEY STREET G.8 44
LINDSAY ROAD A.11 40
LINKS AVENUE A.5 38
LINKS CLOSE A.5 38
LINTOCK ROAD B.8 39
LINTON CLOSE A.11 40
LINTON CRESCENT A.11 40
LISHMAN ROAD B.12 41
LISLE ROAD D.2 37
LITTLE ARMS STREET D.6 38
LITTLE BETHEL STREET E.8 39
LITTLE JOHN ROAD H.7 44
LITTLE PADDOCK STREET D.7 39
LIVINGSTONE STREET D.6 38
LLOYD ROAD D.10 40
LOCKSLEY ROAD H.7 44
LODDON ROAD H.10 45
LODGE FARM DRIVE M.8 46
LODGE LANE M.8 46
LODGE PLACE E.12 41
LODORE AVENUE N.6 46
LOLLARDS PIT E.9 40
LOLLARDS ROAD E.9 40
LONDON STREET E.8 39
LONE BARN ROAD B.10 40
LONG JOHN HILL G.9 45
LONG ROW C.8 39
LONGBOW CLOSE H.7 44
LONGDEL HILLS B.1 37
LONGFIELDS ROAD C.13 41
LONGLAND CLOSE N.8 46
LONGMEAD G.8 44
LONGWATER LANE B.1 37
LORRAINE GARDENS B.8 39
LOSINGA CRESCNET B.7 39
LOTHIAN STREET D.7 39
LOUIS CLOSE N.8 46
LOUND ROAD E.5 38
LOVELACE ROAD F.4 43
LOVELSTAITHE E.9 40
LOW ROAD, HELLESTON A.4 38
LOWER CLARENCE ROAD E.9 40
LOWER CLOSE E.9 40
LOWER GOAT LANE E.8 39
LOWES YARD D.8 39
LOWESWATER GARDENS E.4 38
LOWTHER ROAD H.6 43
LOXWOOD M.8 46
LUBBOCK CLOSE E.5 38
LUCAS COURT C.14 41
LUCERNE CLOSE A.9 40
LUKE CLOSE C.1 37
LUSHER DRIVE D.4 38
LUSHERS LOKE A.9 40
LUSHINGTON CLOSE D.3 37
LYHART ROAD H.7 44
LYNN CLOSE C.14 41
LYON WOOD ROAD D.11 40

MAGDALENE CLOSE D.8 39
MAGDALENE ROAD D.8 39
MAGDALENE STREET D.8 39
MAGPIE ROAD D.8 39
MAID MARIAN ROAD H.7 44
MAIDA VALE F.7 44
MAIDENS CLOSE C.14 41
MAIDSTONE ROAD E.9 40
MALBROOK ROAD D.3 37
MALLORY ROAD N.8 46
MALTBY COURT C.9 40
MALTHOUSE ROAD F.8 44
MALVERN ROAD E.9 40
MALZY COURT D.8 39
MANBY ROAD C.11 40
MANCHESTER PLACE E.7 39
MANCROFT WALK D.7 39
MANDELA CLOSE D.8 39
MANSEL DRIVE B.8 39
MANSFIELD LANE H.8 44
MANTHORPE CLOSE H.8 44
MANTLE CLOSE A.11 40
MAPLE DRIVE D.6 38
MARDLE STREET E.1 37
MARGARET CLOSE N.4 46
MARGARET CRESCENT D.13 41
MARGARET PASTON AVE. C.6 38
MARGARET ROAD B.3 37
MARGETSON AVENUE D.11 40
MARINERS LANE F.9 45
MARION ROAD E.10 40
MARIONVILLE ROAD B.8 39
MARK LEMMON CLOSE J.4 43
MARKET AVENUE F.8 44
MARKHAM TOWER B.6 38
MARLBOROUGH COURT B.10 40
MARLBOROUGH ROAD D.8 39
MARLOW COURT B.9 40
MARLPIT LANE D.4 38
MARRIOT CLOSE D.7 39
MARRYAT ROAD C.11 40
MARSHALL CLOSE C.3 37

MARSHALL ROAD B.6 38
MARSTON LANE J.5-J.6 43
MARSTON MOOR D.14 41
MARTIN CLOSE A.11 40
MARTINEAU LANE H.9 45
MARVELL GREEN C.14 41
MARY CHAPMAN CLOSE E.14 41
MASON ROAD A.7 39
MASSINGHAM ROAD C.9 40
MATLOCK ROAD E.10 40
MAUD STREET E.6 38
MAVISH WAY E.2 37
MAYES CLOSE D.3 37
MAYFIELD AVENUE A.7 39
MEADOW CLOSE B.2 37
MEADOW CLOSE G.10 45
MEADOW FARM DRIVE J.3 42
MEADOW GARDENS A.9 40
MEADOW LANE E.13 41
MEADOW RISE AVENUE F.6 43
MEADOW RISE CLOSE F.6 43
MEADOW RISE ROAD F.6 43
MEADOW ROAD B.2 37
MEADOW SWEET A.8 39
MEADOW VALE B.2 37
MEADOW WAY N.6 46
MEADOWBROOK CLOSE G.9 45
MEADWAY J.3 42
MELBOURNE COTTAGES F.7 44
MELROSE ROAD G.6 43
MENDHAM CLOSE G.8 44
MERCHANT WAY A.6 38
MEREDITH ROAD N.5 46
MERITON ROAD D.6 38
MERLIN AVENUE A.11 40
MERLIN CLOSE A.11 40
MERROW GARDENS H.5 43
METCAFF CLOSE C.5 38
METEOR CLOSE M.8 46
MIDDLETON CLOSE B.7 39
MIDDLETON COURT A.5 38
MIDDLETON CRESCENT B.1 37
MIDDLETON LANE A.5 38
MIDDLETONS LANE N.6 46
MIDLAND STREET D.7 39
MIDLAND WALK D.7 39
MILE CROSS LANE A.7 39
MILE CROSS ROAD C.7 39
MILE END CLOSE G.6 43
MILE END ROAD G.6 43
MILESTONE CLOSE B.1 37
MILL CLOSE F.8 44
MILL HILL ROAD E.7 39
MILL LANE D.8 39
MILLCROFT C.8 39
MILLCROFT CLOSE C.1 37
MILLENIUM AVENUE N.5 46
MILLERS LANE WEST C.8 39
MILTON CLOSE G.8 44
MILTON STREET G.8 44
MILVERTON ROAD G.9 45
MINION CLOSE D.14 41
MINNS COURT D.8 39
MITCH COURT D.2 37
MITRE COURT B.6 38
MONS AVENUE D.10 40
MONTCALM ROAD E.10 40
MONTGOMERY CLOSE D.1 37
MONTROSE COURT D.14 41
MOORE AVENUE A.9 40
MOORLAND CLOSE B.10 40
MORELLO CLOSE F.4 43
MORGAN WAY C.1 37
MORLEY STREET D.9 40
MORNINGTON ROAD F.6 43
MORRIS CLOSE C.3 37
MORSE AVENUE D.11 40
MORSE ROAD D.11 40
MOSSFIELD CLOSE D.10 40
MOTTRAM CLOSE E.4 38
MOTURN ROAD D.4 38
MOUNT PLEASANT F.7 44
MOUNTENEY CLOSE A.9 40
MOUNTERGATE E.9 40
MOUNTFIELD AVENUE A.6 38
MOUSEHOLD AVENUE D.9 40
MOUSEHOLD HOUSE E.10 40
MOUSEHOLD LANE B.10 40
MOUSEHOLD STREET D.9 40
MUNNINGS ROAD C.12 41
MURIEL ROAD F.6 43
MURRAYFIELD ROAD N.7 46
MURRELL'S COURT E.9 40
MUSIC HOUSE LANE F.9 45
MUSKETEER WAY D.14 41
MUSLEY COURT G.6 43
MUSPOLE STREET D.8 39
MYRTLE AVENUE A.2 37

NAPIER PLACE D.7 39
NAPIER STREET D.7 39
NASEBY WAY D.14 41
NASMITH ROAD G.4 43
NAYLOR ROAD C.6 38
NELSON COURT F.4 43
NETHERWOOD GREEN G.9 45
NEVILLE CLOSE B.9 40
NEVILLE ROAD B.9 40
NEVILLE STREET E.7 39
NEW COSTESSEY ; C.2 37
NEW MILLS YARD D.8 39
NEW ROAD D.1 37
NEWARK CLOSE D.14 41
NEWBEGIN CLOSE D.11 40
NEWBEGIN ROAD D.10 40
NEWBURY WAY D.14 41
NEWCASTLE CLOSE C.14 41
NEWFOUND DRIVE H.3 42
NEWMARKET ROAD J.3 42
NEWMARKET STREET F.7 44
NEWTON CLOSE, NR4 H.7 44
NEWTON CL., TRWS. NWTN. G.10 45
NEYLOND CRESCENT N.5 46
NICHOLAS COURT C.8 39
NICHOLAS MEWS D.6 38
NIGHTINGALE COTTAGES G.9 45
NIGHTINGALE LANE D.9 40

NILE STREET D.7 39
NINHAM STREET G.8 44
NOBLE CLOSE C.12 41
NOOT ALLEY D.3 37
NORFOLK ROAD F.3 42
NORFOLK STREET F.7 44
NORFOLK TERRACE F.3 42
NORGATE ROAD G.5 43
NORMAN DRIVE M.9 46
NORMAN ROAD C.8 39
NORMANS BUILDINGS E.8 39
NORTH GATE N.6 46
NORTH PARK AVENUE F.4 43
NORTH PARK DRIVE F.5 43
NORTH VIEW ROAD C.3 37
NORTH WALSHAM ROAD A.9 40
NORTHCOTE ROAD C.8 39
NORTHFIELDS F.5 43
NORTHGAGE CLOSE A.11 40
NORTHGATE B.14 41
NORTHSIDE E.14 41
NORTHUMBERLAND ST. D.6 38
NORTON DRIVE H.6 43
NORVIC DRIVE H.4 43
NORWICH LIVE STCK MRKT J.7 44
NORWICH RD, NR9 J.1 42
NORWICH RD, NW. CSTSSY. B.3 37
NOTRIDGE ROAD D.2 37
NOTYKIN STREET C.2 37
NURSERY LANE A.2 37
NUTFIELD CLOSE H.5 43

OAK CLOSE B.2 37
OAK HOUSE D.1 37
OAK LANE A.8 39
OAK LODGE E.11 40
OAK ROAD D.13 41
OAK STREET D.8 39
OAK TREE DRIVE B.10 40
OAKFIELD CLOSE J.4 43
OAKFIELDS ROAD J.4 43
OAKLANDS DRIVE H.3 42
OFFLEY COURT D.2 37
OLD BARGE YARD F.9 45
OLD CATTON ; M.8 46
OLD COSTESSEY ; A.1 37
OLD FARM LANE C.7 39
OLD GROVE COURT B.8 39
OLD HALL CLOSE G.10 45
OLD HALL ROAD J.7 44
OLD LAKENHAM HALL DR. H.9 45
OLD LAUNDRY COURT C.6 38
OLD LIBRARY MEWS E.9 40
OLD NORWICH ROAD L.7 46
OLD PALACE ROAD D.7 39
OLD RECTORY CLOSE E.12 41
OLD SCHOOL COURT F.9 45
OLD WATTON ROAD E.2 37
OLIVE CLOSE C.3 37
OLIVE ROAD B.3 37
ONLEY STREET F.7 44
OPIE STREET E.8 39
ORCHARD CLOSE D.11 40
ORCHARD DRIVE B.4 38
ORCHARD STREET D.7 39
ORFORD HILL E.8 39
ORFORD PLACE E.8 39
ORWELL CLOSE F.4 43
ORWELL ROAD G.7 44
OSBERT CLOSE H.8 44
OSBORNE ROAD G.4 43
OULTON ROAD N.7 46
OVAL AVENUE C.3 37
OVAL ROAD C.3 37
OVERBURY ROAD A.6 38
OXFORD STREET E.7 39
OXNEAD ROAD B.7 39

PADDOCK STREET D.7 39
PADGATE A.14 41
PAGE ROAD C.5 38
PAGG LANE E.8 39
PAINE ROAD C.11 40
PALACE STREET E.9 40
PALMER CLOSE B.7 39
PALMER ROAD B.7 39
PARADISE PLACE F.8 44
PARAGON PLACE E.7 39
PARANA CLOSE A.11 40
PARANA COURT A.11 40
PARANA ROAD A.11 40
PARK CLOSE A.8 39
PARK LANE E.7 39
PARK ROAD C.6 38
PARK WAY N.5 46
PARKER ROAD E.7 39
PARKLAND CRESCENT B.9 40
PARKLAND ROAD B.9 40
PARKSIDE DRIVE A.8 39
PARKSIDE DRIVE N.8 46
PARLIAMENT COURT D.14 41
PARMENTER ROAD G.5 43
PARMENTERGATE COURT E.9 40
PARR ROAD C.6 38
PARSONS MEAD H.5 43
PARTRIDGE WAY A.8 39
PASTON WAY C.13 41
PATRICIA ROAD G.8 44
PATTESON CLOSE J.3 42
PATTESON ROAD C.8 39
PAXTON PLACE F.7 44
PEACOCK STREET D.8 39
PEARCEFIELD C.9 40
PECK CLOSE C.1 37
PECKOVER ROAD G.5 43
PELHAM ROAD C.8 39
PEMBREY CLOSE B.8 39
PEMBROKE ROAD E.6 38
PENN GROVE C.7 39
PENNY ROYAL N.8 46
PENRYN CLOSE G.6 43
PENSHURST MEWS H.5 43
PERCIVAL CLOSE F.5 43
PEREGRINE CLOSE A.11 40
PEREGRINE MEWS A.11 40
PEREGRINE ROAD A.11 40
PETERKIN ROAD H.7 44

PETERSON ROAD B.6 38
PETO COURT D.3 37
PETTUS ROAD G.5 43
PEVERELL ROAD D.3 37
PHELPS ROAD D.13 41
PHILADELPHIA LANE C.7 39
PIKEMAN PLACE C.14 41
PILLING PARK ROAD E.10 40
PILLING ROAD D.11 40
PINDER CLOSE C.6 38
PINDER ROAD C.6 38
PINE CLOSE G.6 43
PINE COURT B.12 41
PINE ROAD C.12 41
PINETREES ROAD B.12 41
PINEWOOD CLOSE A.5 38
PIPER ROAD C.12 41
PIPPIN GREEN E.4 38
PITCHFORD ROAD E.4 38
PITT STREET D.8 39
PLAFORD ROAD B.10 40
PLANTATION DRIVE B.12 41
PLANTATION ROAD N.5 46
PLANTSMAN CLOSE G.7 44
PLAYERS WAY N.9 46
PLEASANT CLOSE N.4 46
PLUMSTEAD ROAD D.10 40
PLUMSTEAD ROAD EAST D.11 40
POCKTHORPE GATE D.9 40
POINTER WAY D.5 38
POLLYWIGGLE CLOSE E.2 37
POPLAR AVENUE H.5 43
POPLAR CLOSE B.1 37
PORSON ROAD C.11 40
PORTERS LOKE B.9 40
PORTERSFIELD ROAD F.6 43
PORTLAND STREET F.6 43
PORTWAY PLACE D.7 39
POST MILL CLOSE B.9 40
POTTERGATE E.8 39
POUND LANE C.14 41
PRESS LANE C.7 39
PRESSGATE E.8 39
PRIDE WAY C.14 41
PRIMROSE COURT E.13 41
PRIMROSE CRESCENT E.13 41
PRIMROSE PLACE F.7 44
PRIMROSE ROAD E.10 40
PRIMULA DRIVE E.4 38
PRINCE ANDREWS CL N.7 46
PRINCE EDWARD CLOSE D.13 41
PRINCE OF WALES ROAD E.9 40
PRINCE RUPERT WAY C.14 41
PRINCES STREET E.8 39
PRINCESS BEATRICE CL B.4 38
PRINE ANDREWS ROAD N.6 46
PRIOR ROAD C.13 41
PRIORS DRIVE N.8 46
PRISCILLA CLOSE E.4 38
PROVIDENCE PLACE E.10 40
PURDANCE CLOSE C.1 37
PURLAND ROAD C.11 40
PURTINGAY CLOSE H.6 43
PYM CLOSE C.14 41
PYRFORD DRIVE H.5 43

QUAKERS LANE D.8 39
QUAYSIDE E.8 39
QUEBEC CLOSE J.3 42
QUEBEC ROAD E.10 40
QUEEN ELIZABETH CLOSE D.9 40
QUEEN STREET E.8 39
QUEENS CLOSE G.6 43
QUEENS ROAD F.8 44
QUELPH ROAD E.10 40

RACECOURSE ROAD C.12 41
RACHEL CLOSE E.4 38
RACKHAM ROAD B.8 39
RAFEMAN CLOSE D.1 37
RAINSBOROUGH RISE C.14 41
RALEIGH COURT E.8 39
RAMPANT E.8 39
RAMSEY CLOSE G.4 43
RANDLE GREEN C.3 37
RANDOLF ROAD H.8 44
RANGOON CLOSE A.11 40
RANSON ROAD E.10 40
RANWORTH ROAD D.4 38
RAWLEY ROAD C.2 37
RAYMOND CLOSE M.5 46
RAYMOND ROAD M.5 46
RAYNHAM STREET D.7 39
RECORDER ROAD E.9 40
RECREATION GROUND RD A.10 40
RECREATION ROAD C.6 38
RECTORY CLOSE B.8 39
RED COTTAGE CLOSE C.6 38
RED LION STREET E.8 39
REDFERN CLOSE C.12 41
REDFERN ROAD C.12 41
REDWELL STREET E.8 39
REDWOOD LODGE G.6 43
REEPHAM STREET A.6 38
REGENCY COURT D.10 40
REGINA ROAD F.8 44
RENSON CLOSE A.7 39
REPTON AVENUE M.8 46
REYDON CLOSE D.2 37
RHODA TERRACE B.7 39
RICE WAY B.11 40
RICHENDA CLOSE E.4 38
RICHMOND COURT E.12 41
RICHMOND ROAD C.1 37
RILEY CLOSE C.12 41
RIMER CLOSE E.2 37
RIMINGTON ROAD A.9 40
RING ROAD D.13 41
RIPLEY CLOSE E.5 38
RISEWAY CLOSE D.10 40
RIVER LANE D.9 40
RIVER VIEW BUNGALOWS C.4 38
RIVERSIDE F.9 45
RIVERSIDE CLOSE B.4 38
RIVERSIDE ROAD E.9 40
ROBBERDS WAY C.1 37
ROBERT GYBSON WAY E.8 39

35 Norwich....*maps on pages 37 to 46*

ROBIN HOOD ROAD H.7 44
ROBSON ROAD E.3 37
ROCELIN CLOSE B.8 39
ROCKINGHAM ROAD E.3 37
ROCKLAND DRIVE E.11 40
ROGERS CLOSE D.3 37
ROLLESTON CLOSE D.3 37
ROMANY ROAD C.9 40
ROPEMAKER ROW C.7 39
ROSARY ROAD E.9 40
ROSE AVENUE E.8 39
ROSE LANE E.9 40
ROSE VALLEY F.7 44
ROSE YARD D.8 39
ROSEACRE CLOSE G.7 44
ROSEBAY CLOSE A.8 39
ROSEBAY CLOSE N.8 46
ROSEBAY COURT E.14 41
ROSEBERY ROAD C.8 39
ROSEDALE CRESCENT E.10 40
ROSEMARY LANE D.8 39
ROSEMARY ROAD A.10 40
ROSEVILLE CLOSE F.10 45
ROSSLARE G.6 43
ROSTWOLD WAY B.8 39
ROTARY COURT C.5 38
ROUEN ROAD E.8 39
ROUNDHEAD COURT D.14 41
ROUNDTREE CLOSE B.10 40
ROUNDTREE WAY C.10 40
ROUNDWAY DOWN D.14 41
ROUNDWELL ROAD C.1 37
ROWAN CT, NEW COSTESSEY C.2 37
ROWAN CT, SPROWSTON ...A.12 41
ROWINGTON ROAD F.8 44
ROWLAND COURT F.8 44
ROWTON HEATH D.14 41
ROXLEY CLOSE E.13 41
ROYALIST DRIVE D.14 41
RUGGE DRIVE G.4 43
RUNCTON CLOSE D.3 37
RUPERT STREET F.7 44
RUSHMORE CLOSE A.10 40
RUSHMORE ROAD A.10 40
RUSKIN RD, EARLHAM F.4 43
RUSKIN RD, HELLESDON ...C.3 37
RUSSELL AVENUE B.10 40
RUSSELL STREET D.7 39
RUSSELL TERRACE H.10 45
RUSSET GROVE E.4 38
RUTLAND STREET F.7 44
RYDAL CLOSE E.3 37
RYE AVENUE B.6 38
RYE CLOSE B.7 39
RYRIE COURT G.5 43

SADLER ROAD M.5 46
SAFFRON SQUARE B.8 39
SAKER CLOSE D.14 41
SALE ROAD B.12 41
SALHOUSE ROAD A.11 40
SALISBURY ROAD F.10 45
SALTER AVENUE E.4 38
SAMSON ROAD A.6 38
SAMUEL ROAD D.10 40
SANDHOLME CLOSE D.10 40
SANDRINGHAM ROAD E.6 38
SANDY LANE H.8 44
SARACEN ROAD N.5 46
SARAH WILLIMAN CLOSE ...E.3 37
SAUNDERS COURT E.10 40
SAVERY CLOSE D.3 37
SAWYERS CLOSE C.1 37
SAYERS STREET D.7 39
SCARLETT ROAD H.7 44
SCARNELL ROAD E.4 38
SCEPTRE CLOSE A.6 38
SCHOOL AVENUE E.13 41
SCHOOL LA., COLNEY F.1 42
SCHOOL LA., OLD CATTON ..A.9 40
SCHOOL LA., T. ST ANDRW. .E.12 41
SCOTT ROAD F.10 45
SEABROOK COURT D.2 37
SEAMAN TOWER B.6 38
SECOND CLOSE B.9 40
SEDMAN WALK D.2 37
SEWELL ROAD C.8 39
SHEEP MEADOW CLOSE C.1 37
SHEPHERD CLOSE E.4 38
SHEPHERDS BUILDINGS C.9 40
SHERBOURNE PLACE F.9 45
SHERWELL ROAD M.5 46
SHERWOOD ROAD H.7 44
SHIPFIELD B.9 40
SHIPSTONE ROAD C.8 39
SHORNCLIFFE AVENUE C.7 39
SHORNCLIFFE CLOSE C.7 39
SIDELL CLOSE J.3 42
SIDNEY ROAD A.2 37
SIGISMUND ROAD F.8 44
SILVER ROAD C.9 40
SILVER STREET D.9 40
SKELTON ROAD C.11 40
SKIPPON WAY C.14 41
SKONER ROAD D.3 37
SKYE CLOSE C.2 37
SLEAFOED GREEN C.8 39
SMEAT STREET D.3 37
SMITHDALE ROAD C.3 37
SMITHFIELD ROAD G.9 40
SOFTLEY DRIVE G.4 43
SOLEME ROAD C.6 38
SOMERLEYTON GARDENS ...F.7 44
SONYA TERRACE D.10 40
SORREL HOUSE D.2 37
SOTHERTON ROAD G.5 43
SOUTH AVENUE E.12 41
SOUTH HILL CLOSE D.13 41
SOUTH HILL ROAD C.13 41
SOUTH PARK AVENUE G.5 43
SOUTH WALK B.14 41
SOUTHER WOOD N.8 46
SOUTHGATE CLOSE A.11 40
SOUTHGATE LANE F.9 45
SOUTHWELL STREET F.8 44
SOVEREIGN WAY D.8 39
SPAR ROAD A.7 39

SPARHAWK AVENUE A.11 40
SPARHAWK CLOSE A.11 40
SPEEDWELL WAY E.2 37
SPEKE STREET D.6 38
SPELMAN ROAD F.6 43
SPENCER ROAD N.7 46
SPENCER STREET C.9 40
SPINDLE ROAD A.8 39
SPINNEY CLOSE D.13 41
SPINNEY ROAD D.12 41
SPITALFIELDS D.9 40
SPITFIRE ROAD N.7 46
SPIXWORTH ROAD A.9 40
SPRINGBANK G.8 44
SPRINGFIELD ROAD C.12 41
SPROWSTON ROAD C.8 39
SPROWSTON: A.11 40
SPYNKE ROAD A.7 39
ST. ALBANS ROAD G.8 44
ST. ANDREW STREET E.8 39
ST. ANDREWS AVENUE E.13 41
ST. ANDREWS CLOSE E.13 41
ST. ANDREWS COURT E.12 41
ST. ANDREWS DRIVE H.5 43
ST. ANDREWS ROAD N.4 46
ST. ANDREWS SQUARE E.14 41
ST. ANNE'S LANE F.9 45
ST. AUGUSTINE STREET D.8 39
ST. BARTHOLOMEWS CL ...D.7 39
ST. BENEDICT ALLEY E.7 39
ST. BENEDICT STREET E.7 39
ST. CATHERINES CLOSE F.8 44
ST. CATHERINES ROAD D.13 41
ST. CLEMENTS HILL C.8 39
ST. CRISPINS ROAD D.8 39
ST. DAVIDS DRIVE B.14 41
ST. EDMUNDS CLOSE C.4 38
ST. FAITHS LANE E.9 40
ST. GEORGE STREET D.8 39
ST. GILES STREET E.7 39
ST. HELEN'S SQUARE E.9 40
ST. JAMES CLOSE D.9 40
ST. JAMES COURT D.9 40
ST. JOHN ST., NORWICH E.8 39
ST. JOHN'S STREET E.9 40
ST. JOHNS CLOSE G.8 44
ST. JULIANS ALLEY F.9 45
ST. LAWRENCE DRIVE H.3 42
ST. LEONARDS CRESCENT ..E.10 40
ST. LEONARDS ROAD E.10 40
ST. LEONARDS TERRACE ...E.10 40
ST. MARTIN LANE D.8 39
ST. MARTIN ROAD D.8 39
ST. MARTINS CLOSE D.8 39
ST. MARYS PLACE D.8 39
ST. MARYS ROAD D.8 39
ST. MATTHEW ROAD E.9 40
ST. MILDREDS ROAD D.3 37
ST. OLAVES ROAD C.9 40
ST. PAULS CLOSE N.6 46
ST. PETER STREET E.8 39
ST. PETERS CLOSE J.4 42
ST. PHILIP ROAD E.6 38
ST. PHILIPS CLOSE E.7 39
ST. SAVIOUR'S LANE D.8 39
ST. STEPHEN ROAD F.8 44
ST. STEPHEN SQUARE F.8 44
ST. STEPHEN STREET F.8 44
ST. SWITHINS ROAD E.7 39
ST. THOMAS ROAD E.6 38
ST. WILLIAMS WAY D.11 40
STACY ROAD D.8 39
STAFFORD AVENUE C.1 37
STAFFORD STREET E.6 38
STAN PETERSEN CLOSE E.10 40
STANFORD COURT E.5 38
STANLEY AVENUE E.11 40
STANMORE ROAD E.12 41
STANNARD ROAD F.5 43
STARLING ROAD D.8 39
STATHAM CLOSE G.7 44
STATION APPROACH E.9 40
STATION ROAD E.9 40
STEEPGREEN CLOSE D.11 40
STEEPING LANE E.8 39
STEPPINGS WAY B.14 41
STEVENSON ROAD D.3 37
STEWARD STREET D.9 40
STILLINGTON CLOSE B.10 40
STOKE ROAD H.9 45
STONE BRECK B.1 37
STONE ROAD C.7 39
STONEHOUSE ROAD A.10 40
STONES BUILDINGS C.8 39
STRACEY ROAD F.10 45
STRANGERS COURT E.8 39
STRATFORD CLOSE G.9 45
STRATFORD CRESCENT G.3 42
STRATFORD DRIVE G.9 45
STUART GARDENS E.9 40
STUART ROAD F.9 45
SUCKLING AVENUE B.6 38
SUFFIELD CLOSE J.4 42
SUFFIELD COURT C.8 39
SUFFOLK ROAD F.4 43
SUFFOLK TERRACE F.3 42
SUFFOLK WALK F.4 43
SUKEY WAY E.2 37
SUMPTER COURT G.5 43
SUN LANE C.8 39
SUNCROFT F.7 44
SUNNINGDALE G.6 43
SUNNY CLOSE C.3 37
SUNNY GROVE C.3 37
SUNNY HILL D.5 38
SUPPLE CLOSE D.11 40
SURREY CLOSE A.11 40
SURREY GROVE F.8 44
SURREY STREET F.8 44
SURSHAM AVENUE A.9 40
SUSSEX STREET D.8 39
SUTHERLAND AVENUE A.8 39
SWAFIELD STREET D.2 37
SWALLOWTAIL CLOSE E.2 37
SWANSEA ROAD E.6 38

SWANSGATE N.9 46
SWANTON ROAD C.6 38
SWEET BRIAR ROAD D.5 38
SWINBOURNE CLOSE B.8 39
SWINDELLS CLOSE B.2 37
SYCAMORE CRESCENT D.5 38
SYLVAN CLOSE N.5 46

TALBOT SQUARE D.8 39
TALEWORTH CLOSE D.2 37
TAMARIND MEWS H.5 43
TANAGER CLOSE B.8 39
TANNERS COURT D.7 39
TANSY CLOSE A.8 39
TAVERNERS SQUARE D.9 40
TAYLOR AVENUE J.3 42
TAYLOR ROAD E.3 37
TAYLORS BUILDINGS C.8 39
TAYLORS LANE C.8 39
TELEGRAPH LANE EAST ...E.10 40
TELEGRAPH LANE WEST ...E.10 40
TELFORD CLOSE C.6 38
TEMPLE ROAD C.8 39
TEMPLEMERE B.9 40
TEN BELL COURT E.7 39
TEN BELL LANE E.8 39
TENISON COURT H.5 43
TERENCE AVENUE A.9 40
TERRACE WALK F.9 45
THE AVENUES F.5 43
THE BUTTS D.1 37
THE CEDARS F.7 44
THE CHANTRY E.8 39
THE CLOSE E.9 40
THE COLUMBINE A.8 39
THE COTTAGE DRIVE D.12 41
THE CRESCENT F.7 44
THE CROFT A.2 37
THE CROFTS D.1 37
THE DENES E.11 40
THE DRIVE C.3 37
THE ELMS, NR2 ....E.7 39
THE ELMS, OLD CATTON ...N.8 46
THE GLADE A.2 37
THE HEDGEROWS D.2 37
THE HEIGHTS E.10 40
THE KERRIDGES C.1 37
THE LANE B.6 38
THE LATHES D.8 39
THE LOANIN G.9 45
THE LOKE, CRINGLEFORD ..H.4 43
THE LOKE, HELLESDON D.5 38
THE LOKE, NEW COSTESSEY B.1 37
THE MEWS F.7 44
THE OLD BARLEY MARKET ..E.8 39
THE OVAL C.3 37
THE PADDOCK H.10 45
THE PARADE F.6 43
THE PINELODGES E.11 40
THE PLANTATION E.7 39
THE RIDGEWAY D.10 40
THE RIDINGS J.4 42
THE RUNNEL E.2 37
THE SHRUBLANDS E.7 39
THE SPINNEY D.14 41
THE SQUARE F.4 43
THE STEPS F.7 44
THE ST., OLD COSTESSEY ...A.1 37
THE ST., TROWSE NEWTON .G.10 45
THE SWALE D.1 37
THE TERRACE E.10 40
THE WALNUTS G.6 43
THE WARREN A.9 40
THE WATERING D.7 39
THEATRE STREET E.8 39
THEOBALD ROAD J.8 44
THIRD CLOSE B.9 40
THISTLE CLOSE E.2 37
THOMAS VERE ROAD D.13 41
THOMPSON ROAD D.13 41
THOR CLOSE D.12 41
THOR LOKE D.12 41
THOR ROAD D.12 41
THORN LANE F.8 44
THORNHAM CLOSE B.10 40
THORNHAM DRIVE B.10 40
THORNHAM ROAD B.10 40
THORPE AVENUE D.12 41
THORPE CLOSE D.13 41
THORPE END B.14 41
THORPE HALL CLOSE E.11 40
THORPE HEIGHTS E.9 40
THORPE MEWS E.13 41
THORPE ROAD E.9 40
THORPE ST. ANDREW ; E.12 41
THORPE STATION E.9 40
THREE MILE LANE C.2 37
THREE SCORE ROAD E.1 37
THREE TOWERS COURT B.6 38
THROCKMORTON YARD D.8 39
THUNDER LANE D.12 41
THURLBY ROAD D.1 37
THURLING LOKE C.12 41
THURLING PLAIN C.12 41
THURLOW CLOSE C.1 37
THURSTON CLOSE D.2 37
TIERCEL AVENUE A.11 40
TILLETT ROAD C.9 40
TILLETT ROAD EAST C.9 40
TILLS CLOSE A.9 40
TILLS ROAD A.9 40
TIMBERHILL STREET E.8 39
TIMOTHY CLOSE D.10 40
TIPPETT CLOSE E.2 37
TOFTES PLACE C.3 37
TOLLGATE WAY E.2 37
TOLLHOUSE ROAD D.5 38
TOLWIN WALK C.9 40
TOLYE ROAD D.1 37
TOMBLAND E.8 39
TOTTINGTON CLOSE C.2 37
TOWER HILL E.11 40
TOWN HOUSE ROAD A.1 37
TOWNCLOSE ROAD G.7 44
TOWNSEND ROAD H.7 44
TRACEY ROAD C.12 41
TRAFALGAR STREET F.8 44

TRAFFORD ROAD G.8 44
TRAVERSE STREET C.8 39
TREMAIN CLOSE C.4 38
TRENDALL ROAD A.11 40
TRIDENT DRIVE D.10 40
TRILITHON CLOSE C.4 38
TRINITY STREET F.7 44
TRIX ROAD F.7 44
TRORY STREET E.7 39
TROWSE NEWTON; H.10 45
TRUMAN CLOSE E.4 38
TUCKSWOOD LANE H.7 44
TUDOR COURT F.8 44
TUNGATE CRESCENT J.4 42
TUNSTALL CLOSE D.2 37
TURNER ROAD D.6 38
TURNHAM GREEN D.14 41
TURNHOUSE LANE B.3 37
TUSTING CLOSE A.9 40
TWICKENHAM ROAD N.7 46

UNION PLACE F.4 43
UNION STREET F.7 44
UNIVERSITY DRIVE E.4 38
UNTHANK ROAD G.5 43
UPLANDS COURT G.6 43
UPPER BRECKLAND ROAD ..C.2 37
UPPER CLOSE E.9 40
UPPER GOAT LANE E.8 39
UPPER GREEN LANE D.8 39
UPPER KING STREET E.8 39
UPPER ST. GILES STREET ...E.7 39
UPPER STAFFORD AVENUE .C.2 37
UPTON CLOSE G.6 43
UPTON ROAD G.6 43

VALE GREEN C.6 38
VALENTINE STREET E.7 39
VALLEY ROAD C.3 37
VALLEY SIDE ROAD D.11 40
VALLEY VIEW CRESCENT ...B.2 37
VALPY AVENUE C.6 38
VANCOUVER ROAD D.11 40
VANE CLOSE E.14 41
VARVEL AVENUE A.11 40
VARVEL CLOSE A.11 40
VAUXHALL STREET E.7 39
VENABLES CLOSE D.10 40
VERA ROAD A.6 38
VICARAGE COURT B.10 40
VICARAGE ROAD C.7 39
VICTORIA STATION F.8 44
VICTORIA STREET F.8 44
VICTORIA WAY B.3 37
VINCENT ROAD D.10 40
VIOLET ELVIN COURT E.5 38
VIOLET ROAD C.9 40
VIRGINIA CLOSE A.11 40
VULCAN ROAD A.7 39
VULCAN ROAD SOUTH A.7 39

WADDINGTON STREET D.7 39
WAGON & HORSES LANE ...E.8 39
WAKEFIELD ROAD E.3 37
WAKEHURST CLOSE H.6 43
WALCOT CLOSE D.2 37
WALDECK ROAD G.6 43
WALDEMAR AVENUE A.6 38
WALDEMAR PARK A.7 39
WALDEMAR ROAD A.6 38
WALDERGRAVE D.2 37
WALES SQUARE E.9 40
WALL LANE D.9 40
WALL ROAD B.8 39
WALLER CLOSE C.14 41
WALPOLE CLOSE E.7 39
WALPOLE GARDENS E.7 39
WALPOLE STREET E.7 39
WALTON ROAD G.8 44
WAR MEMORIAL COTT. B.10 40
WARD LANE F.10 45
WARING ROAD D.3 37
WARNETT ROAD C.12 41
WARREN AVENUE A.6 38
WARREN CLOSE A.9 40
WARWICK STREET F.7 44
WATER LA., CRINGLEFORD ..H.4 43
WATER LA., NORWICH E.8 39
WATER LA., TP. ST ANDRW. .E.11 40
WATERLOO PARK AVENUE ..C.7 39
WATERLOO PARK CLOSE ...C.7 39
WATERLOO ROAD D.8 39
WATERMANS ROAD D.5 38
WATERWORKS ROAD D.6 38
WATKIN ROAD J.7 44
WATLING ROAD C.11 40
WATSON GROVE D.7 39
WATTON ROAD F.1 42
WAVENEY ROAD F.4 43
WAVENEY TERRACE F.4 43
WAVERLEY ROAD G.6 43
WEATHERBY ROAD D.1 37
WEBDELL COURT H.9 45
WEBSTER CLOSE D.3 37
WELL LAKE A.7 39
WELLESLEY AVENUE D.10 40
WELLESLEY AVE. NORTH ...E.10 40
WELLESLEY AVE. SOUTH ...E.10 40
WELLINGTON GREEN E.7 39
WELLINGTON LANE E.7 39
WELLINGTON ROAD E.6 38
WELSFORD ROAD H.7 44
WENDENE D.2 37
WENMAN COURT D.2 37
WENSUM CRESCENT A.4 37
WENSUM STREET E.8 39
WENSUM VALLEY CLOSE ...A.4 37
WENTWORTH GREEN G.6 43
WESSEX STREET F.7 44
WEST CLOSE B.2 37
WEST END A.1 37
WEST END STREET D.6 38
WEST PARADE E.7 39
WEST POTTERGATE E.7 39
WEST ROAD B.2 37
WESTACRE DRIVE M.8 46
WESTERN AVENUE E.12 41

WESTGATE CLOSE F.6 43
WESTON ROAD B.7 39
WESTON ROAD IND. EST. ...A.7 39
WESTON WOOD CLOSE E.12 41
WESTON WOOD ROAD E.12 41
WESTWICK STREET E.8 39
WESTWOOD DRIVE N.4 46
WHEATLEY ROAD D.5 38
WHEELER RD, HELLESDON ..C.6 38
WHERRY ROAD E.9 40
WHIFFLER ROAD B.6 38
WHITE FARM LANE E.11 40
WHITE HORSE LANE H.9 45
WHITE HORSE MEWS H.10 45
WHITE HOUSE COURT B.7 39
WHITE LION STREET E.8 39
WHITE ROSE CLOSE C.4 38
WHITEBEAM COURT D.4 38
WHITEFRIARS D.9 40
WHITEGATES C.1 37
WHITEHALL ROAD F.6 43
WHITETHORN CLOSE A.8 39
WHITETHORN CLOSE N.8 46
WHITING ROAD H.8 44
WHITLEY CLOSE N.8 46
WHITLINGHAM LANE G.10 45
WHTLNGHM. LA., T. S. ANDRW F.13 46
WHITWELL ROAD D.10 40
WILBERFORCE ROAD E.3 37
WILBY ROAD H.8 44
WILD ROAD C.8 39
WILKINS COURT D.3 37
WILLHIRE WAY N.7 46
WILLIAM STREET E.7 39
WILLIAM WHITE PLACE E.7 39
WILLIAMS LOKE D.12 41
WILLIAMSON CLOSE C.11 40
WILLIS STREET D.8 39
WILLOW LANE E.8 39
WILSON ROAD F.10 45
WINCEBY CLOSE D.14 41
WINCHCOMB ROAD D.5 38
WINDMILL COURT B.9 40
WINDMILL LANE A.2 37
WINDMILL ROAD B.9 40
WINDSOR ROAD N.6 46
WINGATE WAY D.7 39
WINGFIELD ROAD D.8 39
WINKLE ROW F.9 45
WINSFORD WAY C.4 38
WINSTANLEY ROAD D.14 41
WINTER ROAD E.6 38
WITARD CLOSE C.12 41
WITARD ROAD C.12 41
WOBURN STREET E.7 39
WODEHOUSE STREET D.9 40
WOLFE ROAD E.10 40
WOLFSON CLOSE F.4 43
WOMERSLEY CLOSE D.10 40
WOMERSLEY ROAD D.10 40
WOOD STREET F.8 44
WOOD VIEW ROAD N.5 46
WOODCOCK CLOSE B.8 39
WOODCOCK ROAD B.7 39
WOODCROFT CLOSE B.13 41
WOODFORDE ROAD C.12 41
WOODGATE J.3 42
WOODGROVE PARADE B.8 39
WOODHAM LEAS N.9 46
WOODHILL RISE C.3 37
WOODLAND CLOSE N.4 46
WOODLAND DRIVE N.8 46
WOODLAND ROAD A.5 38
WOODLAND ROAD N.4 46
WOODLANDS ROAD B.2 37
WOODLANS CRESCENT C.14 41
WOODROW PLACE E.10 40
WOODRUFF CLOSE N.8 46
WOODS CLOSE B.6 38
WOODSIDE ROAD B.12 41
WOODVIEW COURT B.2 37
WOODWARD ROAD B.7 39
WORDSWORTH ROAD E.3 37
WORTHAM CLOSE D.2 37
WREN CLOSE G.4 43
WRENCH ROAD E.4 38
WROXHAM ROAD B.10 40
WYCLIFFE ROAD F.4 43
WYRNER STREET E.7 39

YARE COURT E.12 41
YARE VALLEY DRIVE G.4 43
YARMOUTH ROAD E.12 41
YARN MEWS D.8 39
YARRINGTON WAY C.1 37
YAXLEY WAY D.2 37
YELVERTON CLOSE N.4 46
YEW COURT A.12 41
YORK STREET F.7 44

ZOBEL CLOSE C.6 38

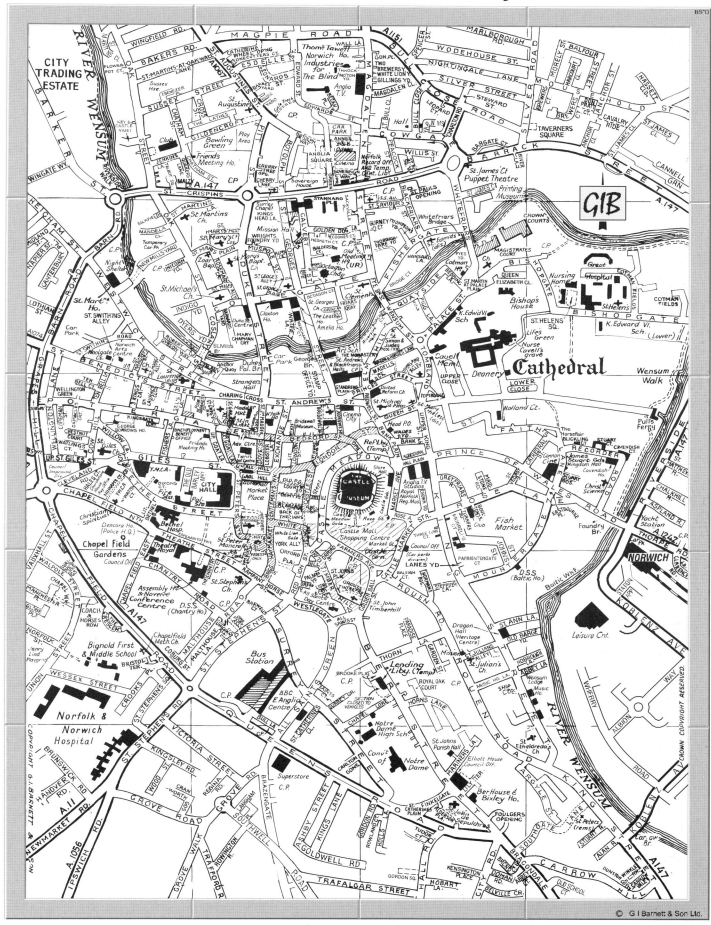

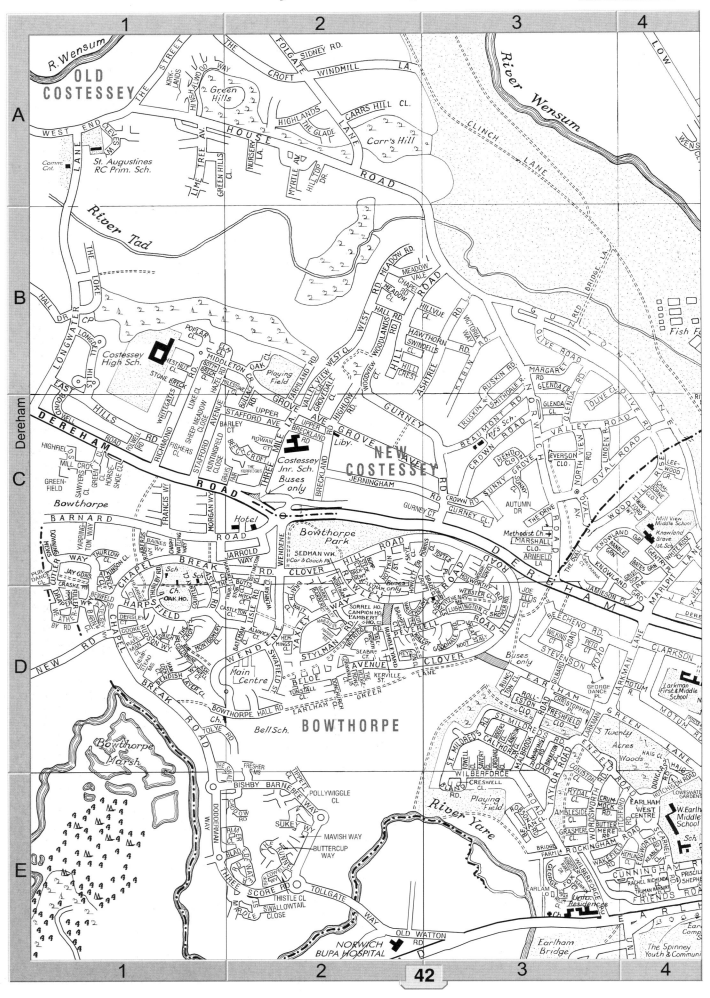

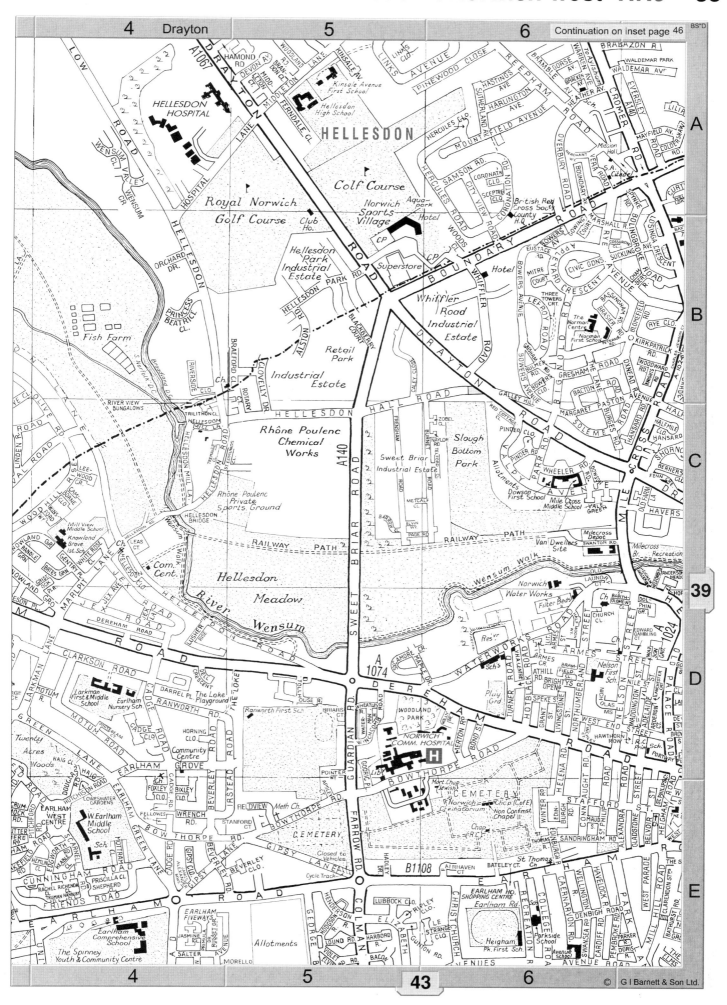

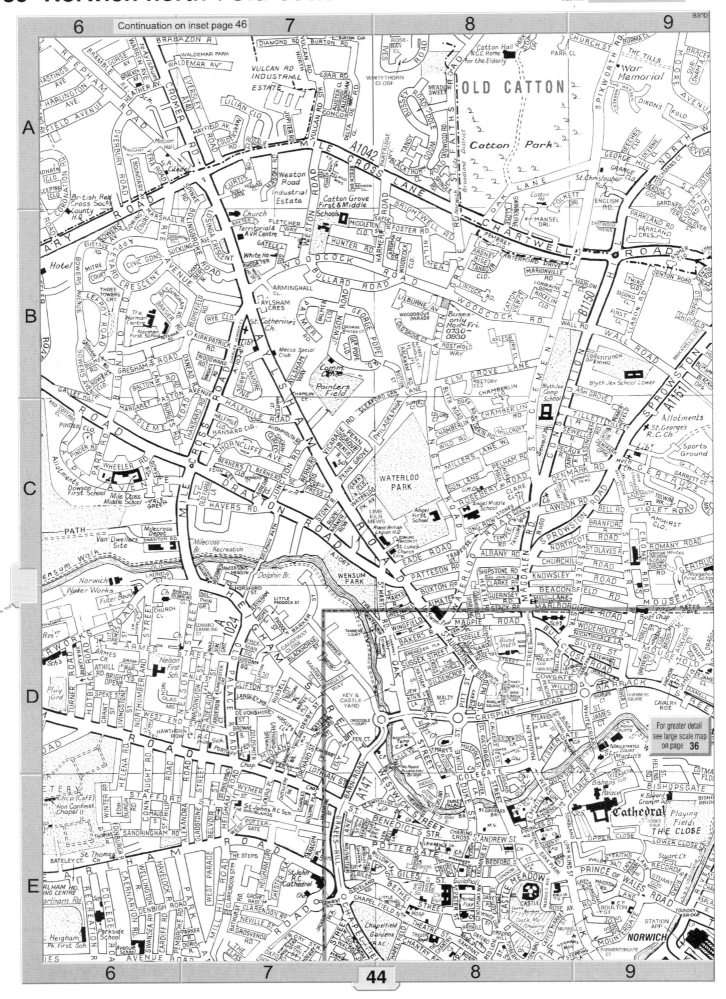

Continuation on inset page 46

OLD CATTON

Catton Park

Waterloo Park

Wensum Park

For greater detail
see large scale map
on page 36

Cathedral

THE CLOSE

PRINCE OF WALES

NORWICH

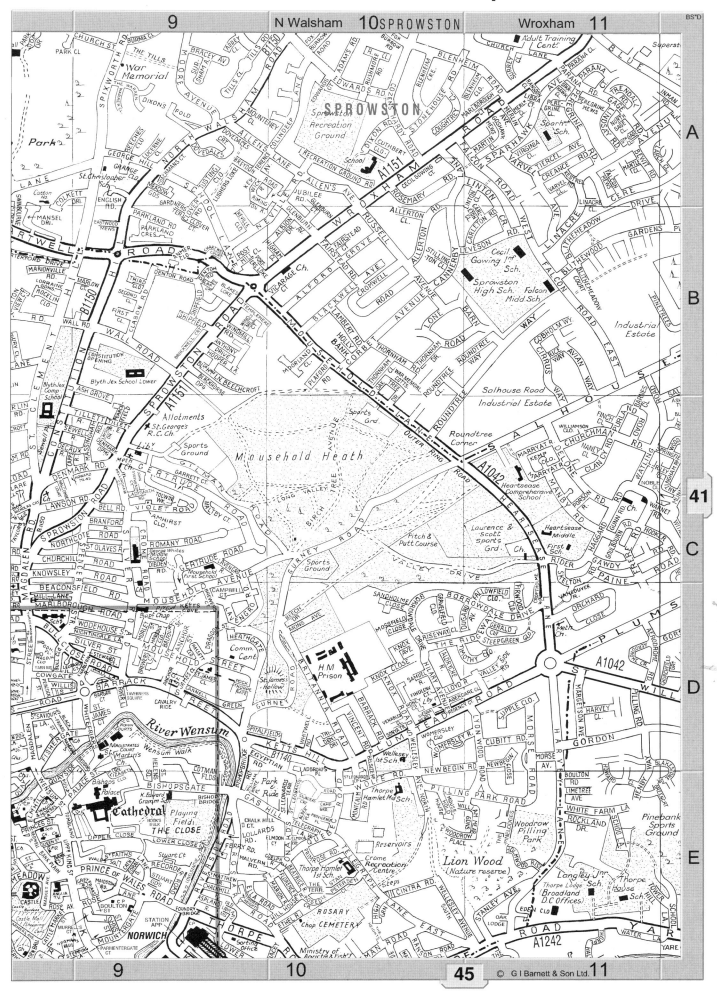

© G I Barnett & Son Ltd.

0.5 Km
0.25 Mile

BS"D

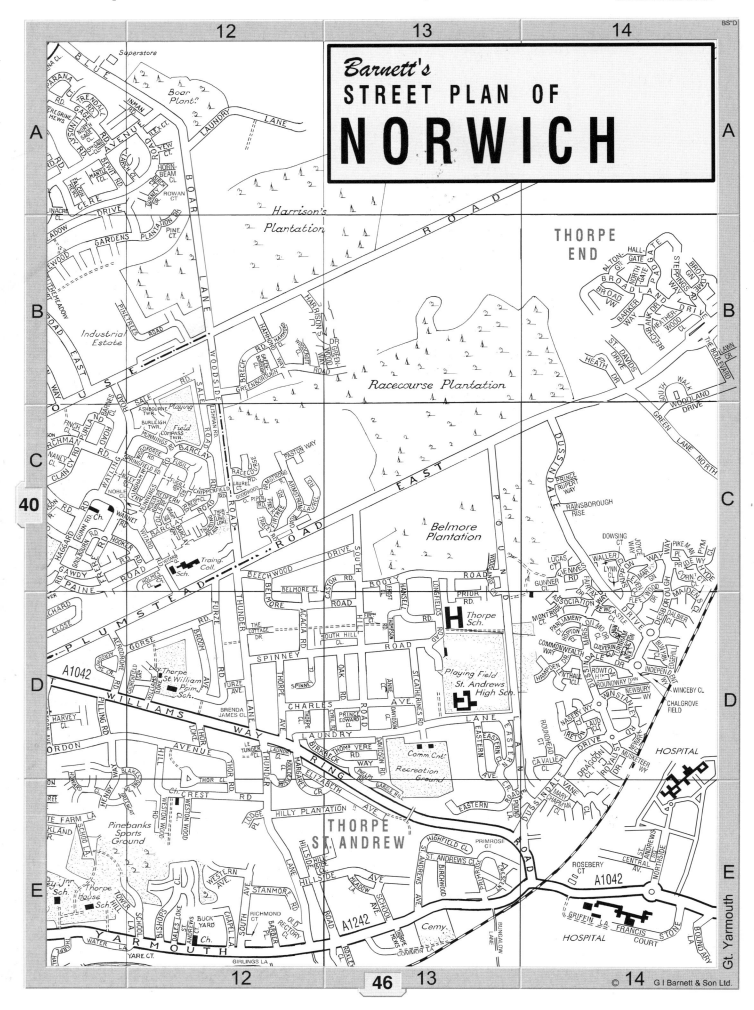

Barnett's
STREET PLAN OF
NORWICH

THORPE END

THORPE ST. ANDREW

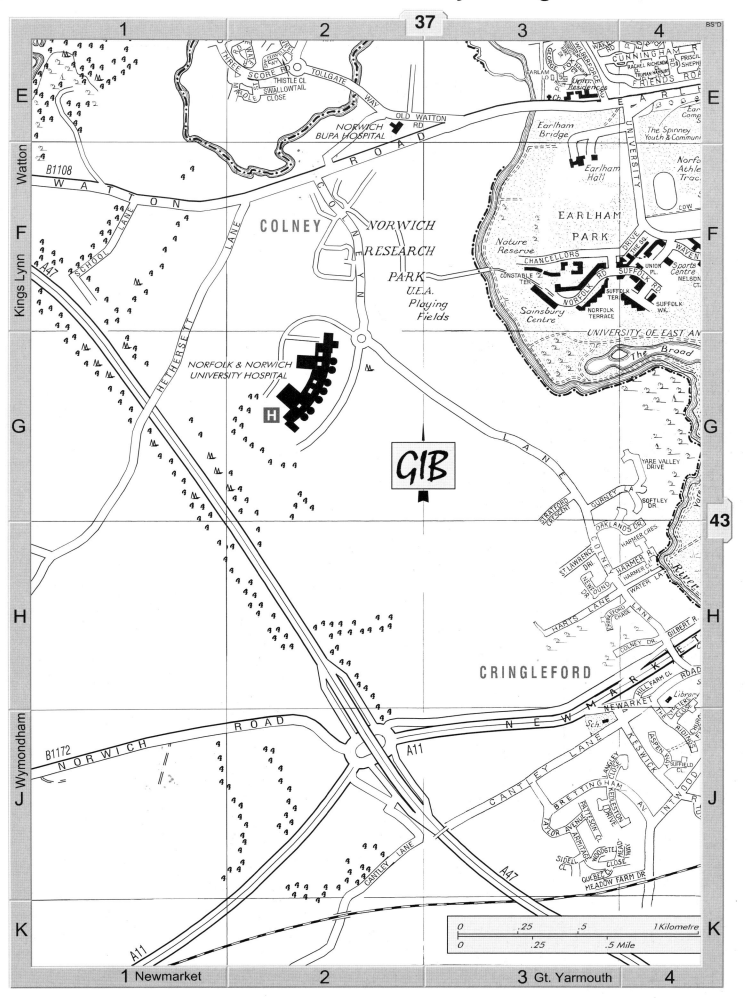

BS"D

1 **2** **3** **4**

E

Watton

WATTON RD
THREE SCORE RD
TOLLGATE WAY
THISTLE CL
SWALLOWTAIL CLOSE
MARDLE
OLD WATTON RD
NORWICH BUPA HOSPITAL

GEORGE
WILBERFORCE RD
WAKE CL
CUNNINGHAM RD
RACHEL RICHENDA
TRUMAN HARBURY
PRISCILLA SHEPHE
FRIENDS ROAD
EARLAM
FOX
Univ. Residences
Ch

EARLHAM BRIDGE
The Spinney Youth & Communi
Norfo
Athle
Trac
EARLHAM UNIVERSITY
Earlham Hall

F

Kings Lynn
B1108
WATTON
SCHOOL LANE
A47
HETHERSETT LANE

COLNEY
NORWICH RESEARCH PARK
U.E.A. Playing Fields

COLNEY LANE

EARLHAM PARK
Nature Reserve
CHANCELLORS
CONSTABLE TER.
NORFOLK RD
SUFFOLK RD
UNION PL.
THE SQ.
WAVEN
Sports Centre
NELSON CT.
NORFOLK TERRACE
SUFFOLK TER.
SUFFOLK WK.
Sainsbury Centre

COW
DRIVE

G

NORFOLK & NORWICH UNIVERSITY HOSPITAL
H

UNIVERSITY OF EAST AN
The Broad

GIB

YARE VALLEY DRIVE
SOFTLEY DR.
River Yare

43

STRATFORD CRESCENT
GURNEY LA.
OAKLANDS DR.
HARMER CRES
COLNEY LANE
ST LAWRENCE DRI.
NEWFOUND DR.
HARMER LANE
HARMER CL.
WATER LA.

H

CRINGLEFORD

HARTS LANE
STRATFORD CHASE
PRIORY LANE
COLNEY DR.
GILBERT R.

NEWMARKET ROAD
NEW MARKET ROAD
A11

Library
HILL FARM CL
ST PETERS CLOSE
THE RIDINGS
CHURCH
Sch.

J

Wymondham
B1172
NORWICH ROAD

CANTLEY LANE
CANTLEY LANE
A11
A47

BRETTINGHAM
TAYLOR AVENUE
ARMITAGE
PATTISON CL
KENLESTON DRIVE
LANGLEY CLOSE
KESWICK
ASPEN WAY
SUFFIELD CL
INTWOOD R
WOODGTE
HEAD WAY
SIDELL CL
QUEBEC CL
MEADOW FARM DR

J

K

0   .25   .5   1 Kilometre
0   .25   .5 Mile

K

1 Newmarket   **2**   **3** Gt. Yarmouth   **4**

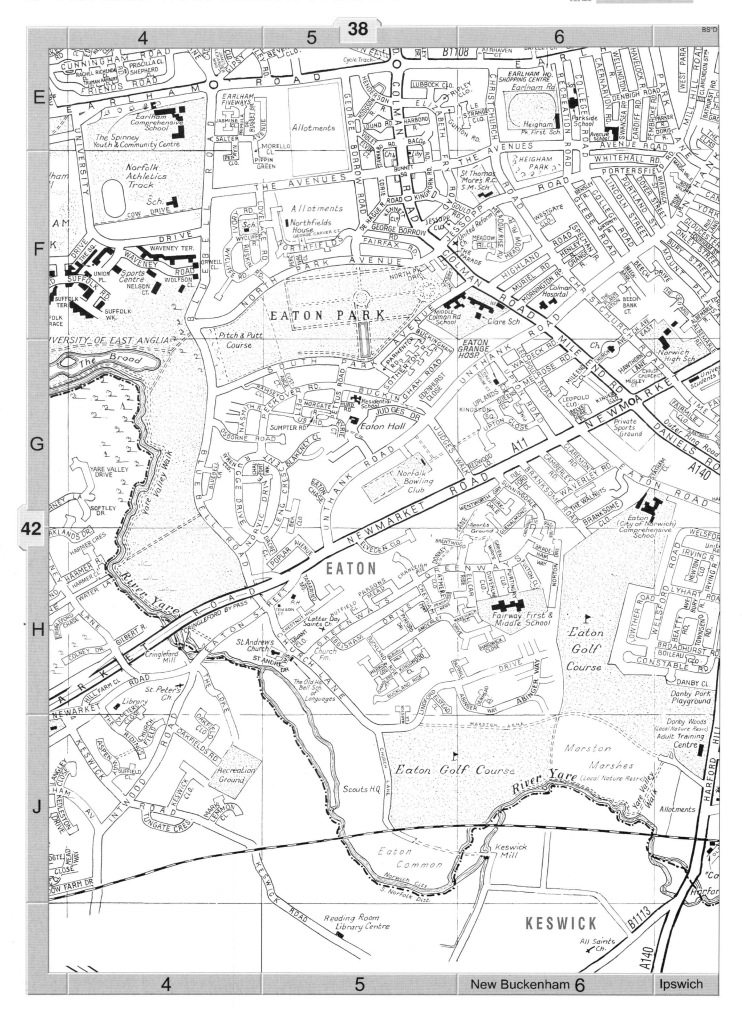

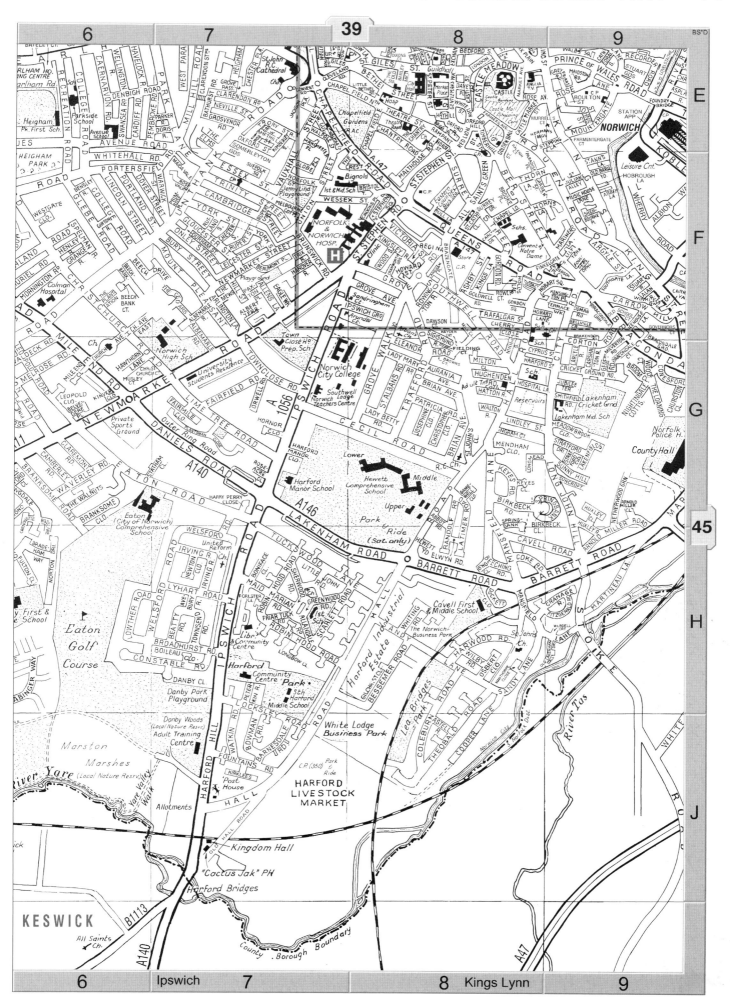

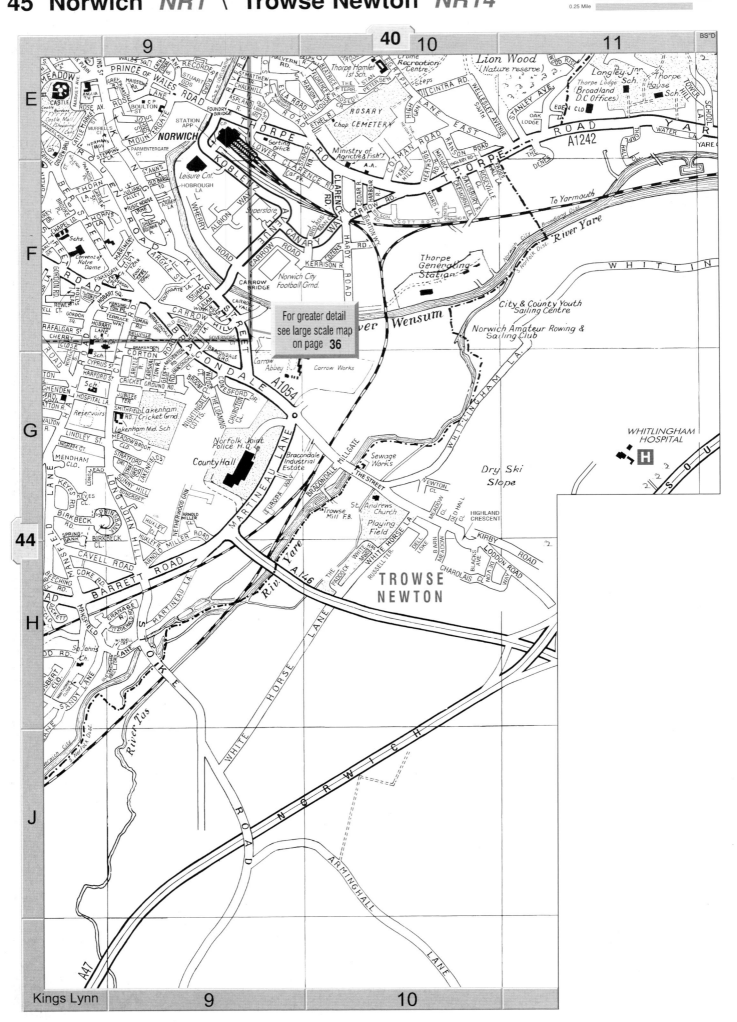

For greater detail
see large scale map
on page **36**

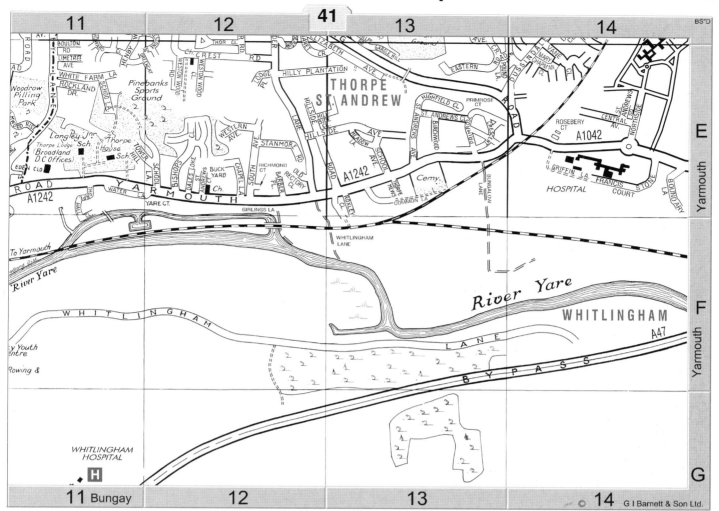

**Continuation nortwards
from pages 38,39 & 40**

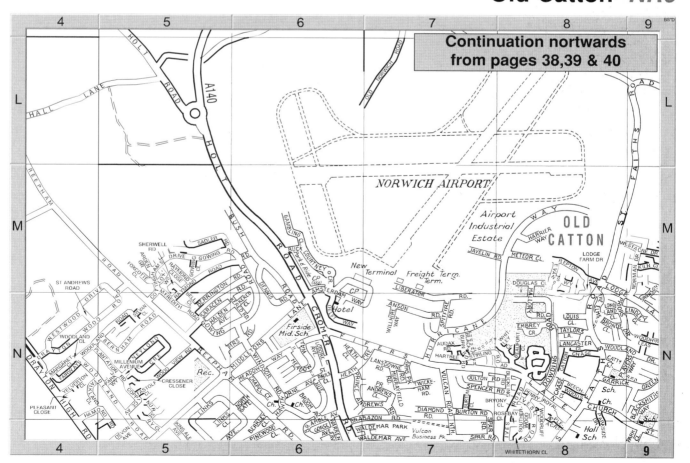

1 Km
0.5 Mile

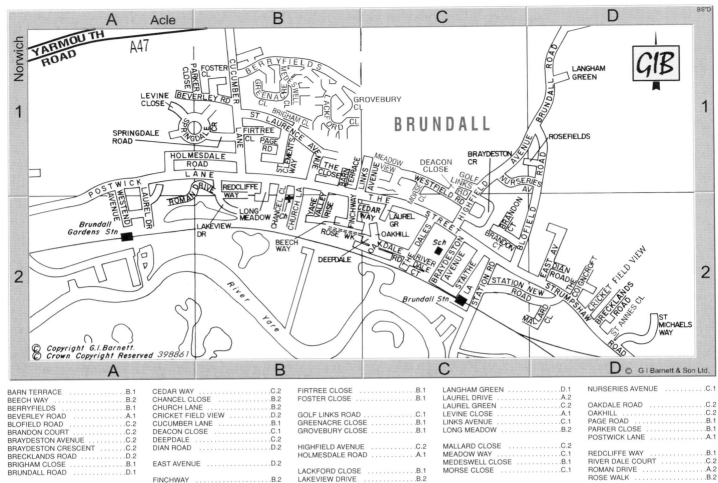

BARN TERRACE B.1
BEECH WAY B.2
BERRYFIELDS B.1
BEVERLEY ROAD A.1
BLOFIELD ROAD C.2
BRANDON COURT C.2
BRAYDESTON AVENUE C.2
BRAYDESTON CRESCENT C.2
BRECKLANDS ROAD D.2
BRIGHAM CLOSE B.1
BRUNDALL ROAD D.1

CEDAR WAY C.2
CHANCEL CLOSE B.2
CHURCH LANE B.2
CRICKET FIELD VIEW D.2
CUCUMBER LANE B.1
DEACON CLOSE C.1
DEEPDALE C.2
DIAN ROAD D.2

EAST AVENUE D.2

FINCHWAY B.2

FIRTREE CLOSE B.1
FOSTER CLOSE B.1

GOLF LINKS ROAD C.1
GREENACRE CLOSE B.1
GROVEBURY CLOSE B.1

HIGHFIELD AVENUE C.2
HOLMESDALE ROAD A.1

LACKFORD CLOSE B.1
LAKEVIEW DRIVE B.2

LANGHAM GREEN D.1
LAUREL DRIVE A.2
LAUREL GREEN C.2
LEVINE CLOSE A.1
LINKS AVENUE C.1
LONG MEADOW B.2

MALLARD CLOSE C.2
MEADOW WAY C.1
MEDESWELL CLOSE B.1
MORSE CLOSE C.1

NURSERIES AVENUE C.1

OAKDALE ROAD C.2
OAKHILL C.2
PAGE ROAD B.1
PARKER CLOSE B.1
POSTWICK LANE A.1

REDCLIFFE WAY B.1
RIVER DALE COURT C.2
ROMAN DRIVE A.2
ROSE WALK B.2

ROSEFIELDS D.1

ST. ANNES CLOSE D.2
ST. CLEMENTS WAY B.1
ST. LAURENCE AVENUE ...B.1
ST. MICHAELS WAY D.2
SPRINGDALE CRESCENT ...A.1
SPRINGDALE ROAD B.1
STAITHE LANE C.2
STATION NEW ROAD C.2
STATION ROAD C.2
STRUMPSHAW ROAD D.2

THE CLOSE B.1
THE COIGNCROFT D.2
THE DALES C.2
THE STREET C.2

WESTEND AVENUE A.2
WESTFIELD ROAD C.1

YARE VALLEY RISE B.2
YARMOUTH ROAD A.1

0.5 Km
0.25 Mile

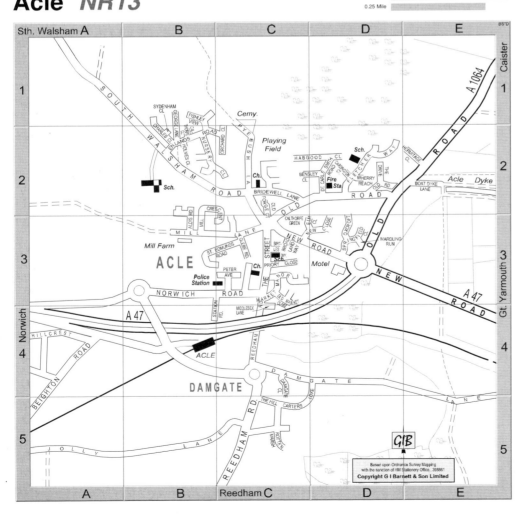

Acle

ALDIS ROAD B.3
BEIGHTON ROAD .....A.S
BENSLEY CLOSE C.2
BIRTLES WAY C.3
BOAT DYKE LANE E.2
BRIDEWELL LANE C.2
BROADLAND WAY C.3

CALTHORPE CLOSE ...B.2
CALTHORPE GREEN ...C.3
CARDINGTON COURT .D.2
CARTERS LOKE C.5
CHARLES CLOSE B.2

DAMGATE CLOSE C.4
DAMGATE LANE C.4
DE CARLE SMITH RD ..D.2

ELM CLOSE D.3
ENLANDS ROAD B.2

FISHLEY VIEW B.1
FLEYCHER WAY D.2

GEORGE LANE B.1
GLEBE ROAD C.3

HABGOOD CLOSE ...C.2
HERMITAGE CLOSE ..E.2
HILLCREST A.4
HOLMES CLOSE B.2

JOLLY LANE A.5

MARDLING RUN D.3

MARKET MANOR......C.3
MIDDLESEX LANE C.4
MILL CRESCENT B.3
MILL LANE B.3

NEW CLOSE D.3
NEW ROAD C.3-E.4
NORWICH ROAD B.3
NURSERY CLOSE B.2

OLD FORGE CT. C.2
OLD MARKET CL. C.3
OLD ROAD C.2-D.3
OXCROFT D.3

PETER AVENUE.......C.3
PRIORY CLOSE C.3
PYEBUSH LANE C.2

REEDHAM ROAD C.5
ROTTEN MARSH C.5

SOUTH WALSHAM RD .A.1
SPRINGFIELD CLOSE .D.3
ST. EDMUNDS ROAD ..C.3
STATION ROAD C.4
SYDENHAM CLOSE ...B.2

THE DRIVE..........D.2
THE HILL C.5
THE STREET C.3

WHERRY REACH D.2

0.5 Km
0.5 Mile

ALDER CLOSE B.4
ALL SAINTS ROAD C.3
ALSTON CLOSE C.3

BARRI CLOSE B.4
BAYNES CLOSE B.4
BEECH WALK C.2
BELLAMY WAY B.4
BIRKBECK CLOSE A.2
BLACKTHORN WAY ...B.3
BLIGH CLOSE C.3
BOUNDARY WAY B.2
BRAMBLE WAY C.3
BRICKLE LOKE A.2
BRICKLE ROAD A.2
BROOKS MEADOW C.3
BUNGAY ROAD B.4
BURGATE LANE C.3

CAISTOR LANE B.1
CAROL CLOSE B.2
CARR LANE A.4
CAWSTONS MEADOW ..B.3
CHHANDLER ROAD ...A.2
CHURCH CLOSE B.3
CLEARVIEW DRIVE ...B.2
CRITOPH CLOSE B.4
CROMES OAK CLOSE ..B.3

DEVLIN DRIVE B.3

ELIZABETH ROAD B.3

FALL GREEN B.3
FALLOWFIELD C.3
FITZGERALD ROAD ...C.3
FORGE CLOSE B.3

GLENN ROAD B.4
GREENACRES DRIVE ..B.2

HADDEN CLOSE B.3
HALL ROAD C.3
HARDESTY CLOSE ...B.3
HIGHGROVE COURT ..B.1
HIGHLAND B.1
HILLSIDE B.2
HORNBEAM DRIVE ...B.3
HOWE LANE A.4

IVY CLOSE C.3

JOHN DREWRY CL C.3

LEAFYOAK LANE A.4
LONG LANE A.2
LONG ROAD B.2

MALTEN CLOSE B.3
MEADOW WAY B.3
MILL CLOSE B.2

NORWICH ROAD B.2

OAK AVENUE B.2
OAKCROFT DRIVE B.2
OAKLANDS B.2
OLD MILL ROAD B.2
OVERTONS WAY B.3

PAGE CLOSE B.3
PIGOT LANE B.2
PINE LOKE A.2
PORINGLAND ROAD ...A.2

RECTORY LANE B.3
RIGBY CLOSE C.3
ROMANY WALK B.2
ROSEBERY AVE. C.3

SAXONFIELDS B.3
SHOTESHAM RD ...A.3-B.4
SOUTH WOOD DR A.1
SPRINGFIELDS B.3
SPRUCE CR. B.3
SPUR LANE C.2
ST. ANDREWS CL. ...C.3
ST. ANNES ROAD C.3
ST. EDMUND CLOSE ..B.1
ST. MARY'S ROAD ...B.3
STOKE ROAD A.2
SUNNYSIDE AVENUE ..B.3

THE FOOTPATH B.3
THHE RIDINGS B.2
THE STREET B.2-B.3
TULIP TREE DRIVE ...B.2

UPGATE C.3

WHITE HOUSE GDS ...C.3
WINDMILL CLOSE B.3

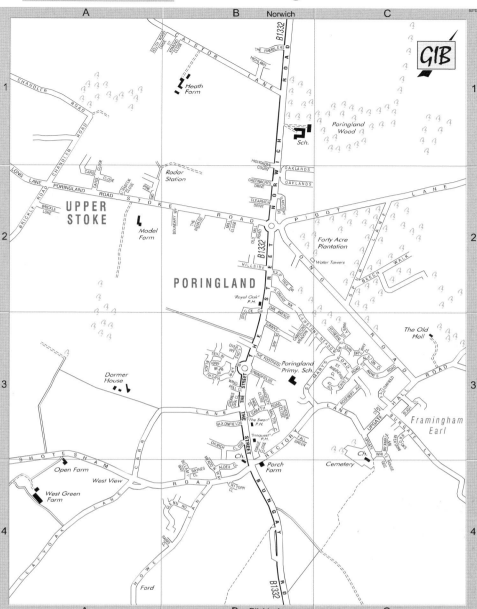

0.5 Km
0.25 Mile

BROADLAND CL. B.1

CHAPEL FIELD B.1
CHURCH DAM B.1
CHURCH RD. A.1
CHURCH VIEW CL. B.1
CLIFF CL. A.1

FERRY RD. A.1
FREETHORPE RD. A.1

HOLLY FARM RD. B.2

LOW COMMON B.1

MIDDLE HILL B.2
MILL RD. B.1

NEW RD. B.1

POTTLE'S LA. A.1

RIVERSIDE A.2

SCHOOL HILL B.2
STATION DR. A.1
STATION RD. A.1

THE HAVAKER A.2
THE HILLS A.2

WITTON CL. A.1
WITTON GREEN A.1

YARE VIEW CL. A.1

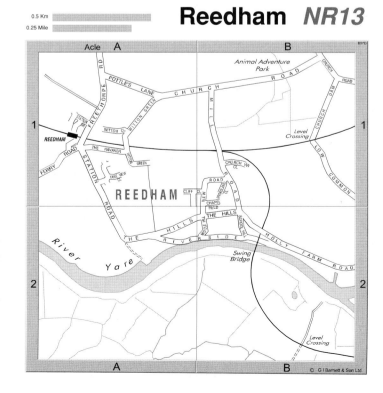

1 Km
0.5 Mile

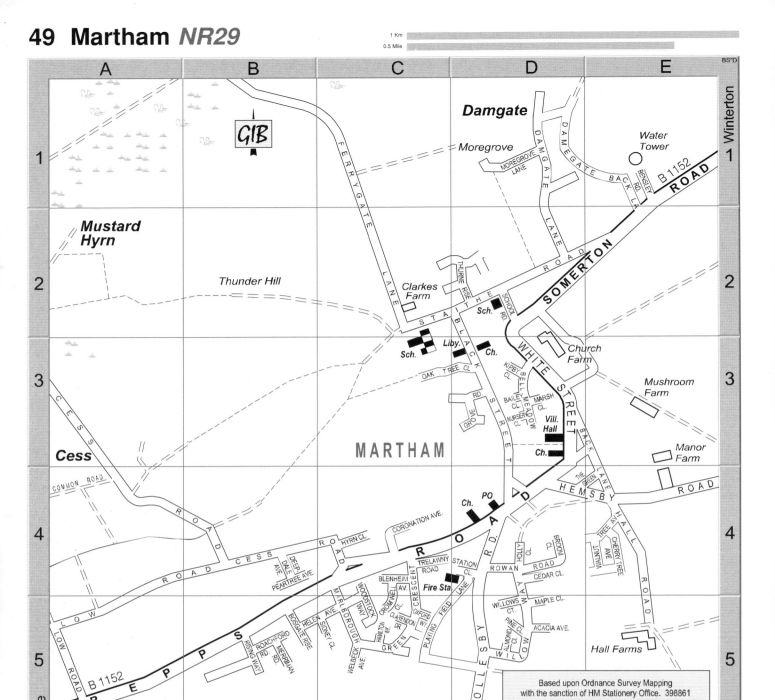

ACACIA AVENUE D.5	DAMGATE BACK LANE D.1	MARLBOROUGH GREEN CR. . . .C.5	SCHOOL ROAD D.2
ALMOND CLOSE D.5	DAMGATE LANE D.1	MARSH CLOSE D.3	SIDNEY CLOSE C.5
	DEEPDALE AVENUE B.4	MERRIMAN ROAD B.5	SOMERTON ROAD D.2
BACK LANE E.3		MOREGROVE LANE D.1	STAITHE ROAD C.2
BAILEY CLOSE D.3	FERRYGATE LANE C.1		STATION CLOSE D.4
BELL MEADOW D.3		NURSERY CLOSE D.3	SYCAMORE AVENUE E.4
BENSLEY ROAD E.1	GROVE ROAD D.3		
BLACK STREET D.2		OAK TREE CLOSE C.3	THE GREEN E.4
BLENHEIM AVENUE C.4	HALL ROAD E.4	OXFORD WAY C.5	THURNE RISE D.2
BOSGATE RISE B.5	HAMILTON WALK C.5		TRELAWNEY ROAD C.4
BROOM CLOSE D.4	HELEN AVENUE B.5	PEARTREE AVENUE B.4	
	HEMSBY ROAD D.4	PINE CLOSE D.5	WALNUT TREE AVENUE E.4
CEDAR CLOSE D.4	HOLLY CLOSE D.4	PLAYING FIELD LANE C.5	WELBECK AVENUE C.5
CESS ROAD A.3	HYRN CLOSE C.4		WHITE STREET D.3
CHERRY TREE AVENUE E.4		REPPS CLOSE A.5-D.4	WILLOW WAY D.5
CLARENDON DRIVE C.5	KIRBY CLOSE D.3	RISING WAY B.5	WILLOWS COURT D.5
COMMON ROAD A.4		ROACHFORD ROAD B.5	WOODSTOCK WAY C.5
CORONATION AVENUE C.4	LOW ROAD A.5	ROLLESBY ROAD D.5	
CROMWELL CLOSE C.5	MAPLE CLOSE D.5	ROWAN ROAD D.4	

0.5 Km
0.25 Mile

ACKLAND CLOSE B3

BACK PATH B2
BACK ROAD B2
BEACH ROAD C2
BLACK STREET A2
BULMER LANE A2-B4
BUSH ROAD C3

DUNE COURT A2

EDWARD ROAD B4
EMPSONS LOKE A2

GEORGE BECK ROAD B3
GREEN COURTS B3

HILLVIEW DRIVE D3

KING STREET B2

LAVENDER COURT A3
LOW ROAD A2

MARKET PLACE B2
MARINE CRESCENT B.2

NORTH MARKET ROAD B1
OLD CHAPEL ROAD B2

SANDPIPER COURT B.2
SOMERTON ROAD A2
SPINDRIFT CLOSE B2

THE COBBLEWAYS B3
THE CRAFT B3
THE HOLWAY B3
THE LANE B2
THE LOKE B2

WINMER AVENUE B2

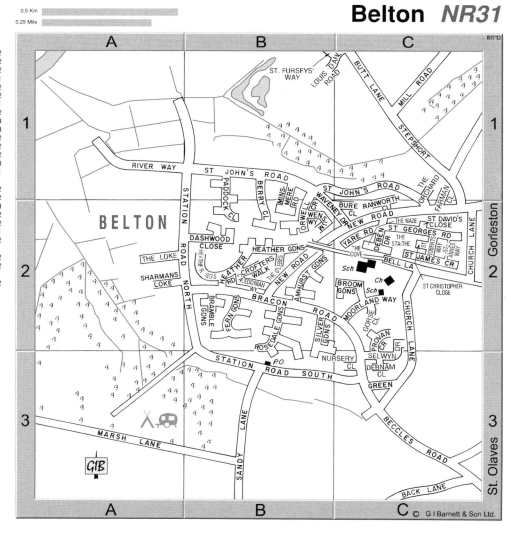

0.5 Km
0.25 Mile

AMHURST GARDENS . . .B.2

BACK LANE C.3
BECCLES ROAD C.3
BELL LANE C.2
BERRY CLOSE B.1
BRACON ROAD B.2
BRAMBLE GDS B.2
BROOM GARDENS C.2
BURE CLOSE C.2
BUTT LANE C.1

CALEDONIAN WAY B.2
CHURCH LANE C.2
CROFTERS WALK B.2

DASHWOOD CL. B.2
DEBEN DRIVE C.2
DEBNAM CLOSE C.3

FARMAN CLOSE C.1
FERN GARDENS B.2

GORSE CLOSE C.2

HEATHER GDS B.2
HEATHER ROAD B.2

LOUIS DAHL ROAD B.1

MARSH LANE A.3
MILL ROAD C.1
MINSMERE ROAD B.1
MOORLAND WAY C.2

NEW ROAD B.2
NURSERY CLOSE C.3

ORWELL CRESCENT . . .B.2

PADDOCK CLOSE B.1
PROVAN CRESCENT . . .C.2

RANWORTH CLOSE C.2
RIVER WAY A.1
ROSEDALE GDS B.2

ST. ANNES WAY C.2
ST. CHRISTOPHER CL. .C.2
ST. DAVID'S CL. C.2
ST. FURSEY'S WAY B.1
ST. GEORGES ROAD . . .C.2
ST. JAMES CR. C.2
ST. JOHN'S ROAD B.1
ST. ROBERT'S WAY C.2
SANDY LANE B.3
SELWYN DRIVE C.3
SHARMANS LOKE A.2
SILVER GARDENS B.2
STATION RD N. B.2
STATION RD S. B.3
STEPSHORT C.1

THE COVE C.2
THE GLEBES B.2
THE GREEN C.3
THE LOKE A.2
THE NAZE C.2
THE ORCHARD C.1
THE STAITHE C.2

WAVENEY DRIVE B.2
WENSUM WAY B.2

YARE ROAD C.2

0.5 Km
0.5 Mile

BS"D

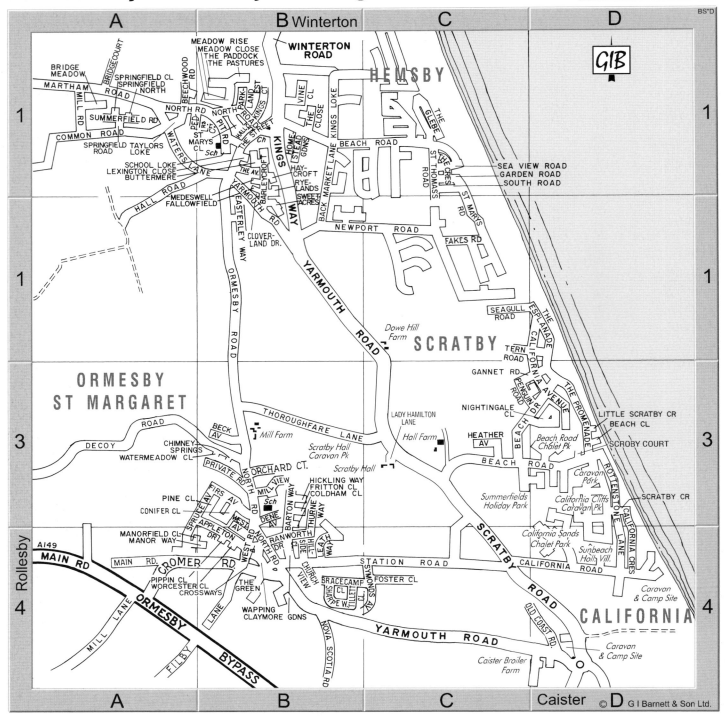

APPLETON DRIVE B.3

BACK MARKET LANE B.1
BARLEYCROFT B.1
BARTON WAY B.3
BEACH CLOSE D.3
BEACH DRIVE C.3
BEACH ROAD, HEMSBY B.1
BEACH ROAD, SCRATBY C.3
BECK AVENUE B.3
BEECHWOOD ROAD A.1
BRACECAMP CLOSE B.4
BRIDGE MEADOW A.1
BRIDGECOURT A.1
BUTTERMERE B.1

CALIFORNIA D.4
CALIFORNIA AVENUE D.2
CALIFORNIA CRESCENT D.3
CALIFORNIA ROAD D.4
CHIMNEY SPRINGS B.3
CHURCH VIEW B.4
CLAYMORE GARDENS B.4
CLOVERLAND DRIVE B.1
COLDHAM CLOSE B.3
COMMON ROAD A.1
CONIFER CLOSE B.3
CROMER ROAD A.4
CROSSWAYS B.4

DECOY ROAD A.3
DENE AVENUE B.3

EASTERLEY WAY B.2

FAKES ROAD C.2
FALLOWFIELD B.1
FILBY LANE A.4
FIRS AVENUE B.3
FOSTER CLOSE C.4
FRITTON CLOSE B.3

GANNET ROAD C.3
GARDEN ROAD C.1

HALL CLOSE B.1
HALL ROAD A.2
HAYCROFL B.1
HEATHER AVENUE C.3
HICKLING WAY B.3
HILLSIDE CLOSE B.4
HOMESTEAD GARDENS B.1

KINGS COURT B.1
KINGS LOKE B.1
KINGS WAY B.1

LADY HAMILTON LANE C.3
LEATH WAY B.4

LEXINGTON CLOSE B.2
LITTLE SCRATBY CRESCENT ...D.3

MAIN ROAD A.4
MANOR WAY A.4
MANORFIELD CLOSE A.4
MARTHAM ROAD A.1
MEADOW CLOSE B.1
MEADOW RISE B.1
MEDESWELL B.1
MILL LANE A.4
MILL ROAD A.1
MILL VIEW B.3

NEWPORT ROAD B.2
NIGHTINGALE CLOSE D.3
NORTH ROAD B.3
NOVA SCOTIA ROAD B.4

OLD COAST ROAD D.4
ORCHARD COURT B.3
ORMESBY BY-PASS A.4
ORMESBY ROAD B.2
ORMESBY ST MARGARET A.3

PARKLAND ESTATE B.1
PEDLARS CROFT A.1
PENGUIN ROAD C.3
PINE CLOSE B.3

PIPPIN CLOSE B.4
PIT ROAD B.1
PRIVATE ROAD B.3

RANWORTH DRIVE B.4
ROTTENSTONE LANE D.3
RYELANDS B.1

ST. MARYS CLOSE B.1
ST. MARYS ROAD C.2
ST. THOMAS'S ROAD C.1
SCHOOL LOKE B.1
SCRATBY C.2
SCRATBY CRESCENT D.3
SCRATBY ROAD C.4
SCROBY COURT D.3
SEA VIEW ROAD C.1
SEAGULL ROAD C.2
SHARPE WAY B.4
SOUTH ROAD C.1
SPRINGFIELD CLOSE A.1
SPRINGFIELD NORTH A.1
SPRINGFIELD ROAD A.1
SPRUCE AVENUE A.3
STATION ROAD C.4
SUMMERFIELD ROAD A.1
SWEETACRES B.2
SYMONDS AVENUE C.4

TAYLORS LOKE A.1
TERRA ROAD C.2
THE AVENUE B.1
THE CLOSE B.1
THE CRESCENT C.1
THE ESPLANADE D.2
THE GLEBE C.1
THE GREEN B.4
THE PADDOCK B.1
THE PASTURES B.1
THE PROMENADE D.3
THE STREET B.1
THOROUGHFARE LANE B.3
THURNE WAY B.3
TILLETT CLOSE B.4

VINE CLOSE B.1

WAPPING B.4
WATERMEADOW CLOSE B.3
WATERS LANE A.1
WEST AVENUE B.3
WEST ROAD B.4
WINTERTON ROAD B.1
WORCESTER CLOSE B.4

YARMOUTH ROAD, SCRATBY ..B.2
YARMOUTH ROAD, CALIFORNIA C.4

© G I Barnett & Son Ltd.

ALEXANDRA CLOSE A.1
ALLENDALE ROAD C.4
AMBROSE ROAD C.5
ARNOLD AVENUE B.1
ARTHUR AVENUE B.1
ASHWOOD CLOSE B.3

BEACH ROAD C.4
BEAUCHAMP PLACE B.2
BEELEIGH WAY A.2
BEELSTEAD AVENUE B.4
BERESFORD ROAD C.5
BIISCAY GARDENS A.3
BLYTH ROAD A.4
BRADDOCK ROAD C.4
BRANFORD ROAD B.2
BREYDON WAY B.3
BROOKE AVENUE B.3
BUILDINGS ROAD C.5
BULLOCKS LOKE C.5
BULTITUDES LOKE C.5
BURE CLOSE B.3
BURGESS CLOSE B.3
BYRON WAY B.3

CAISTER SANDS AVENUE B.1
CARTER CLOSE B.1
CEDAR WAY C.2
CHAPEL LANE A.5
CHAPMAN AVENUE C.4
CHARLES BURTON CLOSE B.2
CHARLES CLOSE C.4
CHURCH CLOSE B.4
CLAY ROAD D.4
CLIFFORD AVENUE B.4
CLUB HOUSE ROAD C.6
COAST GUARD ROAD D.4
CONY PRIORS B.3
COOPER CLOSE C.4
COVENT GARDEN ROAD A.2
COXWAIN READ WAY B.5
CROFT ROAD C.4
CROMARTY WAY A.4

DIANA WAY A.3
DODD CLOSE B.2
DOVER COURT A.4
DRIFT ROAD A.2

EAST END CLOSE B.1
EASTERN AVENUE C.3-D.4
EASTERN CLOSE C.4
EDINBURGH CLOSE C.4
ELIZABETH CRESCENT C.3
ELM ROAD C.5

FAEROES DRIVE A.3
FAIRISLE DRIVE A.4
FAIRWAY C.6
FASTNET WAY A.3
FINISTERRIE RISE A.3
FORTH CLOSE A.3
FORTIES CLOSE A.3

GARFIELD TERRACE C.5
GAYWOOD DRIVE B.4
GEDGE ROAD C.3
GILBERT ROAD C.3
GLENMORE AVENUE B.1
GRAET CLOSE D.4
GRANGE ROAD B.4
GREEN LANE C.5

HALES CLOSE B.4
HALT ROAD B.2
HAMPTON CLOSE A.4
HANLEY COURT B.3
HARVEY LANE C.5
HAYLETT CLOSE C.4
HEBRIDES WAY A.3
HIGH STREET C.4
HONEYMOON LOKE D.5
HUMBER WAY A.4
HURRELL ROAD B.3

JACK PLUMMER WAY A.1
JOHN NEVILLE CLOSE B.2
JOHN ROAD C.2
JOHN WOODHOUSE DRIVE . . .A.2
JORDAN ROAD C.3
JUBILEE TERRACE C.5

KINGSTON ROAD C.4
KIPLING CLOSE B.3

LACON ROAD C.4
LAWNSWOOD DRIVE B.4
LINKS CLOSE C.5
LONGFELLOW ROAD B.4

MALLIN COURT A.3
MANOR ROAD D.4
MARINE DRIVE B.1
MARRAM DRIVE B.1
MEADOW CROFT B.1
MIDLAND CLOSE D.4
MIRIAM CLOSE B.1
MORSE COURT B.3
MOUNTBATTEN WAY B.3

NELSON COURT D.5
NELSON ROAD D.5
NEWARK ROAD B.1
NORTHERN CLOSE D.4
NORWICH ROAD A.4

OLD MILL ROAD D.4
ORCHID CLOSE C.5
ORMESBY ROAD B.2
OXMEAD DRIVE A.1

PASTON DRIVE A.1
PEGASUS CLOSE B.2
PETER CLOSE B.1
PLYMOUTH CLOSE A.3
PRINCE OF WALES ROAD A.3
PRIORY CLOSE B.5
PUMP LANE B.6
PYKE COURT B.2

QUEENSWAY C.4

RECTORY CLOSE C.4
REYNOLDS AVENUE A.1
RIDGEWAY B.1
ROCKALL WAY A.3

ROMAN WAY B.4
ROYAL THAMES ROAD B.2
RUSSELL AVENUE C.4

SAXON GARDENS B.4
SCOTTS COTTAGES C.4
SEABIRD CLOSE B.2
SEAFIELD ROAD B.3
SEAFIELD ROAD NORTH C.3
SEAWARD WALK B.1
SECOND AVENUE B.1
SHANNON DRIVE A.3
SHELLEY CLOSE B.3
SOLENT CLOSE C.4
SOUDAN CLOSE B.2
ST. ANDREWS CLOSE B.2
ST. CHRISTOPHERS CLOSE . . .B.2
ST. GEORGES DRIVE B.2
ST. HILDA CLOSE C.3
ST. HILDA ROAD B.3
ST. JULIAN ROAD C.5

ST. NICHOLAS DRIVE B.2
STONEHILL ROAD B.3

TAN LANE C.5
THAMES WAY A.3
TYNE MEWS A.4

UPLANDS AVENUE B.4
UPPER GRANGE CRESCENT . .B.4

VICTORIA ROAD D.4
VILLAROME A.4

WATERLANDS CLOSE A.2
WATLING CLOSE C.3
WEBSTER WAY B.3
WEST CAISTER ROAD A.5
WEST ROAD B.5
WESTERLEY CLOSE B.5
WESTERLEY WAY B.5
WESTON ROAD B.4

WIGHT DRIVE A.3
WINDSOR ROAD C.3
WINIFRED WAY B.1

YARE CLOSE B.3
YARMOUTH ROAD C.5

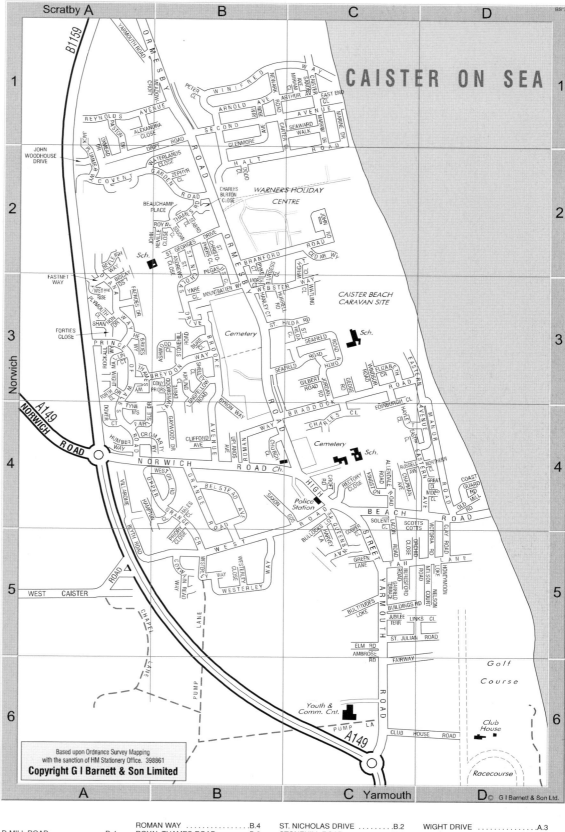

Street	Grid	Page
ABYSSINIA ROAD	G.3	56
ACLE NEW ROAD	J.3	57
ADDISON ROAD	E.2	56
ADMIRALS QUAY	F.2	55,56
ADMIRALTY ROAD	E.3	56
ALBANY CLOSE	G.2	56
ALBANY ROAD	G.3	56
ALBEMARLE RD, GORLESTON	C.2	54
ALBEMARLE RD, GT. Y'RMTH	H.3	56
ALBERT ROAD	F.3	55,56
ALBERT SQUARE	G.3	56
ALBION ROAD	H.3	56
ALDERSON ROAD	J.2	56
ALEXANDRA AVENUE	K.3	57
ALEXANDRA ROAD	G.3	56
ALMA ROAD	G.3	56
ALMOND ROAD	D.1	56
ALPHA ROAD	E.2	55
ALTHAEA GREEN	D.2	55
AMETHYST CLOSE	B.3	54
ANCHOR COURT	F.2	55,56
ANSON ROAD	G.2	56
APOLLO WALK	J.2	57
APSLEY ROAD	G.3	56
ARCHERS ROAD	J.2	57
ARNOTT AVENUE	A.3	54
ARTILLERY SQUARE	H.3	56
ARUNDEL ROAD	J.3	57
ASH GREEN	D.1	56
AUDLEY STREET	H.3	56
AUSTIN ROAD	G.1	56
AVENUE ROAD	D.3	55
AVOCET WAY	D.1	55
AVONDALE ROAD	B.3	54
BACK CHAPEL LANE	D.3	55
BAKER STREET	D.3	55
BALIOL ROAD	C.2	54
BALMORAL AVENUE	K.3	57
BANTING CLOSE	A.2	54
BARHAM COURT	C.3	54
BARKIS ROAD	F.3	55,56
BARNARD AVENUE	K.3	57
BARNARD CLOSE	A.2	54
BARNARD CRESCENT	K.3	57
BARRACK ROAD	F.3	55,56
BATELY AVENUE	A.3	54
BATH HILL TERRACE	G.3	56
BATTERY ROAD	E.3	55
BEACH ROAD	C.3	54
BEACONSFIELD ROAD	J.3	57
BEATTY CLOSE	K.3	57
BEATTY ROAD	K.3	57
BEAUFORT WAY	A.2	54
BEAVANS COURT	G.3	56
BECCLES ROAD	D.1	55
BEEVOR ROAD	E.3	55
BELLS MARSH ROAD	C.3	54
BELLS ROAD	C.3	54
BELVIDERE ROAD	J.3	57
BENDISH AVENUE	B.3	54
BERBERIS GREEN	D.2	55
BERESFORD ROAD	K.3	57
BERMONDSEY PLACE EAST	H.3	56
BERMONDSEY PLACE SOUTH	H.3	56
BERMONDSEY PLACE WEST	H.3	56
BERNARD ROAD	B.3	54
BESSEMER WAY	E.1	55
BIRCH WAY	D.1	55
BLACKFRIARS ROAD	G.3	56
BLACKWALL REACH	D.3	55
BLAKE DRIVE	E.1	55
BLAKE ROAD	J.3	57
BODLEIAN COURT	B.1	54
BOUNDARY ROAD	F.2	55,56
BOWLING GREEN WALK	H.2	56
BRADWELL AVENUE	C.1	54
BRASENOSE AVENUE	B.1	54
BRETT AVENUE	A.3	54
BREWERY PLAIN	H.2	56
BREWERY STREET	H.2	56
BREYDON BRIDGE	H.2	56
BREYDON ROAD	H.2	56
BRIDFORD CLOSE	B.2	54
BRIDGE ROAD, GORLESTON	A.3	54
BRIDGE ROAD, GT. Y'RMTH	G.2	56
BRINELL WAY	E.1	55
BRITANNIA ROAD	H.3	56
BROAD ROW	H.2	56
BROOMFIELD ROAD	E.3	55
BRUSH QUAY	C.3	54
BULLS LANE	D.3	55
BUNNEWELL AVENUE	C.1	54
BUNNS LANE	G.2	56
BURE CLOSE	J.2	57
BURE ROAD	J.2	57
BURGH ROAD	E.1	55
BURLEIGH CLOSE	G.3	56
BURNT LANE	E.2	55
BUSSEYS LOKE	D.1	55
BUXTON AVENUE	A.3	54
BYRON ROAD	K.3	57
CAISTER ROAD	J.3	57
CAMBRIDGE AVENUE	B.1	54
CAMBRIDGE WAY	B.1	54
CAMDEN ROAD	F.3	55,56
CAMELOT ROAD	A.1	54
CAMPERDOWN PLACE	G.3	56
CAMPION AVENUE	B.1	54
CARREL ROAD	A.1	54
CASTLE GREEN	E.1	55
CATALPA WAY	D.1	55
CENTRAL ARCADE	G.2	56
CENTURY ROAD	G.2	56
CHARLES STREET	H.2	56
CHARTER CLOSE	C.1	54
CHAUCER ROAD	F.3	57
CHERRY ROAD	D.2	55
CHERWELL WAY	B.1	54
CHESTNUT AVENUE	C.1	54
CHRISTCHURCH ROAD	C.1	54
CHURCH LANE	D.2	55
CHURCH PLAIN	H.2	56
CHURCH ROAD	D.2	55
CHURCHILL ROAD	J.3	57
CLARE AVENUE	B.2	54
CLARENCE RD, GORLESTON	B.3	54
CLARENCE ROAD, GT. Y'RMTH	G.3	56
CLARENDON CLOSE	G.3	56
CLARKES ROAD	J.2	57
CLARKS ROAD	J.2	57
CLAYDON GROVE	D.1	55
CLIFF AVENUE	B.3	54
CLIFF HILL	C.3	54
CLIFF LANE	A.3	54
CLOVER WAY	C.1	54
COBBS PLACE	H.2	56
COBDEN TERRACE	J.2	57
COBHOLM CLOSE	H.2	56
COBHOLM ISLAND	H.1	56
COLLEGE COURT	H.2	56
COLLINGWOOD ROAD	J.3	57
COLOMB ROAD	D.2	55
COMMON ROAD	E.2	55
CONISTON SQUARE	H.3	56
CONNAUGHT AVENUE	B.2	54
CONSTABLE CLOSE	E.1	55
CONVILLE ROAD	C.1	54
CONWAY ROAD	D.3	55
COPPERFIELD AVENUE	F.3	55,56
CORONATION GREEN	G.2	56
CORONATION ROAD	G.2	56
CORONATION TERRACE	H.2	56
CORONILLA GREEN	C.1	54
COTMAN DRIVE	E.1	55
COTONEASTER GREEN	D.2	55
CRAB LANE	D.1	55
CRADOCK AVENUE	K.3	57
CRAYSTREWARD	L.3	57
CRITTENS ROAD	H.2	56
CROMWELL ROAD	F.2	55,56
CROSS ROAD	D.3	55
CROSSTEAD	L.3	57
CROW HALL GREEN	B.2	54
CROWN ROAD	G.3	56
CUNNINGHAM AVENUE	K.3	57
CURIE DRIVE	A.2	54
CURLEW WAY	D.1	55
CYDONIA GREEN	D.1	55
DANBY ROAD	D.2	55
DAPHNE WAY	D.1	55
DEBORAH ROAD	B.2	54
DENE SIDE	G.3	56
DEVONSHIRE ROAD	J.3	57
DICKENS AVENUE	F.3	55,56
DOCK TAVERN LANE	D.3	55
DOLMAN CLOSE	H.2	56
DORSET CLOSE	D.1	55
DOVE CLOSE	D.1	55
DOWNING COURT	C.2	54
DOWNING ROAD	C.2	54
DRAKE AVENUE	K.3	57
DRUDGE ROAD	C.3	54
DUKE ROAD	D.3	55
DUNCAN ROAD	G.3	56
DURHAM AVENUE	B.1	54
EAST ANGLIAN WAY	D.2	55
EAST ROAD	L.3	57
ECCLESTONE CLOSE	C.1	54
EDEN PLACE	H.2	56
EDINBURGH AVENUE	B.1	54
EDINBURGH PLACE	G.3	56
EDISON WAY	E.1	55
ELDER GREEN	C.1	54
ELM AVENUE	C.2	54
ELMGROVE ROAD	B.2	54
ELMHURST CLOSE	B.2	54
ELSIE ROAD	G.2	56
EMMANUEL AVENUE	B.2	54
EMPRESS ROAD	G.1	56
ENGLANDS LANE	C.3	54
ENTERPRISE COURT	F.1	55,56
ERICA WAY	D.2	55
ESTCOURT ROAD	J.3	57
EUSTON ROAD	H.3	56
EXCALIBUR ROAD	A.1	54
EXCELSIOR TERRACE	E.2	55
EXETER ROAD	C.2	54
EXMOUTH PLACE	F.3	57
EXMOUTH ROAD	F.3	55,56
FACTORY ROAD	H.3	56
FALCON COURT	H.2	56
FALKLAND WAY	C.1	54
FARADAY ROAD	E.1	55
FASTOLFF AVENUE	B.1	54
FEATHERS PLAIN	D.3	55
FENNER ROAD	E.3	55
FERRIER CLOSE	H.3	56
FERRIER ROAD	H.3	56
FERRY HILL	E.3	55
FERRY LANE	G.2	56
FISHER AVENUE	K.3	57
FISHERS OPENING	H.3	56
FISHERS QUAY	E.3	55
FISHWHARF	E.3	55
FISKES OPENING	C.3	54
FITZALAN CLOSE	B.1	54
FORSYTHIA ROAD	D.1	55
FRAMLINGHAM CLOSE	G.2	56
FREDERICK ROAD	H.3	56
FREDRICK ROAD	H.2	56
FREMANTLE ROAD	L.3	57
FRIARS LANE	G.3	56
FULLERS HILL	H.2	56
GABLEHURST COURT	C.1	54
GAINSBOROUGH AVENUE	E.1	55
GAPTON HALL ROAD	E.1	55
GAPTON INDUSTRIAL EST.	E.1	55
GARFIELD ROAD	J.3	57
GARNHAM ROAD	D.2	55
GARRISON ROAD	H.2	56
GATACRE ROAD	G.2	56
GEORGE STREET	H.2	56
GIRTON ROAD	B.1	54
GLOUCESTER AVENUE	C.2	54
GORDON ROAD	F.2	55,56
GOURNAY AVENUE	B.3	54
GRANTA WAY	B.1	54
GRANVILLE ROAD	G.2	56
GREBE CLOSE	D.1	55
GREENACRE	F.3	55,56
GREENACRES	B.1	54
GRENVILLE PLACE	K.3	57
GRESHAM CLOSE	B.2	54
GREYFRIARS WAY	G.2	56
HALF MOON	A.2	54
HALL PLAIN	G.2	56
HALL QUAY	H.2	56
HAMILTON ROAD	K.3	57
HAMMOND ROAD	J.3	57
HARBORD CRESCENT	F.3	55,56
HARFREYS INDUSTRIAL EST.	E.1	55
HARFREYS ROAD	E.2	55
HARLEY ROAD	J.3	57
HARTMANN ROAD	D.3	55
HAVELOCK ROAD	F.3	55,56
HAWKINS AVENUE	K.3	57
HAWKINS CLOSE	K.3	57
HAWTHORN ROAD	D.1	55
HAZEL WAY	D.1	55
HEADINGTON CLOSE	C.1	54
HEATH GREEN	D.2	55
HENLEY CLOSE	E.2	55
HERON CLOSE	D.1	55
HERRIES CLOSE	H.2	56
HERTFORD WAY	C.1	54
HEWETT CLOSE	B.3	54
HEWITT ROAD	E.1	55
HIGH MILL ROAD	G.2	56
HIGH ROAD	E.3	55
HIGH STREET	D.3	55
HIGHFIELD ROAD	E.2	55
HILL AVENUE	A.3	54
HOGARTH CLOSE	E.1	55
HOLLY WAY	D.1	55
HORNBEAM CLOSE	D.2	55
HORSLEY DRIVE	A.2	54
HOWARD ST. NORTH	H.2	56
HOWARD ST. SOUTH	G.2	56
HOWE ROAD	K.3	57
HUMBER KEEL	A.2	54
HUMBERSTONE ROAD	D.2	55
ICEHOUSE HILL	D.3	55
INNER RELIEF ROAD	C.2	54
ISAACS ROAD	H.2	56
IVY GREEN	D.1	55
JAMES WATT CLOSE	E.1	55
JASMINE GREEN	D.1	55
JELLICOE ROAD	K.3	57
JEMA CLOSE	K.3	57
JENNER ROAD	A.2	54
JEWS LANE	B.1	54
JOHN ROAD	D.3	55
JONES (GC) WAY	G.1	56
JURY STREET	H.3	56
KALMIA GREEN	D.1	55
KEBLE ROAD	B.1	54
KENNEDY AVENUE	A.2	54
KENT AVENUE	B.2	54
KENT SQUARE	G.3	56
KEPPEL ROAD	C.3	54
KESTREL CLOSE	D.1	55
KEYES AVENUE	K.3	57
KIMBERLEY TERRACE	G.3	56
KING STREET	G.3	56
KINGS ROAD, GORLESTON	G.3	56
KINGS ROAD, GT. YARMOUTH	F.3	55,56
KITCHENER ROAD	J.3	57
LABURNHAM ROAD	C.1	54
LADY HAVEN ROAD	H.2	56
LADY MARGARET'S AVENUE	C.2	54
LANCASTER ROAD	G.3	56
LANCASTER SQUARE	G.3	56
LANGHAM ROAD	H.3	56
LAPWING CLOSE	D.1	55
LARCH DRIVE	D.1	55
LAUGHING IMAGE CORNER	H.2	56
LAWN AVENUE	J.2	57
LAWYER CORYS	A.2	54
LEACH CLOSE	C.1	54
LEICESTER ROAD	C.3	54
LEMAN ROAD	B.2	54
LEYS ROAD	F.2	55,56
LICHFIELD ROAD	F.2	55,56
LIME WAY	D.2	55
LIMEKILN WALK	H.2	56
LIMMER ROAD	C.3	54
LINCOLN AVENUE	B.2	54
LINKS ROAD	A.2	54
LISTER CLOSE	A.2	54
LONG LANE	C.1	54
LOUISE CLOSE	G.3	56
LOVEWELL ROAD	D.2	55
LOWER CLIFF ROAD	C.3	54
LOWER ESPLANADE	B.3	54
LOWESTOFT ROAD	A.2	54
LUCAS ROAD	G.1	56
LYNN GROVE	D.1	55
MADDEN AVENUE	K.3	57
MAGDALEN SQUARE	C.2	54
MAGDALEN WAY	C.2	54
MAGNOLIA GREEN	D.2	55
MAIN CROSS ROAD	E.3	55
MALAKOFF ROAD	G.3	56
MALLARD WAY	D.1	55
MALTHOUSE LANE	E.3	55
MANBY ROAD	H.3	56
MANBY ROAD, GORLESTON	E.2	55
MANOR CLOSE	E.2	55
MANOR ROAD	C.2	54
MAPLE WAY	D.1	55
MARINA LEISURE CENTRE	G.3	56
MARINE CLOSE	A.3	54
MARINE CRESCENT	J.3	57
MARINE PARADE	H.3	56
MARINE PARADE NORTH	H.3	56
MARINE PARADE SOUTH	E.3	55
MARINE PARADE, GORLESTON	A.3	54
MARINE PARK	F.1	55,56
MARINERS CLOSE	A.2	54
MARINERS COMPASS	A.2	54
MARINERS ROAD	G.3	56
MARKET GATES	H.3	56
MARKET PLACE	H.2	56
MARKET ROW	H.2	56
MARLBOROUGH SQUARE	G.3	56
MARLBOROUGH TERRACE	H.3	56
MARSH ROAD	G.1	56
MASQUERS CLOSE	B.2	54
MAUD TERRACE	J.3	57
MAYGROVE ROAD	H.3	56
MEADOW COURT	A.2	54
MERTON AVENUE	C.1	54
MICAWBER AVENUE	F.3	55,56
MIDDLE MARKET ROAD	H.3	56
MIDDLE ROW EAST	F.3	55,56
MIDDLE ROW WEST	F.3	55,56
MIDDLEGATE STREET	G.3	56
MIDDLESTONE CLOSE	C.2	54
MIDDLETON GARDENS	C.2	54
MIDDLETON ROAD	B.2	54
MIDLAND CLOSE	J.3	57
MILL ROAD	G.2	56
MISSION ROAD	H.1	56
MOAT ROAD	C.1	54
MONUMENT ROAD	E.3	55
MORETON PETO ROAD	E.1	55
NAPOLEON PLACE	G.3	56
NELSON ROAD	C.3	54
NELSON ROAD CENTRAL	H.3	56
NELSON ROAD NORTH	H.3	56
NELSON ROAD SOUTH	F.3	55,56
NETTLE HILL	D.1	55
NETTLE HILL EAST	H.3	56
NETTLE HILL WEST	H.3	56
NEW COLLEGE CLOSE	C.1	54
NEWCASTLE ROAD	F.3	55,56
NEWNHAM GREEN	B.1	54
NEWTON CROSS	A.2	54
NILE ROAD	C.3	54
NINE PARISH	A.2	54
NORFOLK SQUARE	H.3	56
NORMAN LANE	H.2	56
NORTH DENES ROAD	H.2	56
NORTH DRIVE	J.3	57
NORTH MARKET ROAD	H.2	56
NORTH QUAY	H.2	56
NORTH RIVER ROAD	J.2	57
NORTH ROAD, GORLESTON	C.3	54
NORTH ROAD, GT. YARMOUTH	J.3	57
NORTHERN CLOSE	J.3	57
NORTHGATE STREET	H.2	56
NOTTINGHAM WAY	G.3	56
NUFFIELD CLOSE	C.1	54
NUFFIELD CRESCENT	C.2	54
NURSERY TERRACE	J.2	57
OAK ROAD	D.2	55
OLD FOUNTAIN	A.2	54
OLIVE ROAD	G.2	56
OLIVER COURT	F.2	55,56
ONSLOW AVENUE	K.3	57
ORDE AVENUE	A.2	54
ORDNANCE ROAD	H.2	55,56
ORFORD CLOSE	G.3	56
ORIEL AVENUE	B.1	54
ORIEL WAY	B.1	54
ORMOND ROAD	J.2	57
OSBORNE AVENUE	K.3	57
OWEN ROAD	F.2	55,56
OXFORD AVENUE	B.1	54
PAGET CRESCENT	A.2	54
PAGET ROAD	H.3	56
PALGRAVE ROAD	J.2	57
PALMER ROAD	B.3	54
PARK ROAD	B.3	54
PARKLAND DRIVE	C.1	54
PASTEUR ROAD	G.2	56
PASTON ROAD	C.2	54
PATTERSON CLOSE	H.2	56
PATTINSONS ROAD	J.2	57
PAVILION ROAD	C.3	54
PEGGOTTY ROAD	F.3	55,56
PEMBROKE AVENUE	C.1	54
PEREBROWN AVENUE	K.3	57
PETERHOUSE AVENUE	C.2	54
PIER GARDENS	C.3	54
PIER PLACE	F.3	55,56
PIER PLAIN	C.3	54
PIER ROAD	C.3	54
PIER WALK	C.3	54
PINE GREEN	C.1	54
PINTAIL DRIVE	D.1	55
PLANE ROAD	D.2	55
PLEVNA TERRACE	G.2	56
PLOVER CLOSE	D.1	55
POMMERS LANE	E.3	55
POPLAR AVENUE	B.2	54
PORTLAND COURT	G.2	56
PORTLAND PLACE	G.2	56
POTTERS FIELD	A.1	54
POUND LANE	B.2	54
PRINCES ROAD	H.3	56
PRIORY GARDENS	H.3	56
PRIORY PLAIN	H.3	56
PRIORY STREET	D.3	55
PURLEY COURT	F.1	55,56
QUAY ANGEL	A.2	54
QUAY MILL WALK	H.2	56
QUAY OSTEND	A.2	54
QUAY ROAD	C.3	54
QUEEN ANNE'S ROAD	E.2	55
QUEEN STREET	G.2	56
QUEEN'S CRESCENT	B.2	54
QUEEN'S ROAD	F.3	55,56
RAINBOW CORNER SQUARE	H.2	56
RALEIGH AVENUE	K.3	57
RAMBOUILLET CLOSE	C.1	54
RAMPART ROAD	H.2	56
RAVEN CLOSE	D.1	55
RECREATION CLOSE	D.2	55
RECREATION ROAD	D.2	55
REGENT ROAD	H.3	56
REGENT STREET	G.2	56
RIVER WALK	K.2	57
RIVERSIDE ROAD	C.3	54
ROBIN CLOSE	D.1	55
RODNEY ROAD	G.3	56
ROMAN PLACE	H.3	56
ROSLYN ROAD	C.2	54
ROWAN WAY	D.1	55
ROYAL ALBERT COURT	C.3	54
ROYAL AVENUE	K.3	57
RUNHAM ROAD	J.2	57
RUNHAM VAUXHALL	J.2	57
RUSKIN AVENUE	B.1	54
RUSSELL AVENUE	B.2	54
RUSSELL ROAD	G.3	56
RUSSELL SQUARE	H.3	56
SACKVILLE CLOSE	G.3	56
SALISBURY ROAD	J.3	57
SALK ROAD	A.2	54
SALMON ROAD	E.3	55
SANDOWN ROAD	H.3	56
SANDPIPER CLOSE	D.1	55
SANDRINGHAM AVENUE	K.3	57
SAWMILL LANE	H.2	56
SAXON ROAD	H.3	56
SCHOOL LANE	D.3	55
SCHOOL ROAD	H.2	56
SCHOOL ROAD BACK	H.2	56
SEAFIELD CLOSE	F.3	55,56
SEAWAKE CLOSE	C.1	54
SEEBY PLACE	F.3	55,56
SEFTON LANE	G.2	56
SELWYN ROAD	C.1	54
SEYMOUR AVENUE	K.3	57
SHADINGFIELD CLOSE	F.3	55,56
SHAKESPEARE ROAD	K.3	57
SHEARWATER DRIVE	E.1	55
SHELDONIAN COURT	C.1	54
SHRUBLANDS WAY	D.2	55
SHUTTLEWORTH CLOSE	E.1	55
SIDNEY CLOSE	G.3	56
SILK MILL ROAD	H.3	56
SINCLAIR COURT	E.1	55
SISKIN CLOSE	D.1	55
SMITHS LOKE	D.1	55
SOMERVILLE AVENUE	B.2	54
SOUTH BEACH PARADE	C.3	54
SOUTH DENES ROAD	C.3	54
SOUTH GARDEN	A.2	54
SOUTH MARKET ROAD	H.3	56
SOUTH QUAY	G.2	56
SOUTH ROAD	L.3	57
SOUTH ROAD, GORLESTON	C.3	54
SOUTHGATES ROAD	F.3	55,56
SOUTHTOWN	F.2	55,56
SOUTHTOWN ROAD	E.2	55
SPENCER AVENUE	D.2	55
SPENS AVENUE	B.2	54
SPRINGFIELD ROAD	C.3	54
ST. ANDREW'S ROAD	D.2	55
ST. ANDREWS CLOSE	D.2	55
ST. ANNE'S CRESCENT	C.1	54
ST. ANTHONYS AVENUE	B.1	54
ST. BENET'S ROAD	C.2	54
ST. CATHERINE'S WAY	C.2	54
ST. EDMUNDS CLOSE	B.1	54
ST. FRANCIS WAY	H.2	56
ST. GEORGES PLAIN	G.3	56
ST. GEORGES ROAD	G.3	56
ST. HILDA'S CRESCENT	C.2	54
ST. HUGH'S GREEN	B.2	54
ST. JOHN'S AVENUE	C.1	54
ST. JOHN'S TERRACE	G.3	56
ST. LUKE'S TERRACE	H.1	56
ST. MARY'S LANE	G.2	56
ST. NICHOLAS ROAD	J.3	57
ST. PAUL'S WAY	B.2	54
ST. PETER'S PLAIN	G.3	56
ST. PETER'S ROAD	G.3	56
STAFFORD ROAD	G.2	56
STANDARD PLACE	G.3	56
STANDARD ROAD	G.3	56
STANLEY AVENUE	B.2	54
STANLEY ROAD	J.3	57
STATION ROAD	H.2	56
STEAM MILL LANE	H.2	56
STEPHENSONS CLOSE	J.3	57
STONE ROAD	J.3	57
STONECUTTERS WAY	H.2	56
STRADBROKE CLOSE	C.2	54
STRADBROKE ROAD	C.2	54
STUART CLOSE	C.2	54
STURDEE AVENUE	K.3	57
STYLES CLOSE	C.1	54
SUFFIELD ROAD	E.3	55
SUFFLING ROAD	E.3	55
SUFFOLK CLOSE	E.2	55
SUFFOLK PLACE	H.3	56
SUFFOLK ROAD	E.2	55
SUSSEX ROAD	E.3	55
SUTTON ROAD	F.3	55,56
SWALLOW CLOSE	D.1	55
SWANSTON ROAD	E.3	55
SWIRLES PLACE	H.3	56
SYCAMORE GREEN	D.1	55
TAMWORTH LANE	G.2	56
TAR WORKS ROAD	J.2	57
TEMPLE ROAD	H.3	56
TENNYSON ROAD	K.3	57
TERN CLOSE	D.1	55
TERN GARDENS	D.1	55
THAMESFIELD WAY	F.2	55,56
THE CLOSE	H.2	56
THE CONGE	H.2	56
THE FAIRWAY	A.2	54
THE LAWNS	K.3	57
THE LEA	J.2	57
THE PASTURES	E.2	55
THE STREET	L.3	57
THE WALK	D.1	55
THE WILLOWS	B.1	54
THEATRE PLAIN	H.3	56
TOLHOUSE STREET	G.3	56
TOLLGATE ROAD	F.2	55,56
TOTTENHAM STREET	H.3	56
TOWN WALL ROAD	H.3	56
TOWNLANDS	E.2	55
TOWNSHEND CLOSE	G.3	56
TRAFALGAR ROAD	G.3	56
TRAFALGAR ROAD EAST	D.3	55
TRAFALGAR ROAD WEST	D.2	55
TRINITY AVENUE	C.1	54
TRINITY PLACE	G.3	56
TRINITY SQUARE	F.3	55,56
TUDOR WALK	A.2	54
TURNER CLOSE	E.1	55
TYRELLS ROAD	H.2	56
TYROLEAN SQUARE	H.2	56
UNION ROAD	H.3	56
UNIVERSITY CRESCENT	C.2	54
UPPER CLIFF ROAD	C.3	54
UPPER ESPLANADE	B.3	54
VANGUARD ROAD	E.1	55
VAUXHALL TERRACE	J.3	57
VERONICA GREEN	D.1	55
VIBURNHAM WAY	D.2	55
VICTORIA GARDENS	G.3	56
VICTORIA RD, GORLESTON	B.3	54
VICTORIA RD, GT. YARMOUTH	G.3	56
VICTORIA STREET	J.3	57
VIKING CLOSE	B.3	54
WADHAM AVENUE	B.2	54
WADHAM ROAD	B.2	54
WAGTAIL CLOSE	D.1	55
WALPOLE ROAD	J.3	57
WATERLOO ROAD	G.3	56
WAUNCI CRESCENT	B.3	54
WAVENEY ROAD	F.2	55,56
WEDGEWOOD COURT	B.2	54
WELL STREET	H.3	56
WELLESLEY ROAD	H.3	56
WELLINGTON PLACE	H.3	56
WELLINGTON ROAD	G.3	56
WEST AVENUE	B.2	54
WEST ROAD	H.3	56
WESTBROOK AVENUE	D.2	55
WESTERN ROAD	C.2	54
WHERRY WAY	K.2	57
WHIMBREL DRIVE	E.1	55
WHITEHORSE PLAIN	H.2	56
WIDGEON CLOSE	D.1	55
WINDSOR AVENUE	K.3	57
WINDSOR WAY	C.2	54
WINIFRED ROAD	G.2	56
WOLLSELEY ROAD	G.2	56
WOODCOCK MEWS	D.1	55
WOODFARM LANE	A.1	54
WOODPECKER MEWS	D.1	55
WORCESTER WAY	C.2	54
WREN DRIVE	D.1	55
YALLOP AVENUE	A.3	54
YARE CLOSE	J.2	57
YARMOUTH WAY	G.3	56
YAXLEYS ROAD	K.2	57
YORK ROAD	G.3	56
YOUELL AVENUE	A.3	54

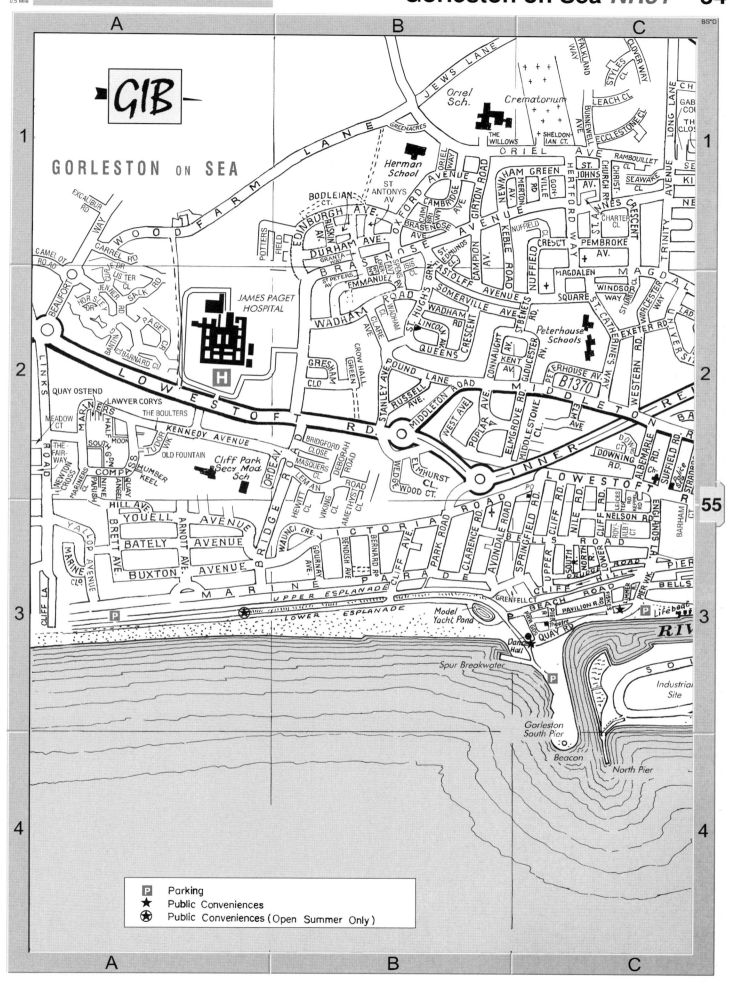

0.5 Km
0.5 Mile

BS"D

GIB

GORLESTON ON SEA

	Parking
P	Parking
★	Public Conveniences
✪	Public Conveniences (Open Summer Only)

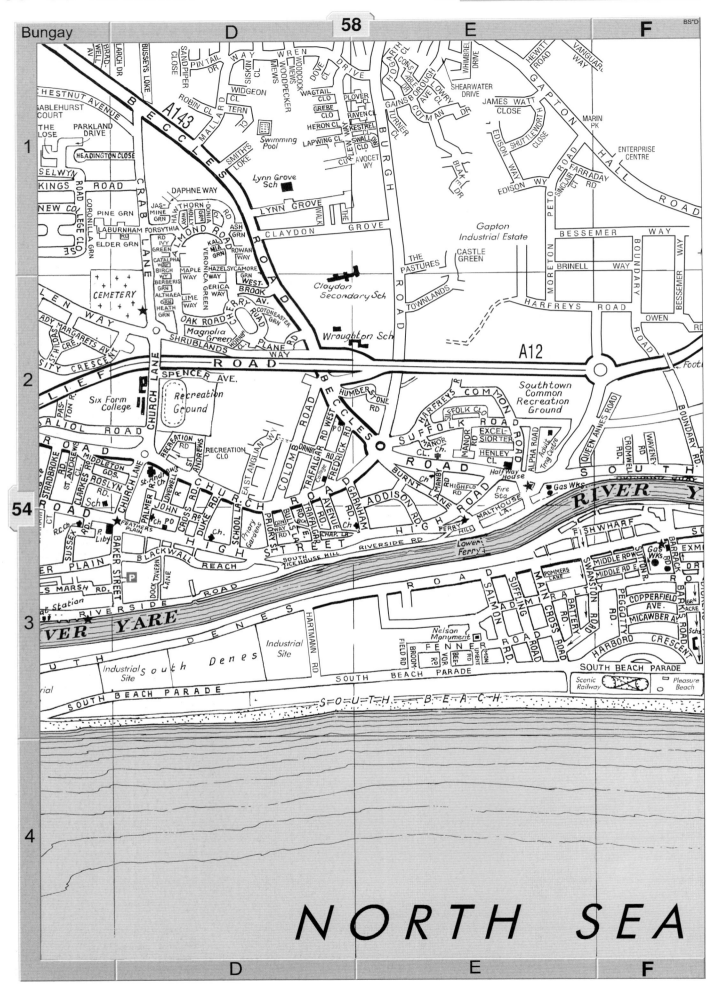

Bungay

58

BS"D

D E F

1

Chestnut Avenue
GABLEHURST COURT
THE CLOSE
PARKLAND DRIVE
HEADINGTON CLOSE
SELWYN
KINGS ROAD
NEW COLLEGE CLO
CORONILLA GRN
PINE GRN
LABURNHAM RD
ELDER GRN

BRAD-WELL AV.
LARCH DR
BUSSEY'S LOKE
SANDPIPER CLOSE
PINTAIL DR
ROBIN CL
MALLARD CL
SISKIN CL
TERN CL
WIDGEON CL
WOODCOCK MEWS
WOODPECKER
WAY
WREN
DOVE CT
WAGTAIL CLO
GREBE CLO
HERON CLO
LAPWING CL
PLOVER CL
RAVEN CL
KESTREL CLO
SWALLOW CLO
AVOCET WY
CURLEW WAY
THE
GAINSBOROUGH AVE
HOGARTH CL
CONSTABLE DR
TURNER CL
COTMAN DR
OWRY CL
SHEARWATER DRIVE
WHIMBREL DRIVE

HEWITT ROAD
VANGUARD WAY
JAMES WATT CLOSE
SHUTTLEWORTH CLOSE
EDISON WAY
PETO ROAD
MORETON
MARINE PK
ENTERPRISE CENTRE
SINCLAIR CT
FARRADAY RD
EDISON WY
HALL ROAD

A143
BECCLES

DAPHNE WAY
JASMINE GRN
HAWTHORN GRN
HOLLY GRN
CATALPA WAY
IVY GRN
BIRCH WY
BERBERIS GRN
ALTHAEA GRN
HEATH GRN
ALMOND ROAD
KALMIA GRN
VERONICA GREEN
MAPLE WAY
LIME WAY
ERICA WAY
HAZEL
ASH RD
ROWAN WAY
SYCAMORE GRN
WEST-BROOK
FORSYTHIA
DONIA GRN
DAPHNE WAY
LYNN GROVE Sch
LYNN GROVE
WALK
CLAYDON GROVE
THE PASTURES
TOWNLANDS
Swimming Pool
CASTLE GREEN
Gapton Industrial Estate
BESSEMER WAY
BRINELL WAY
BOUNDARY
BESSEMER WAY
OWEN
HARFREYS ROAD

2

LEN WAY
LADY MARGARETS AVE
UNIVERSITY CRESCENT
SMITHS CRES
BALIOL ROAD
CEMETERY
OAK ROAD
MAGNOLIA GREEN
SHRUBLANDS
SPENCER AVE.
CHURCH LANE
Recreation Ground
Six Form College
RELIEF ROAD
COTONEASTER GRN
FERRY RD
PLANE WAY
CLAYDON Secondary Sch
Wroughton Sch
A12
A12
Southtown Common Recreation Ground
Footpath

54

STRADBROKE ROAD
ST ANDREWS CL
MIDDLETON GDS
CLARKES RD
ROSLYN RD
Sch
SUSSEX RD
CT
R.Cch
P Liby
FEATHERS PLAIN
BAKER STREET
BLACKWALL REACH
DOCK TAVERN LANE
P
ST ANDREWS ROAD
ST ANDREWS
LOVEWELL RD
PALMER RD
JOHN
CROSS RD
DUKE RD
Ch PO
Ch.
RECREATION RD
RECREATION CLO
EAST ANGLIAN WY
ST ANDREWS
HIGH
PRIORY Gardens
PRIORY ST.
SCHOOL LA.
CHURCH
BULLS LANE
CON WAY
BECCLES
COLOMB ROAD
DANBY
RD WEST
FREDRICK RD
COLLEGE RD
TRAFALGAR
AVENUE
GARNHAM RD
TRAFALGAR RD
Ch
CHAP. LA.
HUMBERSTONE RD
HARFREYS RD
PO
SUFFOLK CLO
MANOR CL.
MANOR Ch.
EXCELSIOR TER
HENLEY CL
MANBY RD
HIGHFLD RD
ALPHA ROAD
Adult Trg Centre
Half Way House
COMMON ROAD
SUFFOLK ROAD
BURNT LANE
ADDISON RD.
HIGH RD
Ch
Fire Sta
MALTHOUSE LA.
Ferry Hill
Lower Ferry
Gas Wks.
FISH WHARF
RIVER Y
QUEEN ANNES ROAD
BOUNDARY ROAD
CROMWELL RD.
WAVENEY RD.
SOUTH

3

VER YARE
Station
RIVERSIDE ROAD
RIVERSIDE RD
SOUTH ICE HOUSE HILL
PLAIN RD.
MARSH RD.
DENES ROAD
HARTMANN RD
Industrial Site
Industrial Site
South Denes
SOUTH DENES
SOUTH BEACH PARADE
FIELD RD
BROOM RD
FENNER RD.
VOR RD
BEE-
URBENT
Nelson Monument
SOUTH BEACH PARADE
SALMON ROAD
SUFFLING RD.
BATTERY RD.
MAIN CROSS ROAD
SWANSTON ROAD
BALTIC RD.
MIDDLE ROW
MIDDLE RD
POMMERS LANE
GARRISON RD
PEGGOTTY RD.
COPPERFIELD AVE.
MICAWBER AV
HARBORD CRESCENT
SOUTH BEACH PARADE
BARRACK RD
SUTTON RD.
GRN ACRE
BARKIS ROAD
Sch
EXM
OR
Gas Wks.
Scenic Railway
Pleasure Beach

4

SOUTH BEACH PARADE
SOUTH BEACH

NORTH SEA

D E F

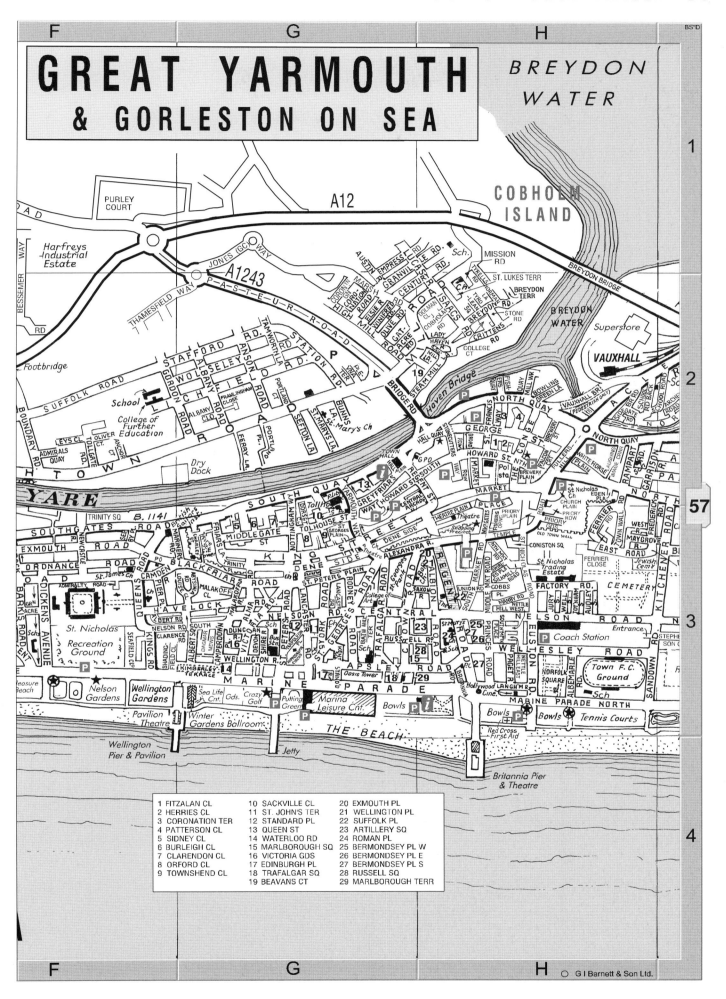

GREAT YARMOUTH
& GORLESTON ON SEA

BREYDON WATER

COBHOLM ISLAND

1	FITZALAN CL	10	SACKVILLE CL	20	EXMOUTH PL
2	HERRIES CL	11	ST. JOHN'S TER	21	WELLINGTON PL
3	CORONATION TER	12	STANDARD PL	22	SUFFOLK PL
4	PATTERSON CL	13	QUEEN ST	23	ARTILLERY SQ
5	SIDNEY CL	14	WATERLOO RD	24	ROMAN PL
6	BURLEIGH CL	15	MARLBOROUGH SQ	25	BERMONDSEY PL W
7	CLARENDON CL	16	VICTORIA GDS	26	BERMONDSEY PL E
8	ORFORD CL	17	EDINBURGH PL	27	BERMONDSEY PL S
9	TOWNSHEND CL	18	TRAFALGAR SQ	28	RUSSELL SQ
		19	BEAVANS CT	29	MARLBOROUGH TERR

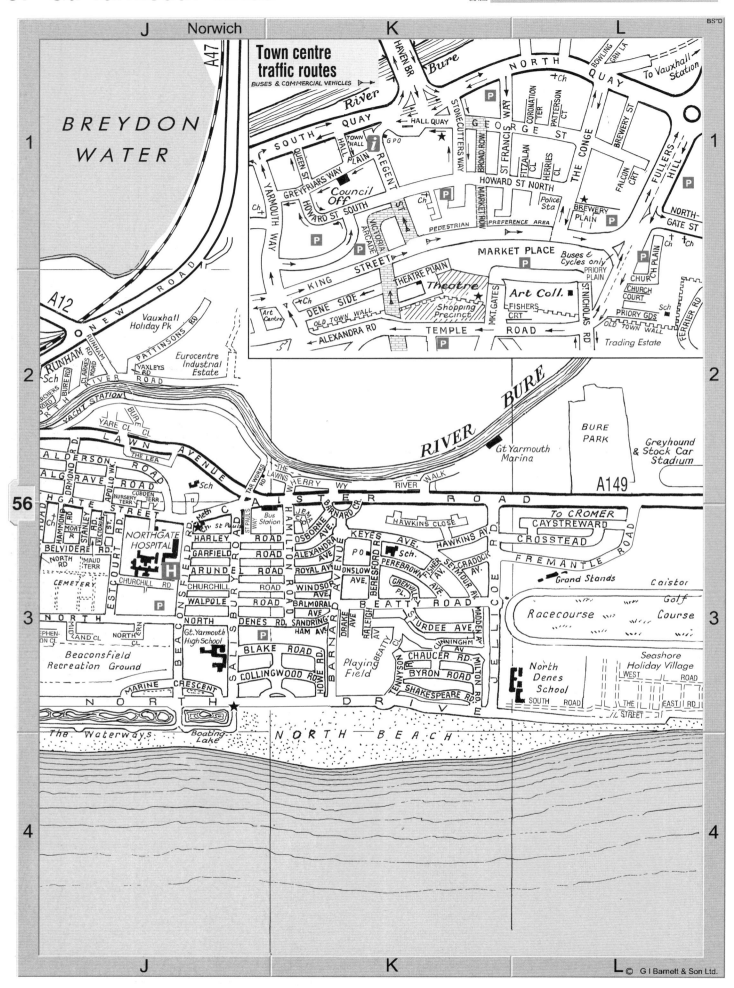

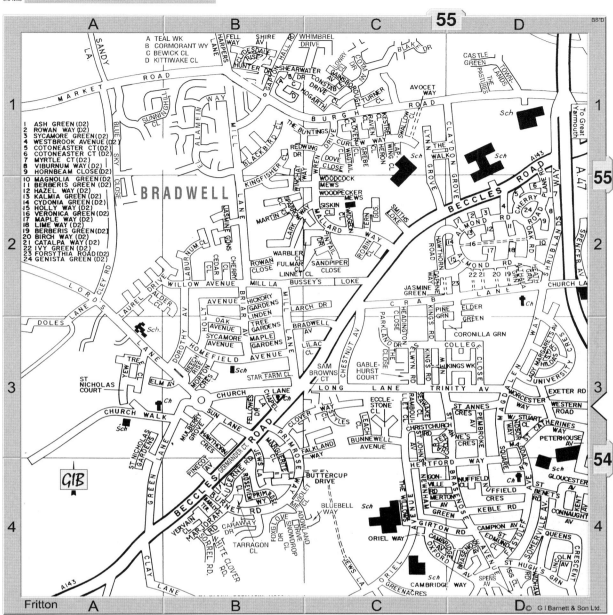

ALDER CLOSE B.2	CLEY ROAD A.2	GREENACRES C.4	LILAC CLOSE C.3	PINTAIL DRIVE C.2	SUNNINGHILL CLOSE ...A.1
ALMOND AVENUE D.2	CLOVER WAY B.3	GONVILLE ROAD C.4	LIME WAY (18) D.2	PLANE ROAD D.2	SWALLOW CLOSE C.1
ALTHAEA GREEN D.2	CLYDESDALE RISE B.1		LINCOLN AVENUE D.4	PLOVER CLOSE C.1	SYCAMORE AVENUE ...B.3
ASH GREEN (1) D.2	COB CLOSE B.1	HARPERS LANE B.1	LINDEN TREE GDS B.3	PRIMROSE WAY B.3	SYCAMORE GREEN (3) .D.2
AVOCET WAY C.1	CONNAUGHT AVE D.4	HAWTHORN CR B.3	LINNET CLOSE B.2		
	CONSTABLE DRIVE ...C.1	HAWTHORN ROAD ...C.2	LONG LANE C.3	QUEENS CR D.4	TARRAGON CLOSE B.4
BARLEY TERRACE B.4	CORMORANT WAY B.1	HAZEL WAY (12) D.2	LORD'S LANE A.2		TEAL WALK B.1
BECCLES ROAD D.2	CORONILLA GREEN ...D.3	HEADINGTON ROAD ..C.3	LOWRY CLOSE C.1	RAMBOUILLET CL C.3	TERN GARDENS C.2
BEECH RISE B.3	COTMAN DRIVE C.1	HEATH GREEN D.2	LUCERNE ROAD B.4	RAVEN CLOSE C.1	THE BUNTINGS B.1
BERBERIS GREEN (19) .D.2	COTONEASTER CT (5) .D.2	HERON CLOSE C.1	LYNN GROVE C.1	REDWING ROAD B.1	THE CLOSE C.3
BERBERIS GREEN (11) .D.2	COTONEASTER CT (6) .D.2	HERTFORD WAY C.4		ROBIN CLOSE C.2	THE PASTURES D.1
BEWICK CLOSE B.1	CRAB LANE C.2	HICKORY GARDENS ...B.2	MAGDALEN SQUARE ...D.3	ROSEVIEW CLOSE B.4	THE WALK C.1
BIRCH WAY (20) B.1	CURLEW WAY C.1	HOGARTH CLOSE C.1	MAGDALEN WAY D.3	ROWAN CLOSE B.2	THE WILLOWS C.4
BLACKBIRD CLOSE B.1	CYDONIA GN (14) D.2	HOLLY AVENUE B.3	MAGNOLIA GREEN (10) .D.2	ROWAN WAY (2) D.2	TOWNLANDS D.1
BLAKE DRIVE C.1		HOLLY WAY (15) D.2	MALLARD WAY C.2		TRINITY AVENUE D.3
BLUE SKY CLOSE A.1	DALES COURT B.1	HOMEFIELD AVENUE ..B.3	MAPLE GARDENS B.3	ST. ANNES CR D.3	TURNER CLOSE C.1
BLUEBELL WAY C.4	DAPHNE WAY C.2	HORNBEAM CLOSE (9) .D.2	MAPLE WAY (17) D.2	ST. BENET'S ROAD ...D.4	
BRADWELL AVENUE ..B.3	DOLES LANE A.3	HUNTER DRIVE B.1	MARGUERITE CLOSE ..B.3	ST. CATHERINES WAY .D.3	UNIVERSITY CRESCENT .D.3
BRASENOSE AVENUE .D.4	DOROTHY AVENUE ...B.3		MARJORAM ROAD B.4	ST. EDMUND CLOSE ..D.4	
BRIAR AVENUE B.2	DOVE CLOSE C.1	ISIS CLOSE D.4	MARKET ROAD A.1	ST. HILDAS CR D.3	VERONICA GREEN (16) ..D.2
BUNNEWELL AVENUE .C.3		IVY GREEN (22) D.2	MARTIN CLOSE C.2	ST. HUGH'S GREEN ...D.4	VERVAIN CLOSE B.4
BURGH ROAD C.1	ECCLESTON CLOSE ...C.3		MEADOWLAND DR B.4	ST. JOHN'S AVENUE ..C.3	VIBURNUM WAY (8) ...D.2
BURNET ROAD B.4	EL ALAMEIN WAY B.1	JASMINE GARDENS ...B.2	MERTON AVENUE C.4	ST. NICHOLAS COURT .A.3	VIOLET CLOSE B.4
BUSSEY'S LOKE C.2	ELDER GREEN D.2	JASMINE GREEN C.2	MILL LANE B.1	ST. NICHOLAS GDS ...A.3	
BUTTERCUP DRIVE ...C.4	ELM AVENUE A.3	JEWS LANE B.3	MORTON CR B.3	SAM BROWNS CT C.3	WADHAM ROAD D.4
	EXETER ROAD D.3	JEWS LANE C.4	MULBERRY GROVE ...B.3	SANDPIPER CLOSE ...C.2	WAGTAIL CLOSE C.1
CAMBRIDGE AVENUE ..C.4			MYRTLE COURT (7) ...D.2	SANDY LANE A.1	WARBLER CLOSE C.2
CAMBRIDGE WAY C.4	FALKLAND WAY C.3	KALMIA GREEN (13) ..D.2		SEAWAKE CLOSE C.3	WESTBROOK AVENUE (4)D.2
CAMPION AVENUE C.4	FASTOLFF AVENUE ...D.4	KEBLE ROAD D.4	NEW COLLEGE CL D.3	SELWYN ROAD C.3	WESTERN ROAD D.3
CARAWAY DRIVE B.4	FELL WAY B.1	KENT AVENUE D.4	NEWNHAM GREEN C.4	SHEARWATER DRIVE ..B.1	WHIMBREL DRIVE C.1
CASTLE GREEN D.1	FELLOWES DRIVE B.3	KESTREL CLOSE C.1	NUFFIELD CLOSE D.4	SHIRE AVENUE B.1	WHITE CLOVER ROAD .B.4
CATALPA WAY (21) ...D.2	FORSYTHIA ROAD (23) .D.2	KINGFISHER CLOSE ...B.2	NUFFIELD CRESCENT ..D.4	SHRUBLANDS WAY ...C.2	WIDGEON CLOSE C.2
CEDAR CLOSE B.2	FOXGLOVE DRIVE B.4	KING'S ROAD C.2		SISKIN CLOSE C.2	WILLOW AVENUE B.2
CHAPEL LANE B.3	FULMAR CLOSE B.2	KING'S ROAD C.3	OAK AVENUE B.3	SMITHS LOKE C.2	WINCHAT WAY B.2
CHARTER CLOSE C.3		KINGS WALK D.3	OAK ROAD C.2	SNOWDROP CLOSE ...B.4	WINDSOR WAY D.3
CHERRY CLOSE B.2	GABLEHURST CT C.3	KITTIWAKE CLOSE ...B.1	ORIEL AVENUE C.4	SOMERVILLE AVENUE .D.4	WOODCOCK MEWS ...C.2
CHERRY ROAD D.2	GAINSBOROUGH AVE ..C.1		ORIEL WAY C.4	SORREL ROAD B.4	WOODPECKER MEWS ..C.2
CHESTNUT AVE B.2	GAPTON HALL RD B.1	LABURNUM CLOSE ...B.2	OXFORD AVENUE C.4	SPARROW CLOSE C.3	WORCESTER WAY D.3
CHRISTCHURCH RD ...C.3	GENISTA GREEN (24) ..D.2	LADY MARGARETS AVE .D.3		SPENCERS AVENUE ...D.2	WREN DRIVE C.1
CHURCH LANE B.3	GERMANDER COURT ..B.3	LAPWING CLOSE C.1	PARKLAND DRIVE C.3	SPENS AVENUE C.4	
CHURCH LANE D.2	GIRTON ROAD C.4	LARCH DRIVE B.2	PEMBROKE AVE D.3	STAR FARM CLOSE ...B.3	YEW TREE CLOSE A.3
CHURCH WALK A.3	GLOUCESTER AVE D.4	LARK WAY B.2	PETERHOUSE AVE D.3	STUART CLOSE D.3	
CLAY LANE A.4	GREBE CLOSE C.1	LAUREL DRIVE A.2	PINE GREEN C.2	STYLES CLOSE C.3	
CLAYDON GROVE D.1	GREEN LANE A.4	LEACH CLOSE C.3	PINECOT AVENUE B.4	SUN LANE B.3	

...continued on next page.....

© G I Barnett & Son Ltd.

0.5 Km
0.5 Mile

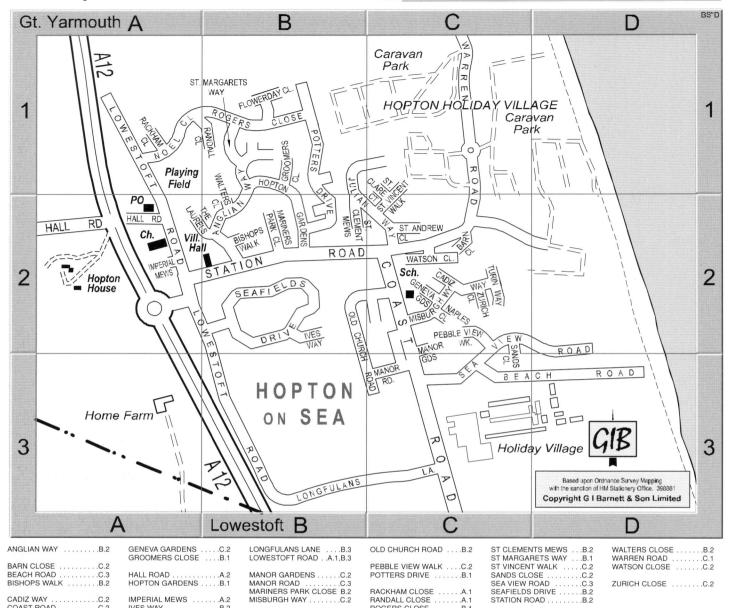

ANGLIAN WAY B.2	GENEVA GARDENS C.2	LONGFULANS LANE B.3	OLD CHURCH ROAD B.2	ST CLEMENTS MEWS ...B.2	WALTERS CLOSE B.2

ANGLIAN WAY B.2

BARN CLOSE C.2
BEACH ROAD C.3
BISHOPS WALK B.2

CADIZ WAY C.2
COAST ROAD C.2

FLOWERDAY CLOSE B.1

GENEVA GARDENS C.2
GROOMERS CLOSE B.1

HALL ROAD A.2
HOPTON GARDENS B.1

IMPERIAL MEWS A.2
IVES WAY B.2

JULIAN WAY B.1

LONGFULANS LANE B.3
LOWESTOFT ROAD ..A.1,B.3

MANOR GARDENS C.2
MANOR ROAD C.3
MARINERS PARK CLOSE B.2
MISBURGH WAY C.2

NAPLES CLOSE C.2
NOEL CLOSE A.1

OLD CHURCH ROAD B.2

PEBBLE VIEW WALK C.2
POTTERS DRIVE B.1

RACKHAM CLOSE A.1
RANDALL CLOSE A.1
ROGERS CLOSE B.1

ST ANDREW CLOSE C.2
ST CLARE COURT C.1

ST CLEMENTS MEWS ...B.2
ST MARGARETS WAY ..B.1
ST VINCENT WALK C.2
SANDS CLOSE C.2
SEA VIEW ROAD C.3
SEAFIELDS DRIVE B.2
STATION ROAD B.2

THE LAURELS A.2
TURIN WAY C.2

WALTERS CLOSE B.2
WARREN ROAD C.1
WATSON CLOSE C.2

ZURICH CLOSE C.2

Feltwell....*map on facing page*

ADDISON CLOSE C.1
ARCHERS AVENUE B.2

BARRETTS LANE C.2
BELL STREET C.2
BIRD VIEW SQUARE B.2
BLACKDYKE CLOSE ...A.3

CAMP CLOSE A.2
CLOUGH DRIVE C.2
CRABBES CLOSE C.2
CURTIS DRIVE A.2

EAST HALL D.1
EDMUND MOUNDEFORD
ROAD C.2

FAIR CLOSE C.2
FALCON ROAD C.2
FAIRFIELD WAY C.2

GREEN LANE B.2

HALL DRIVE C.2
HARVARD ROAD B.2
HAYTILL LANE A.1
HEREWARD WAY A.2
HIGH STREET C.2
HILL STREET ....C 2
HYTHE ROAD ....B 1

LAMBERTS CLOSE ...C. 1
LANCASTER ROAD ...B.2
LEONARDS LANE A.2

LIME KILN LANE B.2
LODGE ROAD D.1
LONG LANE A.2

METHWOLD ROAD .....C 1
MOAT SIDE ....A 2
MULBERRY CLOSE C.2
MUNSONS LANE C.1
MUNSONS PLACE C.1

NEWCOMBE DRIVE C.2
NIGHTINGALE LANE ...C.2

OAK STREET C.2
OLD BRANDON ROAD ..D.2
OXFORD ROAD B.2

PAYNES LANE B.2
PORTAL CLOSE A.2
PROVOST ROAD B.2

RAWLINS WAY C.1

ST. JOHNS WAY C.2
ST. MARYS STREET C.2
ST. NICHOLAS DRIVE ...C 1
SHORT BECK ....B 2
SHORT LANE B.2
SPARKES WAY B.2
STIRLING ROAD B.2

THE BECK C.2
TRENCHARD SQUARE ..A.2

WELLINGTON ROAD B.2
WESTERN CLOSE B.2
WILTON ROAD C.3

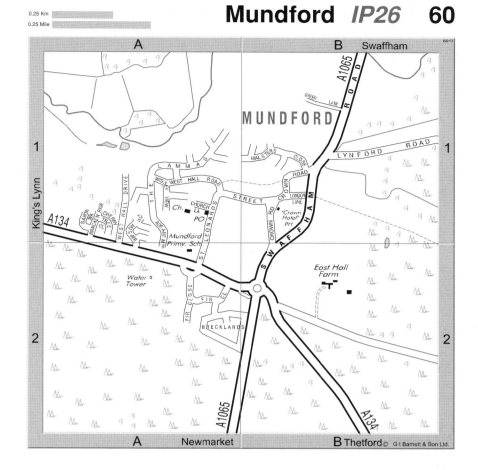

0.25 Km
0.25 Mile

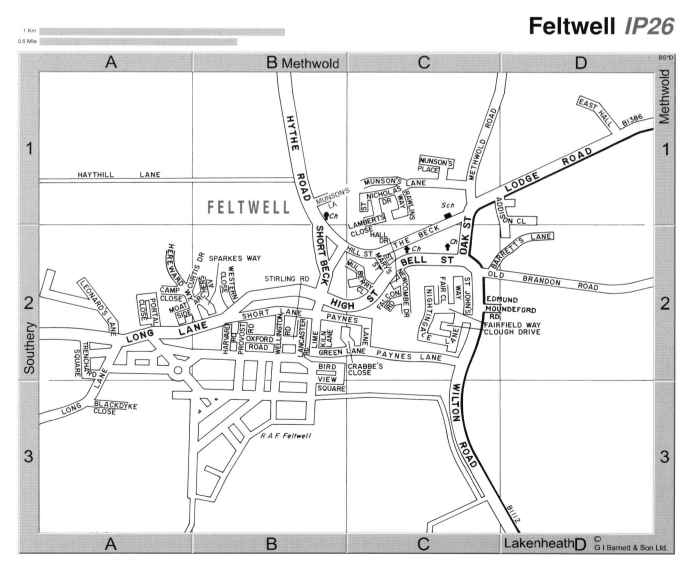

1 Km
0.5 Mile

0.5 Km
0.5 Mile

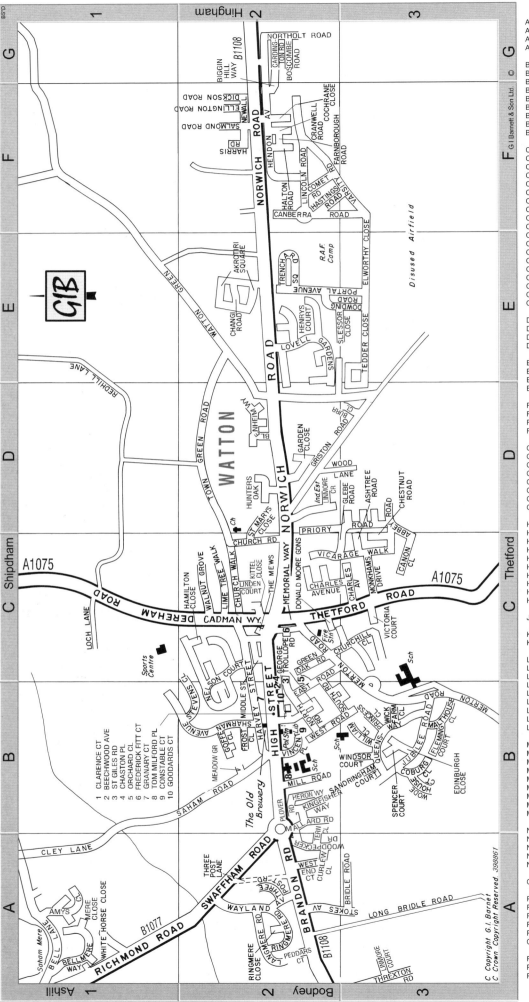

ABBEY ROAD D.3
AKROTIRI SQ E.2
AMYS CL A.1
ASHTREE RD C.3

BEECHWOOD AVE (2) .B.2
BELL LANE A.1
BELLMERE WAY A.1
BIGGIN HILL WAY ...F.2
BLENHEIM WAY D.2
BOSCOMBE RD F.2
BRANDON ROAD A.2
BRIDLE ROAD A.3
BURR CL D.3

CADMAN WAY C.2
CANBERRA RD F.2
CANON CL C.3
CARDINGTON RD F.2
CHANGI ROAD E.2
CHARLES AVE C.2
CHASTON PL (4) C.2
CHESTNUT RD C.3
CHURCH ROAD C.2
CHURCH WALK C.2
CHURCHILL CL C.3
CLARENCE CT (1) ...B.2
CLEY LANE A.1
COBURG CL B.3
COCHRANE CL F.2
COMET ROAD F.2
CONSTABLE CT B.2
CRANWELL RD B.2
CURLEW CL A.2

DEREHAM RD C.2
DICKSON RD F.2
DONALD MOORE GDS .C.2
DOWDING RD E.3

EAST ROAD B.2
EDINGBURGH CT B.3
ELLINGTON RAD F.2
ELWORTHY CL E.3

FARNBOROUGH RD ..F.2
FLEMING CT B.3
FRDRCK. FITT CT (6) .C.2
FROST CL B.2

GARDEN CL D.2
GEO. TROLLOPE RD ..B.2
GLEBE ROAD C.3
GODDARDS CT B.2
GOFFE CL B.2
GRANARY CT B.2
GREEN OAK ROAD ..C.2
GRISTON ROAD D.2

HALTON ROAD F.2
HAMILTON CL C.2
HARRIS ROAD F.2
HARVEY RD B.2
HASTINGS ROAD F.2
HENDON AVE F.2
HENRYS CT E.2
HERON WAY B.2
HIGH STREET B.2
HUNTERS OAK D.2

JUBILEE ROAD B.3

KINGFISHER WAY ...B.2
KITTEL CL C.2

LANGMERE ROAD ...A.2
LIME TREE WALK ...C.2
LINCOLN ROAD F.2
LINDEN CT C.2
LINMORE CT A.3
LINMORE CR. D.2
LOCH LANE C.1
LONG BRIDLE RD ...A.3
LOVELL GARDENS ...E.2

MALLARD ROAD B.2
MALTHOUSE CL B.3
MEADOW GROVE B.2
MEMORIAL WAY C.2
MERE CL A.1
MERTON ROAD B.3
MIDDLE STREET C.2
MILL ROAD B.2
MONKHAMS DRIVE ..C.3

NELSONS CT B.2
NEWALL AVE F.2
NORTH ROAD B.2
NORTHOLT ROAD ...G.2
NORWICH ROAD G.2

ORCHARD CL (5) B.2

PEDDARS CT A.2
PLOVER ROAD B.2
PORTAL AVE E.3
PRINCESS CL B.3
PRIORY ROAD D.2
QUEENS WAY B.3

REDHILL LANE D.1
RICHMOND RD A.1
RINGMERE CL A.2

RINGMERE RD A.2

SAHAM ROAD B.2
SALMOND ROAD F.2
SANDRINGHAM CT ..B.3
SHARMAN AVE B.2
SLESSOR CL E.3
SOUTH ROAD B.2
SPENCER CT B.3
ST. GILES ROAD (3) .B.2
ST. MARY'S CL D.2
STEVENS CL B.2
STOKES AVE A.3
SWAFFHAM RD A.2

TEDDER CL E.3
TERN CL A.2
THE MEWS C.2
THETFORD RD C.2
THREE POST LA A.2
THREE POST RD A.2
THREXTON RD A.2
TOWN GREEN RD ...D.2
TRENCHARD SQ E.2

VARSITY ROAD F.3
VICARAGE WALK ...C.2
VICTORIA CT C.3
VINCENT PLACE B.2

WALNUT GROVE C.2
WATTON GREEN E.2
WAYLAND AVE A.2
WEST END CT A.2
WEST ROAD B.2
WHITE HORSE CL ...A.1
WICK FARM CL B.3
WILLIAM CL B.3
WINDSOR CT B.3
WODE HOUSE CT ..B.3
WOOD LANE D.2
WOODPECKER DR ...A.2